Rise of the Habsburg Empire 1526–1815

VICTOR S. MAMATEY

University of Georgia

ROBERT E. KRIEGER PUBLISHING COMPANY
HUNTINGTON, NEW YORK
1978

Original edition 1971
Reprint 1978

Printed and Published by
ROBERT E. KRIEGER PUBLISHING COMPANY
645 NEW YORK AVENUE
HUNTINGTON, NEW YORK 11743

Library of Congress Cataloging in Publication Data
Mamatey, Victor S
    Rise of the Habsburg Empire, 1526-1851.

    Reprint of the ed. published by Ho, Rinehart and Winston,
New York, in series: Bershire studies in history.
    Reprint of the ed. published by Holt, Rinehart and Wiston,
New York, in series: Berkshire studies in history.
    Bibliography: p.
Includes index.
1,Austria—History.   2. Habsburg, House of.
I. Title.
DB38.M3   1978   943.6'03   77-15525
ISBN 0-88275-639-7

Printed in the United States of America

Preface

FOR FOUR CENTURIES the Habsburg empire constituted an important—sometimes a decisive—
element in the European balance of power, and
its peoples made notable contributions to the development of European civilization. In 1914 it was
second in area (264,204 square miles) and third
in population (about 52 million inhabitants) among
the European states. It was then exceeded in population and area only by the Russian empire, and
in population but not in area by Germany. Vienna,
the imperial capital, was one of Europe's great
cultural centers, often vying with Paris and London
in setting intellectual and artistic trends and fash-
ions. Yet, owing perhaps to its extreme complexity
and diversity, the development of the Habsburg
empire is seldom given its due importance in
general accounts of modern European history.

The treatment given the Habsburg empire in
conventional college textbooks on European history is reminiscent of the manner in which Africa
was dealt with in medieval maps of the "world";
beyond the contours of the North African coast
there was only blank space and a sign, *hic sunt
liones* (here are lions). The formation of the Habsburg empire in the sixteenth century is generally
ignored, and its development in the seventeenth
and eighteenth centuries is usually brought in
only as background material for the study of other

European states or general trends. As a unit, to be studied *per se,* the Habsburg empire is usually brought in only in the nineteenth century, when it was already in decay, and then only to point out that as a multi-national dynastic empire it was an anachronism and anomaly among European nation-states and, consequently, doomed to extinction.

To judge the whole history of the Habsburg empire, with hindsight wisdom, only by its ultimate fate rather than by its significance at the time of its existence is historically questionable. Such an approach distorts not only the history of the Habsburg monarchy but also that of Europe generally. During its four centuries of existence the Habsburg empire affected, for better or for worse, not only the destinies of its own peoples but also those of Europe as a whole. Its history should, therefore, be studied for its own merits and significance in European history. Moreover, it should be judged by the values prevalent at the time of its existence rather than from the vantage point of the democratic and nationalistic twentieth century.

The history of the Habsburg empire offers some parallels with that of West European nation-states and some with that of the East European multinational empires, but for the most part it was *sui generis*. It was unique, for instance, in the sense that until 1804 it did not even exist as a legal entity but was hidden behind the hollow facade of the Holy Roman Empire. Yet at least from the Peace of Westphalia in 1648 it, and not the ghostlike Holy Roman Empire, was the dominant political reality in East Central Europe.

The purpose of this modest study cannot be, of course, to reassess the whole role of the Habsburg empire in European history. It is addressed to the beginning student of European history, and its objective is a limited one. It is to give a general outline of the rise of the Habsburg empire from its formation after the Battle of Mohács in 1526 to the Congress of Vienna in 1815, when for the first time it acted in a great international forum under its own identity as the empire of Austria.

Athens, Ga.   V. S. M.
March 1971

Contents

Preface *iii*
Spelling of Geographic and Personal Names *vii*
Habsburg Dynasty, Fifteenth to Eighteenth
   Centuries *x*

CHAPTER 1
Background *1*
AUSTRIA AND THE HABSBURGS *1*
THE REFORMATION, FRANCE, AND TURKEY *8*
BOHEMIA *11*
HUNGARY *17*
TWILIGHT OF INDEPENDENT HUNGARY AND
   BOHEMIA *22*

CHAPTER 2
Formation of the Habsburg Empire, 1526–1648 28
FERDINAND I AND MAXIMILIAN II *28*
STRUGGLE FOR HUNGARY *31*
PROTESTANT REFORMATION AND CATHOLIC COUNTER-
   REFORMATION *38*
RUDOLF II AND MATTHIAS I *44*
THIRTY YEARS' WAR, 1618–1648 *49*

CHAPTER 3
Consolidation and Expansion, 1648–1739 *58*
AFTERMATH OF THE THIRTY YEARS' WAR *58*
STRUGGLE FOR THE MASTERY OF EUROPE *67*
TRIUMPH IN HUNGARY *74*
FAILURE IN THE BALKANS *79*
COMPROMISE IN THE WEST AND IN HUNGARY *85*

THE LAST HABSBURG   *91*
SUCCESS AND FAILURE IN FOREIGN POLICY   *96*

CHAPTER 4
Reform and Reaction, 1740–1815   *101*
MARIA THERESA   *101*
WAR OF THE AUSTRIAN SUCCESSION   *103*
SEVEN YEARS' WAR   *108*
MARIA THERESA'S REFORMS   *112*
MARIA THERESA AND HUNGARY   *118*
FOREIGN AFFAIRS   *123*
THE REVOLUTIONARY EMPEROR   *127*
WAR AND DIPLOMACY   *136*
LEOPOLD II   *139*
THE HABSBURG EMPIRE AND THE FRENCH
   REVOLUTION   *142*

Bibliographical Note   *161*
Index   *167*

Spelling of Geographic and Personal Names

OWING to its multinational character, nearly every town, river, and mountain in the former Habsburg empire has had two, three, or more national names. To prevent confusion, the present names, that is the official names in the present successor states of the Habsburg empire, will be used in this book with alternate names indicated in parentheses, except for the names of capitals, provinces, rivers, etc., that have well-established English names. Thus, for instance: Alba Iulia (Gyulafehérvár, Karlsburg), but Vienna instead of Wien, Croatia instead of Hrvatska, the Danube instead of Donau, Duna, or Dunaj, etc. For the same reason, the present spelling of personal names will be used, except for the names of sovereigns and a few outstanding personalities that are well established in history under English or latinized names.

V. S. M.

RISE OF THE HABSBURG EMPIRE

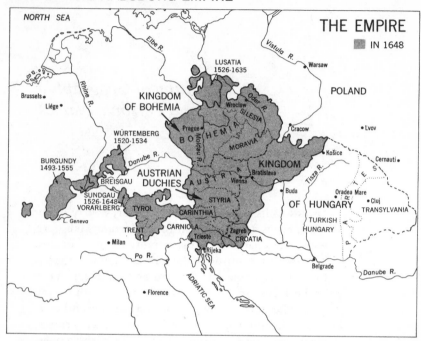

THE EMPIRE

IN 1648

NORTH SEA

Brussels
Liége

Rhine R.

Elbe R.

Vistula R.

Warsaw

POLAND

LUSATIA
1526-1635

KINGDOM
OF BOHEMIA

WÜRTEMBERG
1520-1534

Prague

Wroclaw

Oder R.

SILESIA

Cracow

Lvov

BURGUNDY
1493-1555

Danube R.

MORAVIA

Košice

Cernauti

BREISGAU

SUNDGAU
1526-1648
VORARLBERG

TYROL

Vienna

Bratislava

Buda

Oradea Mare
or

Cluj

TRANSYLVANIA

AUSTRIAN
DUCHIES

STYRIA

OF HUNGARY

KINGDOM

KINGDOM
OF HUNGARY

TURKISH
HUNGARY

CARINTHIA

TRENT

CARNIOLA

L. Geneva

Milan

Trieste

Zagreb

Rijeka

CROATIA

Belgrade

Danube R.

Po R.

ADRIATIC SEA

Florence

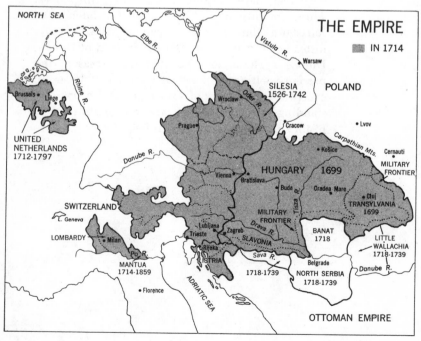

THE EMPIRE

IN 1714

NORTH SEA

Elbe R.

Vistula R.

Warsaw

Brussels
Liége

Rhine R.

Wroclaw

SILESIA
1526-1742

POLAND

UNITED
NETHERLANDS
1712-1797

Prague

Oder R.

Cracow

Lvov

Danube R.

Carpathian Mts.

Cernauti

MILITARY
FRONTIER

Vienna

Bratislava

Buda

Košice

HUNGARY 1699

Oradea Mare

Cluj

TRANSYLVANIA
1699

SWITZERLAND

L. Geneva

LOMBARDY

Milan

Po R.

MANTUA
1714-1859

Ljubljana

Trieste

Zagreb

ISTRIA

Rijeka

MILITARY
FRONTIER

Drava R.

SLAVONIA

Sava R.

Tisza R.

BANAT
1718

LITTLE
WALLACHIA
1718-1739

1718-1739

Belgrade

NORTH SERBIA
1718-1739

Danube R.

ADRIATIC SEA

Florence

OTTOMAN EMPIRE

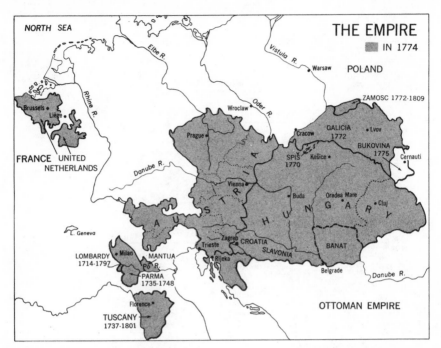

NORTH SEA

THE EMPIRE

▨ IN 1774

Elbe R.

Vistula R.

Warsaw

POLAND

Rhine R.

Wroclaw

Oder R.

ZAMOSC 1772-1809

Brussels

Liége

Prague

Cracow

GALICIA 1772

Lvov

A U S T R I A

SPIŠ 1770

Košice

BUKOVINA 1775

Cernauti

FRANCE UNITED NETHERLANDS

Danube R.

Vienna

Buda

Oradea Mare

Cluj

H U N G A R Y

L. Geneva

Zagreb

CROATIA

Trieste

Rijeka

SLAVONIA

BANAT

LOMBARDY 1714-1797

Milan

MANTUA

Po R.

PARMA 1735-1748

Belgrade

Danube R.

Florence

OTTOMAN EMPIRE

TUSCANY 1737-1801

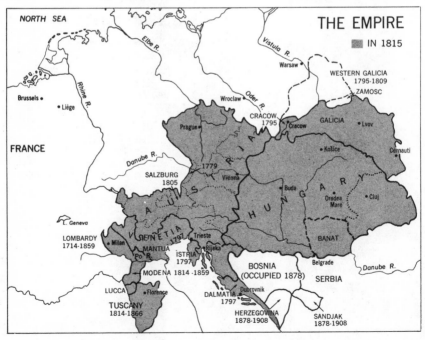

NORTH SEA

THE EMPIRE

▨ IN 1815

Elbe R.

Vistula R.

Warsaw

Rhine R.

Wroclaw

Oder R.

WESTERN GALICIA 1795-1809

ZAMOSC

Brussels

Liége

Prague

CRACOW 1795

Cracow

GALICIA

Lvov

A U S T R I A

Košice

Cernauti

FRANCE

Danube R.

1779

SALZBURG 1805

Vienna

Buda

H U N G A R Y

Oradea Mare

Cluj

L. Geneva

V E N E T I A

1797

Trieste

LOMBARDY 1714-1859

Milan

MANTUA

Po R.

ISTRIA 1797

Rijeka

BANAT

MODENA 1814-1859

Belgrade

Danube R.

LUCCA

Florence

DALMATIA 1797

Dubrovnik

BOSNIA (OCCUPIED 1878)

SERBIA

TUSCANY 1814-1866

HERZEGOVINA 1878-1908

SANDJAK 1878-1908

HABSBURG DYNASTY
Fifteenth to Eighteenth Centuries

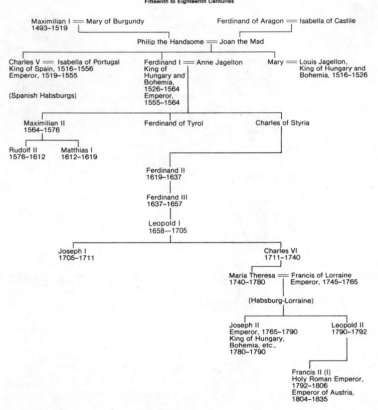

Maximilian I 1493–1519 ═ Mary of Burgundy

Ferdinand of Aragon ═ Isabella of Castile

Philip the Handsome ═ Joan the Mad

Charles V ═ Isabella of Portugal
King of Spain, 1516–1556
Emperor, 1519–1555

(Spanish Habsburgs)

Ferdinand I ═ Anne Jagellon
King of
Hungary and
Bohemia,
1526–1564
Emperor,
1555–1564

Mary ═ Louis Jagellon,
King of Hungary and
Bohemia, 1516–1526

Maximilian II
1564–1576

Ferdinand of Tyrol

Charles of Styria

Rudolf II
1576–1612

Matthias I
1612–1619

Ferdinand II
1619–1637

Ferdinand III
1637–1657

Leopold I
1658—1705

Joseph I
1705–1711

Charles VI
1711–1740

Maria Theresa ═ Francis of Lorraine
1740–1780   Emperor, 1745–1765

(Habsburg-Lorraine)

Joseph II
Emperor, 1765–1790
King of Hungary,
Bohemia, etc.,
1780–1790

Leopold II
1790–1792

Francis II (I)
Holy Roman Emperor,
1792–1806
Emperor of Austria,
1804–1835

CHAPTER ONE

Background

Austria and the Habsburgs

NATURE OF THE EMPIRE If Louis XIV of France could say *l'état c'est moi,* the Habsburgs could say with even greater justice that they *were* the Habsburg empire. It was largely their creation. Unlike the multinational Ottoman or Russian empires, which were, initially at least, products of the expansive energy of the Turks and the Great Russians, respectively, the Habsburg empire was not formed by expansion and conquest of any single people, but rather by association, originally voluntary, of several feudal states, each of which was inhabited by more than one people, under the Habsburg dynasty. The Habsburg monarchy was, and remained throughout its existence, a supranational dynastic empire *par excellence.*

The Habsburgs were a German dynasty. The German Austrians were not only their most numerous subjects but also socially and culturally their most advanced subjects, and of all the peoples of the Habsburg empire the German Austrians identified themselves with the dynasty and the empire the most closely. But the empire was not a product of German-Austrian conquest and expansion. It was formed in 1526 when an Austrian archduke was elected to the vacant thrones of Bohemia and Hungary. Although the Habsburgs already possessed many other European lands, and later acquired more by marriage, diplomacy, and war, their hereditary Austrian lands *(Erblande)* and the lands of the crowns of Bohemia and Hungary remained the core of the Habsburg empire down to its dissolution in 1918.

From the fifteenth century on, the Habsburgs were regularly elected Holy Roman emperors.[1] In a sense, the Habsburg empire grew up under the cracked shell of the Holy Roman Empire, but it was never exclusively a German state. While the Austrian duchies and Slavic Bohemia were associated in the Holy Roman Empire, Hungary was not. Nevertheless, the Habsburgs insisted on keeping one foot in Germany and the other outside of it, even after the extinction of the Holy Roman Empire in 1806 and the wide acceptance of the idea of the nation-state. It was perhaps their inability to decide on a role, whether to be German national rulers or supranational monarchs, that brought about their downfall and the dissolution of their empire.

The union of the Austrian lands with those of Bohemia and Hungary in 1526 did not create a sharp break in their internal development. It seems necessary therefore to explain briefly their earlier history before dealing with that of the Habsburg empire.

AUSTRIAN DUCHIES Austria had its origin in the "Eastern March" *(Ostmark)* established by Charlemagne about 788 in the area of the present provinces of Upper and Lower Austria in the Austrian republic. The function of the Eastern March was to

---

[1] Technically, until the fifteenth century, the German rulers were elected "kings of the Romans" and crowned at Aachen. It was only after another coronation at Rome by the pope that they acquired the imperial dignity.

guard the eastern approach to Charlemagne's empire through the Danube valley against the raids of the Avars, a warlike tribe of nomadic Asian herdsmen then settled in the Pannonian plain (present Hungary). In the ninth century, when the Carolingian empire broke up (843), the Eastern March appears to have been absorbed in Great Moravia, an ephemeral Slavic state in the mid-Danube basin, which was overrun by the Magyars. However, in 955 Emperor Otto the Great (936–976), the founder of the Holy Roman Empire, crushed the Magyars and reestablished the Austrian March. His son Otto II bestowed it as an imperial fief on Leopold of Babenberg, who was the founder of the first Austrian dynasty.

The Babenbergs (976–1346) established their court at Vienna (Roman Vindobona), where they erected the castle *am Hof* (Hofburg) and the Church of St. Stephen. After the extinction of the Babenberg dynasty Austria came under the rule of the king of Bohemia, Přemysl II Ottokar (1251—1278), an ambitious empire-builder. Přemysl II proceeded to acquire the other Alpine duchies—Styria, Carinthia, Carniola, and Istria—that had arisen to the south of Austria. His ambitions, however, provoked the fear and jealousy of other princes of the Holy Roman Empire. In 1273 when he sought the imperial crown, they elected instead Rudolf I Habsburg (1273–1291), until then a relatively obscure South German (Swabian) duke.[2] In an effort to weaken his Bohemian rival, Rudolf reclaimed Austria, Styria, Carinthia, and Istria as imperial fiefs and drove Přemysl II from them by force (1276). Two years later, when the Bohemian king sought to recover them, he was defeated and slain in a battle on the Marchfeld near Vienna.

Rudolf ended a long period of anarchy (the "Great Interregnum," 1254–1273) in Germany and reestablished the imperial authority. His ambitions provoked, in turn, the jealousy of the German princes. When he died, they denied the imperial crown to his son. However, Austria and the Alpine duchies associated with it were linked to the fortunes of the ambitious and grasping Habsburg dynasty until 1918.

[2] Rudolf's ancestral castle was Habsburg (a contraction of *Habichtsburg*—hawk's castle) in the present Swiss canton of Aargau.

HOUSE OF AUSTRIA With the increasing feudalization and decentralization of the Holy Roman Empire, the Habsburgs conducted themselves as independent sovereigns, making treaties with foreign powers and annexing possessions of weaker feudal lords. In 1356 Rudolf IV (1339–1365), who was the first Habsburg to style himself archduke, proclaimed the indivisibility of the Habsburg hereditary possessions. Henceforth the Habsburg *Erblande* were usually referred to as Austria and the Habsburg dynasty as the "House of Austria" *(Domus Austriae)*. Until the seventeenth century, when the number of male Habsburgs declined, it was customary for the head of the Habsburg dynasty to award Styria and other Austrian duchies to younger sons as appanages. The practice, however, never led to a permanent division of the Habsburg hereditary possessions. Unlike many other European feudal dynasties, the Habsburgs showed remarkable family cohesion and solidarity. In time, Habsburg family traditions and policies acquired a dynamic of their own which overrode the predelictions of individual members of the family.

Austria reached the peak of its medieval efflorescence in the fourteenth century. Vienna then became one of the richest and most important German cities. In 1365 the University of Vienna was founded and soon became an important German cultural center. The Church of St. Stephen was rebuilt as a cathedral in Gothic style, which it preserves to this day, although Vienna did not become a seat of an archbishop until 1469. Rudolf IV added the Tyrol (1363) to the Habsburg possessions, and his successor, the port of Trieste (1382) and part of Istria. The former gave the Habsburg a direct link to Italy and the latter an outlet to the sea. Originally Styria, Carinthia, and Carniola had a predominantly Slavic (Slovene) character. In time, however, owing to German colonization, which the Habsburgs encouraged, the nobles and townsmen in the duchies became largely German, and the indigenous Slovenes were reduced in status and numbers to a peasant people.

Although the Habsburgs were strong feudal lords, they were not absolute monarchs but were forced to share power with the feudal classes, or "estates" *(Stände)*. As with other German states in the fifteenth century, the Austrian duchies evolved into "states of the estates" *(Ständestaaten)*, that is corporate states, in which the privileges and duties of the three estates—clergy *(Prälatenstand)*, nobles *(Herrenstand)*, and townsmen *Bürgerstand)*—were defined by law or custom. As in most of Europe at the time, the peasants, who constituted the most numerous segment of the population, stood outside the medieval concept of *populus* (people) and did not constitute an estate. Generally enserfed,[3] they were considered chattel whose function was to provide for the material needs of feudal society. From about 1400 the estates of the Austrian duchies began to meet in "diets" *(Landtage)*, at first only on special occasions but later regularly. The estates generally sat apart, Subsequently, the noble estate was divided into the estates of the great titled lords and the small "knights" *(Ritter)*.

AUSTRIAE EST IMPERARE ORBI UNIVERSO In the thirteenth century the Habsburgs had risen from obscurity to prominence in German affairs; in the fifteenth century they achieved importance on the European scene. Rudolph IV dreamed of building an empire. In 1364 he concluded a family compact with Emperor Charles IV (1347–1378) of the Luxemburg dynasty, who was also king of Bohemia. Under its terms either dynasty, Habsburg or Luxemburg, was to succeed to the possessions of the other upon its extinction. In 1438, on the death of the last Luxemburg, Emperor Sigismund I (1410–1437), who had come into possession also of Hungary, the German electors, as well as the estates of Bohemia and Hungary, elected his brother-in-law Albrecht of Austria to their vacant thrones.

This first combination of Germany, Austria, Bohemia, and Hungary under a Habsburg prince, was short-lived. Emperor Albrecht II (1438–1439) died a year after his accession of a sickness incurred while fighting the Turks. The Habsburg claim to Bohemia and Hungary lapsed with the death, also premature, of his son Ladislav Posthumus. In Germany, however, Albrecht's election had set a permanent trend. On his death, the German

---

[3] An exception were the peasants in the Tyrol. They were free and in return for their freedom provided military service, developing the proud bearing of men free and used to bearing arms.

electors chose his cousin Duke Frederick of Styria to succeed him. From 1438 until the end of the empire in 1806, with only a brief interruption in the eighteenth century, Habsburgs were regularly elected German emperors.

Emperor Frederick III (1440–1493) was the last German ruler to undertake the pilgrimage to Rome for imperial coronation. During his long reign the disintegration of the Holy Roman Empire moved apace. Although indolent and impecunious, he was the first Habsburg to use the initials A.E.I.O.U. of the proud Habsburg motto *Austriae est imperare orbi universo* (Austria is destined to rule over the whole world). The real founder of the Habsburg fortunes, however, was Frederick's son and successor Maximilian I (1493–1519), who was elected king of the Romans during his father's lifetime (1486) but was barred from going to Rome for an imperial coronation by the hostility of Venice. In 1508 he had himself designated "emperor elect" and was crowned without the assistance of the pope. He also significantly modified the name of the Holy Roman Empire by adding to it "of the German nation" (*sacrum imperium Romanum nationis Teutonicae*). Maximilian's successor Charles V was still crowned by the pope, but at Bologna rather than at Rome. All subsequent German rulers were designated emperors elect and crowned in Germany without the assistance of the pope.

BELLA GERUNT ALII   Maximilian's talent for promoting profitable marriages inspired the jocular aphorism, *Bella gerunt alii, tu, felix Austria, nubes!* (Where others have to wage wars, you, lucky Austria, marry!). Maximilian himself had in 1477 married Mary of Burgundy, the heiress of the dukes of Burgundy, who possessed not only the duchy of Burgundy in France but also the Netherlands. Although his bride died prematurely and he remarried, Maximilian successfully defended the Habsburg claim to the Netherlands and the Free County (*Franche-Comté*) of Burgundy[4] against the kings of France. Next, Maxi-

---

[4] The duchy of Burgundy itself reverted to France.

milian arranged the marriage of his son by Mary, Philip the Handsome, to Joan the Mad, daughter of Ferdinand of Aragon and Isabella of Castile, thus establishing the Habsburg claim to Spain and its possessions in Italy (Milan, Naples, and Sicily) and the New World. The offspring of this marriage provided Maximilian with additional brides and grooms for more matchmaking and fortune hunting.

In 1515, at an ostentatious conference at Vienna, Maximilian negotiated a family compact with the Jagellon rulers, Vladislav of Bohemia and Hungary and Sigismund of Poland-Lithuania, whereby either dynasty, Jagellon or Habsburg, was to succeed to the lands of the other upon its extinction. The agreement was sealed with a double wedding: Vladislav's son Louis married Maximilian's granddaughter Mary, while he (Maximilian) married Vladislav's daughter Anne *per procuram*, that is, for one of his minor grandsons, Charles or Ferdinand. Eventually (in 1521), it was Ferdinand who married Anne, while Charles married Isabella of Portugal. While the former marriage reestablished the Habsburg claim to Bohemia and Hungary, the latter established the claim to Portugal. Finally, upon the extinction of the counts of Gorizia (1500), Maximilian added their domain to the Habsburg *Erblande*, thus gaining a better approach to Trieste and the Adriatic Sea.

Charles V, king of Spain (1516–1556) and Holy Roman emperor (1519–1555), combined under his rule the inheritances of his four grandparents: the Habsburg *Erblande* in Austria, the Netherlands, and Spain and its Italian and overseas possessions. In 1526 Ferdinand came into possession of Bohemia and Hungary. Association of so many lands under the Habsburg dynasty gave substance to the proud motto that Austria was destined to rule over the whole world. The sun literally never set over the Habsburg empire. However, so vast an agglomeration of lands and peoples under a single monarch proved ungovernable. As early as 1521 Charles found it necessary to hand over to Ferdinand the hereditary Habsburg duchies in Austria, and in 1522 he turned over to him the conduct of German affairs. In 1532, to assure Ferdinand's succession in Germany, Charles

had the German diet elect him German king. This foreshadowed
the division of the Habsburg dynasty into the Austrian and
Spanish branches.

The Reformation, France, and Turkey

CHARLES V AND MARTIN LUTHER   Charles V went to Germany
for the first time in 1520 to preside over the Diet of Worms. The
principal item on the agenda was the religious problem in Germany. Three years earlier, Martin Luther had launched the
Protestant Reformation with the publication of his famous
ninety-five theses at Wittenberg. Now, in 1520, he was summoned before the Diet of Worms to justify himself. When he
refused to recant, he was placed under a ban of the empire and
his doctrines were forbidden, but Luther's followers refused to
accept the decision. Germany then became embroiled in a bitter
civil-religious conflict.

The religious revolt in Germany presented Charles V with
an insoluble dilemma. He was a faithful son of the Catholic
Church. The matter, however, was not only one of conscience
for him but also of political expediency. To concede tolerance
to the German Lutherans, let alone to adopt Lutheranism himself, would have alienated his Catholic subjects in Spain and
Italy. Whether he cared to or not, he had to make himself the
leader of the Counter-Reformation. Moreover, a true son of
his age, Charles V was a believer in royal absolutism. If he were
to be absolute monarch in Germany, the state would have to be
united, both politically and religiously, for in the sixteenth
century a dissident religious group automatically constituted a
dissident political party. On the other hand, the German Protestants had to defend feudal decentralization, not necessarily
out of conviction but because the "ancient German liberty" (the
feudal rights of the princes or state rights) was the best safeguard
of their religious freedom. Moreover, the secularization of the
Church lands, which accompanied the religious reform, created
a vested interest for the Lutheran princes in defending the Reformation. In 1531 the Lutheran princes and imperial cities

formed the Schmalkaldic League to defend themselves against the Habsburgs.

PEACE OF AUGSBURG In 1546, profiting from a respite in foreign wars, Charles V returned to Germany determined to crush the Schmalkaldic League and restore the unity of church and empire. In the ensuing Schmalkaldic War (1546–1547) he was successful against the Protestant princes, but French intervention prevented him from exploiting his victory. In 1555 he was forced to accept the Peace of Augsburg in Germany, which postulated the famous principle *cuius regio, eius religio* (He who rules, determines religion), thus allowing the German princes to determine their religion and that of their subjects (*jus reformandi*). The Protestant cause was saved in northern Germany, where most of the princes had adopted Lutheranism. Calvinism, on the other hand, which emanated from Switzerland, was not recognized or protected in Germany. Politically, the Peace of Augsburg marked a triumph of royal absolutism within the individual German states, but it dealt a blow to absolutism in Germany as a whole. It left the Holy Roman Empire a hollow shell. Under this shell, however, there rose new sovereign dynastic states, of which Austria was the most important.

DIVISION IN THE HOUSE OF HABSBURG In 1555, discouraged by his failure in Germany, Charles V abdicated as Holy Roman emperor in favor of his brother Ferdinand I (1555–1564) and in the following year as king of Spain in favor of his son Philip II (1556–1598). The division of the House of Habsburg was thus consummated. Henceforth, like the doubleheaded black eagle in the imperial coat of arms, the Habsburgs had two heads, at Vienna and at Madrid, looking east and west.

The Austrian and Spanish Habsburgs remained closely related. Members of the two families frequently intermarried, and they coordinated their policies. Spanish and Italian cultural influences were prominent in Vienna, and Castilian etiquette long prevailed at the court of the Austrian Habsburgs. Until the middle of the seventeenth century the Spanish Habsburgs were the senior branch of the family. In the long run, however, the Austrian Habsburgs were the most successful. They established an empire that endured until 1918. It is with the Austrian Habsburg empire alone that we shall be concerned in this short study.

FRENCH "EASTERN BARRIER" With the accession of Charles V in the Netherlands, Spain, Italy, and Germany, France was encircled by Habsburg possessions. The European balance of power was seriously upset, and efforts were soon made to redress it. To break the ring of Habsburg possessions around them, the kings of France, who since the crusades had borne the proud title "Most Christian kings," concluded an alliance with the Moslem sultans of the Ottoman empire against their fellow-Catholic monarchs, the Habsburgs, much to the consternation of Catholic Europe.

The Franco-Turkish alliance forced the Habsburgs to fight on many fronts: in Hungary against the Turks; in Italy, on the Rhine, in the Netherlands, and in the Pyrenees against the French; and in the Mediterranean against the Turks, their North African vassals (the Barbary pirates), and the French. To outflank the Habsburgs further, France sought friendly relations with Poland and in the seventeenth century with Sweden, thus erecting the famous French *barrière à l'est* (eastern barrier). The Habsburgs, also acting on the principle "The enemy of my enemy is my friend," sought in turn, though less successfully, to outflank the French eastern allies by establishing relations with Muscovite Russia and Safavi Persia. Finally, to weaken the Habsburgs, the French kings supported every element of dissension in the Habsburg possessions, notably the German Protestants, even while suppressing Protestantism at home. For over two centuries the struggle between the House of France and the House of Austria, with its many ramifications, was the crux of European international relations.

TURKISH MENACE The Ottoman empire began in extremely modest circumstances as a domain of the Osmanli[5] Turks in

---

[5] The word Ottoman resulted from Westerners' distortion of "Osman" (Uthman), the name of the legendary leader of the Osmanli Turks and the founder of their dynasty.

western Asia Minor in the thirteenth century. It spread, however, with extraordinary dynamism, at first expanding west-
ward at the expense of the decaying Byzantine empire. The
Turks gained a foothold in Europe in the 1350s when one of
the contestants for the Byzantine throne invited them to cross
the Dardanelles to assist him. After the conflict they did not
return to Asia. Instead, they swept into the Balkans, by-passing
Constantinople for the moment, for its walls were still too much
of a challenge for them. After destroying medieval Serbia[6]
(1389) and Bulgaria (1393), they tightened their vise on the Byzantine empire, reducing it gradually to Constantinople, a small
frontage in Europe, and a few islands. In 1453, under the redoubtable Sultan Mehmet (Mohammed) the Conqueror (1451—
1481), they laid siege to the imperial city and succeeded in cap-
turing it by using artillery on an unprecedented scale to breach
its walls. Under the name of Istanbul, the ancient "City of Constantine" became the capital of the Ottoman empire, which was
to endure, like the Habsburg empire, until 1918.

At the beginning of the sixteenth century the Turks stood
poised to invade Hungary and overrun the heart of Europe.
The various dynastic combinations of Austria, Bohemia, Hungary, and Poland that occurred in the fifteenth century were
in part inspired by fear of the Turks and the realization by the
various dynasties that they had better pool their resources if
they were to escape the fate of the Balkan states.

Bohemia

THE CZECHS In the second half of the sixth century, during
the Great Migration of European peoples, Slavic tribes settled
in Bohemia in the wake of the Germanic Markomans, who had
departed for the Roman empire. One of the tribes was called
the Czechs. Thanks to their central location in the Bohemian
quadrangle, the Czechs gave the other Slavic tribes their name
and also the first Bohemian dynasty, the Přemyslids.

---

[6] In northern Serbia, by leaning on Hungary, a vestigial Serbian "despotate"
survived until 1459.

About 805 Charlemagne invaded Bohemia and forced the Slavic tribes to recognize him as their suzerain and to pay him a tribute, according to Czech national tradition, of 120 oxen and 300 talents of silver. After the division of the Carolingian empire (843), Bohemia passed under the control of the Great Moravian empire. While attached to Great Moravia, the Czechs were brought within the fold of Christianity by Byzantine missionaries—the "Slavic Apostles" St. Cyril (Constantine) and St. Methodius. About 874 the Přemyslid prince Bořivoj and his wife Ludmila (later sainted for her great piety) were baptized by St. Methodius under the Eastern (Slavic) rite. However, after the destruction of Great Moravia by the Magyars (about 895) Bohemia reverted to dependence on the German empire and was permanently oriented toward the Latin rite and Western culture.

ST. VENCESLAS A grandson of Bořivoj, Venceslas (Václav) was a devout Christian prince who zealously spread Christiantiy in Bohemia. However, the spread of Western Christianity was accompanied by an increase in German influence, which provoked a nativist reaction led by Venceslas' brother Boleslav. In 929 Venceslas was assassinated by the nativist party. Because of his Christian zeal and martyrdom, he was canonized and became enshrined in Czech national legend as Bohemia's patron saint. Bohemia and its dependencies became known as the Lands of the Crown of St. Venceslas. At the end of the tenth century Bohemia became an important focus of Christian missionary effort directed toward Hungary and Poland.

In the meantime Venceslas' brother and successor, Boleslav I (929–967), a very warlike prince, asserted his control over all the Slavic tribes of Bohemia and brought adjoining Moravia (a vestigial remnant of Great Moravia) as well as Silesia and Cracow in Poland under Bohemian sway. Except for a few short periods, Moravia was permanently attached to Bohemia. Silesia, however, became a permanent bone of contention between the Bohemian and Polish rulers.[7]

---

[7] Unless otherwise stated, the term Bohemia will be used here to mean all the possessions of the Bohemian crown, not the province of Bohemia alone.

BOHEMIA AND THE EMPIRE   Boleslav defied the German empire, but in 950 Emperor Otto the Great invaded Bohemia and forced him to recognize German suzerainty and pay a tribute. From then until the dissolution of the Holy Roman Empire in 1806, Bohemia was an imperial fief. During this long period of time the relationship of Bohemia to Germany naturally varied. At first, Bohemian dependence on Germany was close. Later, with the growing decentralization of the empire, it became tenuous.

As vassals of the Holy Roman emperors, the Bohemian princes had to provide troops for the emperor, including an honor guard of 300 mounted men for imperial coronations in Rome. In 1156, in return for Bohemian services, Emperor Frederick Barbarossa awarded Prince Vladislav II (1140–1173) a royal crown. Until the eighteenth century the Bohemian kings were the only princes of the empire to have a royal crown. When the empire became an elective monarchy, they became imperial electors. This function as well as the relatively large size and growing wealth of their possessions strengthened their position vis-à-vis the emperors and assured them practical independence.

GERMAN COLONIZATION   The social organization of Bohemia followed the feudal pattern of Germany. Bohemian society was organized along conventional feudal lines into clergy, nobility, and peasantry. The discovery of silver in Bohemia in the thirteenth century led to the development of mining and trade and the growth of a class of townsmen, mainly German in origin.[8] Other German settlers were invited by the Bohemian kings and nobles to clear the forests and develop agriculture in the hilly and sparsely populated border districts of the country. Many German clerics and noblemen likewise found employment and fortune in Bohemia. By the end of the thirteenth century, as a result of steady German immigration, Bohemia had a substantial German minority. The German colonists contributed greatly to the material and cultural development of Bohemia, but they threatened to destroy its Slavic identity.

[8] Modern Czech and German nationalist historians have argued heatedly whether the Germans of Bohemia were descendants exclusively of German colonists of the late Middle Ages (the Czech view) or also of the pre-Slavic Germanic tribes in Bohemia (the German view).

THE LUXEMBURGS   In 1306 the Přemyslid dynasty became extinct. There followed a period of confusion during which the Habsburgs made an early but unsuccessful bid for the Bohemian crown. In 1310 the estates (clergy and nobility) of Bohemia and Moravia elected John of Luxemburg, son of Emperor Henry VII, their king. As the price of his election, they exacted confirmation of their privileges. Under the last Přemyslids the estates had met occasionally in diets. Under John, who was frequently absent from the kingdom, the diets of Bohemia and Moravia began to meet regularly. On special occasions the two diets met jointly, but usually they met and acted separately.

The Luxemburg dynasty (1310–1437) greatly enhanced the prestige of Bohemia. King John (1310–1346) was one of the most famous knights errant of feudal Europe. He spent most of his reign fighting abroad. Fittingly, he died on the battlefield of Crécy (1346), fighting, though aged and blind, in the ranks of the French knights against the English. Although he neglected domestic affairs, he added Silesia and Upper Lusatia to his kingdom and made Bohemia a power to be reckoned with.

FATHER OF THE COUNTRY   The reign of John's son Charles I (IV) (1346–1378) marked the golden age of feudal Bohemia. An astute statesman, Charles preferred to gain his objectives by diplomacy rather than war. He concluded a family compact with Rudolf IV Habsburg[9] and maintained friendly relations with the kings of Poland and Hungary. Elected German emperor in 1347,[10] he sought to halt the growing anarchy in Germany by proclaiming, in the famous Golden Bull of 1356, an orderly system of imperial elections.[11] Knowing, however, that his imperial power depended on the strength of his personal possessions, he devoted most of his energies to them. He decreed the indissoluble unity of the lands of the Crown of St. Venceslas,

---

[9] See p. 4.

[10] It was as Holy Roman emperor that he was Charles IV. As king of Bohemia, he was Charles I.

[11] The electors were the archbishops of Mainz, Trier, and Cologne, the count palatine of the Rhine, the duke of Saxony, the margrave of Brandenburg, and the king of Bohemia.

to which he added Lower Lusatia (1370) and Brandenburg (1373), and spared no effort to develop their economic resources.

Charles, who had spent his youth at the court of the Capetian kings in Paris, introduced French cultural influence in Bohemia. French architects and artisans in his service rebuilt Prague, which during his reign was the political and intellectual center of the Holy Roman Empire. They built the Gothic Charles Bridge over the Vltava (Moldau) River and began construction of the great Gothic cathedral of St. Vitus in the castle of Prague, both of which still adorn Prague. In 1348 Charles established the University of Prague (Charles University), the first European university east of the Rhine and north of Italy. For his many services to Bohemia, he has won in modern Czech historiography the admiring accolade, "father of the country."

THE HUSSITE MOVEMENT In 1378, the year in which Charles died, Catholic Europe was torn by the Great Schism (1378–1417) in the papacy. Beginning in 1403, Jan (John) Hus (1369–1415), a professor of theology at the University of Prague, made Bohemia a center of agitation for the reform of the Church. Influenced by the teaching of John Wycliffe of Oxford, he attacked the sale of indulgences, challenged the primacy of the popes, and emphasized the supreme authority of the Bible in matters of religious doctrine. A popular preacher in the Czech vernacular, he gathered a dedicated following.

In 1415 Hus was summoned by the Council of Constance (1414–1417) to justify himself. Eager for vindication, he went to Constance under a safeconduct from Emperor Sigismund (1410–1437). In violation of the safeconduct he was imprisoned, and when he refused to recant he was condemned for heresy and burned at the stake (July 6, 1415). His martyrdom outraged his followers in Bohemia. In 1419 Sigismund, who was a younger son of Charles I, succeeded his brother on the throne of Bohemia. However the Hussites, who held Sigismund responsible for the death of their prophet, absolutely refused to accept him as king. They took up arms in defense of their cause, and for over a decade beat off one crusade after another that was launched against Bohemia.

The Hussite wars (1420–1434) had aspects of civil as well as religious wars. The Hussites stressed the divine law as Holy Writ. They administered Holy Communion to the laity "in both species" (*sub utraque specie*)—that is, the cup as well as the wafer—and used the Czech vernacular in the liturgy. Hussitism, in addition to being a religious movement, had strong nationalist and social overtones. In part, it represented a Czech national reaction against the germanization of Bohemia and a social protest of the lower classes against feudalization. Perhaps for this reason it never gained much support abroad, although it did produce echoes in Hungary, Poland, and even as far as Moldavia.

In 1436 the Hussites accepted a compromise worked out at the Council of Basel (1431–1436). The "Compacts of Basel" recognized them as true sons of the Church and conceded them the cup in Holy Communion. At last, the Hussites accepted Sigismund as king. Hussitism survived until the sixteenth century when it was merged with the main stream of the Protestant Reformation, for which it had served as a dress rehearsal.

THE AFTERMATH The Hussite wars left a long heritage of religious, political, and social tensions between the Bohemian kings, the nobility, the townsmen, and the peasantry. For seventeen years, while the Hussites defied Sigismund, Bohemia and Moravia had been without a king. Consequently, royal authority was greatly weakened there. In 1421 the royal towns were admitted to the diets. At the same time the clergy were excluded from them. The wars had resulted in much destruction and impoverishment. The great lords generally fared better than the small nobles. The latter often lost their lands and became retainers of the great lords or professional soldiers. For a generation after the Hussite wars Czech mercenaries served in armies throughout Europe. The growing economic and social differences between the great and lesser nobles was reflected in the legal division of the estate of the nobility into the estates of the lords and the knights.

The Hussite wars had resulted in partial reslavicization of Bohemia and Moravia, where the Hussite movement had centered. On the other hand, the movement had alienated the outlying, largely germanized provinces of Silesia and the Lusatias, which had remained loyal to Sigismund and the Catholic Church. Although they were reunited with Bohemia and Moravia after the wars, their loyalty to the Bohemian crown had been undermined. In 1415 Brandenburg was lost altogether; Sigismund had pawned it to, and never redeemed it from, Albrecht Hohenzollern, then an obscure South German feudal lord who, as events turned out, was the founder of the fortunes of the Hohenzollerns of future Prussia.

With Sigismund's death in 1437, only a year after the Compacts of Basel, the Luxemburg dynasty came to an end. The dynasty had brought the Bohemian kingdom prestige and prosperity in the fourteenth century but left it internally troubled and externally weakened in the fifteenth.

Hungary

THE MAGYARS   The origins of Hungary date from the end of the ninth century when a federation of Magyar tribes under their mythical leader Árpád moved from the steppes of southern Russia to the mid-Danube area. Nomad horsemen of Ugro-Finnish origin, the Magyars were a warlike people. They destroyed Great Moravia and subjected its Slavic population, and then, like the Huns and Avars before them, they raided their neighbors until 955 when Otto the Great inflicted a crushing defeat on them on the Lechfeld near Augsburg. With their offensive power broken, the Magyars turned from the life of nomad herdsmen to that of settled farmers. The country was open to Christian missionaries from Bohemia and Germany; this determined its cultural alignment with Western Catholic Europe.

ST. STEPHEN   A descendant of Árpád, Vajk by name, married a Bavarian princess and was baptized under the name of István (Stephen). He is regarded as the true founder of the Hungarian kingdom. In the year 1000 he was crowned king with a crown sent him, according to Hungarian national tradition, by Pope

Sylvester II. King Stephen (997–1038) suppressed the remnants of paganism in his kingdom, and endowed Catholic churchmen who flocked to the country with large estates. He organized the administration of the country into counties (*comitas*) under counts (*ispán*), who together with high dignitaries of the Church formed his royal council. For his many services to the Church he was canonized in 1083; he is enshrined in Hungarian national legend as the patron saint of the country.

King Stephen and his successors rounded out Hungary to its "natural frontier": the foothills of the Alps in the west, the summits of the Carpathian Mountains in the north and east, and the Drava and Danube rivers in the south. The northern area (present Slovakia and Ruthenia) was annexed outright, but Transylvania in the east became an autonomous principality. In 1102 the kingdom of Croatia was brought into a personal union with Hungary that endured until 1918. Although the nature of the union naturally varied during the long period of its existence, Croatia never lost its identity among the lands of the Crown of St. Stephen.[12] Dalmatia, one of the three provinces of the "triune" kingdom of Croatia, was long disputed with Venice, which in the fifteenth century acquired it. Slavonia, another province, was lost by Croatia to Turkey in the sixteenth century.

COLONIZATION To develop the resources of Hungary and augment revenues, the Hungarian kings, like the Bohemian monarchs, invited foreign settlers, especially after the great Mongol (Tartar) invasion in 1241, which left the country devastated and depopulated. The Szekels, a people kindred to the Magyars, were settled in eastern Transylvania to guard the Carpathian passes against eastern marauders. The Cumans, another Asian people dispersed by the Mongol invasion, were· allowed to settle in eastern Hungary. Uninvited and scarcely noticed, Ruthenians (Ukrainians), fleeing from Mongol rule in Russia, settled in northeastern Hungary. Of greater economic

[12] Unless otherwise stated, Hungary will be used here as including Transylvania and Croatia.

importance for the country were the "Saxon" settlers (really Germans from the Rhineland), who cleared forests and developed agriculture, mining, and trade in mountainous, sparsely populated northern Hungary (Slovakia) and Transylvania and built towns throughout the kingdom.

By the end of the thirteenth century, whether as a result of the survival of pre-Magyar peoples[13] or the arrival of later colonists, Hungary was a multinational kingdom in which the Magyars were probably a minority. In the nationalistic nineteenth century Hungary's multinational character became a threat to its integrity, but in the thirteenth century this feature scarcely mattered, as the medieval concept of *populus* (people) had a corporate rather than ethnic basis.

FEUDALISM   Aligned with Western Europe, Hungary was exposed to western feudal influences. In 1222, seven years after the English barons obtained the Magna Charta from King John, the Hungarian nobles exacted from King Andrew II (1205–1235) a "Golden Bull" confirming their feudal privileges. It exempted the nobility and clergy from taxation, granted them freedom to dispose of their domains as they saw fit, guaranteed them against arbitrary imprisonment and confiscation of their property, and provided that no land or office was to be given to foreigners or Jews. If the king should violate these privileges, the nobles had the right to "resist and oppose" *(jus resistendi)* his actions, "without imputation of treason."

In 1298 the last Arpád king granted the privileged estates (nobles and clergy) the right to meet in annual diets in order to inquire into the state of the kingdom and the conduct of royal officials. The estates of Transylvania, Croatia, and Slavonia met in their own diets.

---

[13] Modern nationalist Rumanian and Slovak historians, on the one hand, and Magyar historians, on the other, in an effort to establish a prior historical claim to Transylvania and Slovakia, heatedly argue whether the Rumanians were in Transylvania and the Slovaks in Slovakia before the arrival of the Magyars in the ninth century (Rumanian and Slovak theses) or "infiltrated" these areas afterward (Magyar thesis).

THE ANGEVINS With the extinction of the Árpád dynasty in 1301 Hungary was plunged into confusion, which lasted until 1308 when the estates elected as king Charles Robert of the Italian (Neapolitan) branch of the French feudal dynasty of Anjou. The Angevin dynasty (1308–1385) raised Hungary to the peak of its medieval prestige and prosperity. Charles I (1308–1342) and his son Louis (Lajos) the Great (1342–1382) were statesmen of the first order. Charles found Hungary in anarchy. When he died, royal power was fully restored. Louis' will was never challenged. Both Charles and Louis carefully balanced the upper and lower nobility (magnates and gentry) and the towns, and required from each fulfillment of their function in a feudal society. The principal feudal responsibility of the nobility was defense of the country. In time of invasion or great emergencies all nobles were subject to be called for service in the *insurrectio* (general levy). Charles introduced and Louis perfected the banderial military system. By custom the nobles served under the "banner" *(banderium)* of the king, queen, or royal and county officials. Charles required that the wealthy magnates also provide banners, each to consist of fifty mounted ironclad men. To make up a banner, the magnates had to engage the services of lesser nobles, who became their retainers.

The function of the towns was to produce and exchange goods. Both Charles and Louis showed favor to towns and gave careful attention to economic matters. Thanks in part to the great productivity of the gold and silver mines in northern Hungary and Transylvania, the towns and the country as a whole enjoyed great prosperity during the Angevin rule. Charles and Louis were steeped in the chivalric lore of France and Italy. Their courts became scenes of tournaments and chivalric pageantry. Louis' attempt to establish a university at Pécs proved abortive, but he gave the country a fixed capital. Hungarian coronations were traditionally held at Székesfehérvár (Stuhlweissenburg), but the kings held court and the diets met in different towns. Louis set up a resplendent court at Buda on the Danube River, and the capital remained fixed there until the Turkish occupation of Buda in the sixteenth century.

Charles' energies had been absorbed by the task of consolidating his power. His foreign policy was, consequently, relatively peaceful. Louis, on the other hand, was able to launch a grand foreign policy designed to enhance Angevin prestige. He recovered Dalmatia from Venice and reduced Bosnia, Serbia, Wallachia, and Moldavia to client status. He reached the peak of his prestige in 1370 when he was elected king of Poland. Unfortunately, he left no male heirs, and a period of confusion followed his death. Ultimately, Sigismund, son of Emperor Charles IV and husband of Louis' daughter Mary, became king. Louis' other daughter Hedvig (Jadwiga) became queen of Poland, and the personal union of Hungary and Poland was dissolved.

SIGISMUND LUXEMBURG   During the long reign of Sigismund I (1387–1437) Hungary's prestige, so high under the Anjous, entered an eclipse. Alarmed by the Turks' destruction of Serbia and Bulgaria, Sigismund appealed to the pope to proclaim a crusade. In 1396, in response to the papal proclamation, German, French, English, and other knights gathered at Buda to join Sigismund in the holy march against the Turkish infidels. The expedition had barely reached Bulgaria when it was intercepted by the Turks at Nicopolis on the Danube River and totally destroyed. Sigismund barely escaped with his life. The loss of Dalmatia to Venice, this time definite, marked another setback for his foreign policy.

Owing to his preoccupation with a divided Germany, the divided papacy, and the Hussite revolt in Bohemia, Sigismund was frequently absent from Hungary. As a consequence, royal authority declined. The great magnates became turbulent. Always in need of money for his far-flung schemes, Sigismund dissipated the wealth accumulated by the Anjous. He pawned off, and never redeemed, the prosperous German towns of Spiš (Szepes, Zips) in northern Hungary to the king of Poland. The Turkish occupation of the Balkans disrupted old European trade routes through Hungary and contributed to the decline of the towns.

Sigismund's reign in Hungary, the same as his rule in Bohemia, left the country internally troubled and externally weakened at a time when it had to face the rising Turkish threat.

Twilight of Independent Hungary and Bohemia

THE TURKISH MENACE Sigismund joined Hungary and Bohemia in a personal union. Although the union soon lapsed, the destinies of the two countries continued to be closely linked in the fifteenth century. The reign of the first Habsburg, Albrecht II (1438–1439), which continued the Hungarian-Bohemian union, proved but a short interlude. On his death, the Bohemian estates accepted his posthumously born son Ladislav I (1440–1457). However, the Hungarian diet, apprehensive about the prospect of a long and weak regency for Ladislav Posthumus while the Turks loomed menacingly on the southern border, elected the king of Poland, Wladyslaw, as their ruler.

Albrecht's widow decided to contest the Hungarian election. She engaged the services of a Czech soldier of fortune, Jan (John) Jiskra of Brandeis, to enforce her son's claim. With a band of Hussite mercenaries Jiskra occupied northwestern Hungary (Slovakia) and held it for the infant king. Wladyslaw's claim, however, was supported by another *condottiero,* János (John) Hunyadi, a Transylvanian nobleman who had won fame fighting the Turks, and the greater part of the country accepted the Polish king. The Hungarian-Polish union likewise proved shortlived. Wladyslaw (Ulászló) I (1440–1444) died only four years later at Varna on the Black Sea coast in Bulgaria while leading a crusade against the Turks. The Hungarians then accepted Ladislav (László) I Posthumus (1444–1457), and Hunyadi became administrator of the country during his minority.

Hunyadi continued the war with the Turks with varying success. However, in 1456 (only three years after the fall of Constantinople) when Mehmet the Conqueror led the Turks against Belgrade, the great fortress at the confluence of the Danube and Sava rivers that guarded the entry to the Hungarian plain, Hunyadi decisively defeated him. Mehmet then devoted his energies to consolidating the Turkish hold on the Balkans by conquering the remainder of Serbia, Bosnia, and Montenegro, the Albanians, and the Peloponnese and also to rounding out his empire in Asia Minor. For the next sixty-five years the Turks launched no major campaign against Hungary. Unfortunately, the Hungarians failed to put to good use the respite thus offered them.

NATIONAL KINGS   The successful defense of Belgrade was Hunyadi's last service to Hungary. He died of fever incurred during the siege of Belgrade in the same year, and Ladislav Posthumus followed him into the grave, a victim of the plague, in the following year. For the last time in their history both Hungary and Bohemia then chose national kings. While the Hungarians elected Hunyadi's son Mátyás (Matthias)—surnamed Corvinus (after the black raven in his coat of arms)—the Bohemians chose Jiří (George) of Poděbrady, a Czech Hussite nobleman who had served as administrator of Bohemia for Ladislav Posthumus.

Matthias I (1458–1490) was a typical Renaissance prince— brilliant, versatile, a connoisseur and patron of the arts, versed in the new humanistic learning, and completely void of scruple or principle. He introduced printing in Hungary, established a university, and collected a large library. Unfortunately, neither the *Bibliotheca Corvina* nor the university survived him long. An able soldier and statesman, he created, around the nucleus of Hussite mercenaries, the famous professional Black Army as an instrument to keep in check the turbulent great magnates, who tended to regard him as an upstart because of his lack of "royal blood," and also to promote his ambitious foreign policy. As the son of a famous Turk fighter, Matthias was generally expected to continue the struggle against the Turks. However, since the Turks became inactive on the Hungarian border after 1456, he turned his attention to the west. He conceived a bold scheme to seize Austria and Bohemia and to replace the Habsburgs on the imperial throne.

George I (1458–1471), the "heretic king" of Bohemia, though an able soldier and statesman, was a much simpler man than Matthias. A moderate Hussite, he sought to appease the religious, political, and social quarrels that the Hussite wars had left in their wake. In this effort he came between two fires. On the one hand, the Catholics regarded the Compacts of Basel as but a tactical retreat and wished to wipe out the stain of Hussite heresy. On the other, radical Hussites and the new "Unity of (Czech) Brethren" *(Unitas Fratrum)* regarded the Compacts of Basel as insufficient and wished to break with the Catholic Church completely. The Brethren were a pietist sect founded by a lay preacher Peter Chelčický, who accepted the radical religious and social program of the Hussites but laid a stress on the Fifth Commandment "Thou shalt not kill!" Unlike the Hussites, the Czech Brethren were pacifists.

In 1464 the pope excommunicated George and later released the Bohemians from their oath of allegiance to him. Matthias, whose first wife was George's daughter, undertook to enforce the ban against him. During the ensuing war (1468–1478) Matthias succeeded in detaching Moravia, Silesia, and the Lusatias from Bohemia, and was recognized as king of Bohemia in the dissident provinces. He also succeeded in overrunning Lower Austria and detaching it from the Habsburg domains, but he died suddenly at Vienna before completing the schemes.

In the end the conflict was settled when Bohemia and Hungary entered into a personal union again. In 1471, on the death of George I, the Bohemian diet elected Wladyslaw Jagellon, son of the king of Poland, king. In 1491, on the death of Matthias I, the Hungarians likewise chose him. Upon becoming king of Hungary, as Ulászló II, Wladyslaw restored the dissident provinces to Bohemia and Lower Austria to the Habsburgs.

JAGELLON KINGS   Polish nationalist historians are wont to write glowingly of the grandeur of the "Jagellon system," which linked Poland-Lithuania, Bohemia, and Hungary under the Polish dynasty. In fact, however, it was not much of a "system"; the three countries failed to coordinate their policies. Vladislav II proved an exceptionally weak ruler. His Czech subjects nicknamed him "King Dobře" (King Okay) because of his habit of assenting without cavil to any proposal laid before him. His son Louis (1516–1526), known in Bohemia as Ludvík I and in Hungary as Lajos II, died before he had a chance to prove himself.

Jagellon rule in Bohemia and Hungary was marked by an almost complete breakdown of royal authority, the growth of power of the great lords, the impoverishment of the small nobles, the decline of the towns, and the harsh enserfment of the peasants. The transformation of Bohemia and Hungary from feudal monarchies into *Ständestaaten*, that is, states dominated by the privileged estates, which had begun earlier, was completed under the Jagellons. Not all estates, however, were equally privileged. Owing to the peculiar economic conditions at the time,[14] the great lords achieved unprecedented wealth and power. But, the knights in Bohemia were often forced off the land and had to make a living as mercenaries or retainers of the great lords. In Hungary the gentry, though often impoverished, fared better. While the Bohemian lords and knights formed separate estates, the Hungarian magnates and gentry were legally equal and formed a single estate. The magnates and gentry, together with the clergy, sat in a common diet. In 1514 the Hungarian royal towns were given representation in the diet, but owing to their growing economic weakness they never achieved much influence. The peasants, who in Hungary were called, with cruel frankness, *misera plebs contribuens* (wretched taxpaying folk), stood outside the corporate structure of Bohemian and Hungarian society, as they did everywhere else in Europe at the time.

In the late fifteenth century Bohemia was swept by peasant outbreaks. In 1514 nearly all of Hungary was engulfed in a great peasant jacquerie (the Dózsa Rebellion),[15] which ·was attended by terrible excesses and was put down in 1515 only with great difficulty by the Transylvanian *voevod* (prince) János (John) Zápolyai. Thirsting for revenge, the Hungarian diet then decreed the "real and perpetual servitude" *(mera et perpetua servitus)* of all but a few categories of the peasants. Henceforth they were tied to the soil. The new stringent conditions of peasant serfdom were codified and perpetuated in the *Tripartitum*, a

---

[14] See pp. 58–60.

[15] The rebellion was precipitated by a call for a crusade against the Turks. Few nobles responded to the call, but a host of impoverished peasants joined under the banner of a Szekel soldier, György Dózsa. Left to themselves, the peasant crusaders *(kuruc)* turned against the lords instead of the Turks.

compilation of Hungarian customary law published in 1517 by the great jurist István (Stephen) Verböczy.[16] Yet it would be an error to attribute the deterioration of political, economic, and social conditions in Hungary and Bohemia to the Jagellons alone; it was a culmination of a trend that had begun in the late fourteenth century. Nor was it a product of specific Hungarian and Bohemian conditions alone; general European conditions at the time were an important factor.

In foreign affairs the Jagellon rule was one of weakness and drift. The only notable event was the conclusion of the Habsburg-Jagellon family compact at Vienna in 1515.[17] It was only a dynastic arrangement, however, and did not bind possessions of the two families in an alliance.

BATTLE OF MOHÁCS The accession of Sultan Suleiman I (1520–1566) to the Ottoman throne marked the resumption of Turkish expansion in Europe. Suleiman, who was known to the Europeans as the Magnificent and to his own people as the Lawgiver *(el Kanuni)*, was a cultured and sophisticated gentleman of the Renaissance age and an easy match, both as soldier and statesman, for any of his famous contemporaries—Charles V and Ferdinand I, Francis I Valois, Henry VIII Tudor, or Ivan the Terrible. Under his rule the Ottoman empire reached its apogee, stretching from Algiers to the Persian Gulf and from Hungary and the steppes of southern Russia to the cataracts of the Nile. He opened his reign by seizing Belgrade (1521) and Rhodes (1522), both of which Mehmet the Conqueror had attempted to conquer but failed.

In 1525 Charles V of Spain defeated and captured Francis I of France at Pavia. From his captivity at Madrid the French king managed to send a secret envoy to Istanbul to solicit the aid of the sultan. Suleiman agreed to relieve pressure on France by launching a diversionary campaign against the Habsburgs in their rear. In April 1526 he set out from Istanbul at the head of some 200,000 men to invade Hungary. Alarmed, King Louis

---

[16] Although the *Tripartitum* was never formally promulgated by the diet, it was generally accepted as authoritative until 1848.

[17] See p. 7.

appealed to Catholic Europe for help, but there was little response. No help came from his brother-in-law Ferdinand I and only token aid from Poland and Bohemia. Hungary was left to its own devices. Since Vladislav had dissolved Matthias' professional Black Army, the defense of the country depended on the feudal levies. While the nobles' banners were sluggishly assembling at Buda, the Turks reached Belgrade and crossed the Sava and Drava rivers, the natural defense lines of Hungary, without encountering any opposition. In August at the news of their advance into southern Hungary Louis, an inexperienced youth of nineteen, marched south from Buda. The two armies came face to face on the field of Mohács near the Danube. Although his army comprised only about 25,000 men, Louis disregarded advice to await the arrival of a contingent from Transylvania under Zápolyai and one from Croatia and attacked the Turks. In the ensuing encounter the Hungarian army was crushed (August 29, 1526). The king, two archbishops, and the flower of the Hungarian nobility perished in the battle. Two weeks later the Turks entered Buda unopposed. After looting it, they set it on fire and retired from the country.

The battle of Mohács has rightly been called the graveyard of the Hungarian nation. It set off a chain reaction of historical events, the consequences of which Hungary never fully escaped. The death of the childless King Louis at Mohács left vacant the thrones of Hungary and Bohemia and created a dangerous void in East Central Europe. Lest the Turks fill it, the Habsburgs hastened to claim Bohemia and Hungary.

CHAPTER TWO

Formation
of the Habsburg
Empire
1526–1648

Ferdinand I and Maximilian II

ELECTION IN BOHEMIA After the death of his
brother-in-law Louis at Mohács, Ferdinand Habsburg put forth a claim to the crowns of Bohemia and
Hungary on the basis of the Habsburg-Jagellon
agreement of 1515. The Bohemian estates refused
to recognize his hereditary right to the Bohemian
crown and insisted on a free election. On October
22, 1526, the diet of Bohemia duly elected him, and
the diets of Moravia, Silesia, and the Lusatias
quickly followed suit. However, the diets insisted on
guarantees of their corporate privileges and religious freedom. They envisaged not a merger of the
lands of the Bohemian crown with the Habsburg
Erblande in Austria, but a personal union such as
they had entered into with Austria and/or Hungary

in the fifteenth century. A delegation was sent to Vienna to inform Ferdinand of his election and secure the guarantees. He evaded formal agreement to most of the Bohemian demands until his arrival in Prague, where he conceded that he had been freely elected and promised to respect the Compacts of Basel. On February 24, 1527, amidst much pomp, Ferdinand and his wife Anne Jagellon were crowned king and queen of Bohemia. In choosing him, the Bohemian estates could hardly foresee that they had inaugurated 400 years of Habsburg rule in Bohemia, during the course of which their independence would be extinguished.

ELECTION IN HUNGARY   The death of King Louis and most great magnates and high prelates at Mohács left Hungary in complete chaos. János Zápolyai, the Transylvanian prince, who had failed (perhaps intentionally) to reach Mohács in time for the battle, was the only national figure of importance left. He controlled the only substantial body of troops remaining in the country and was regarded as a hero by the Hungarian nobles since he had taken a conspicuous part in suppressing the Dózsa peasant revolt in 1515. It was natural, therefore, that most nobles looked to him for leadership. On November 11, 1526, on the initiative of the jurist Verböczy, a poorly attended diet at Székesfehérvár, the coronation city, elected him king, and on the following day he was crowned.

Meanwhile Ferdinand had advanced his candidacy to the throne through his sister, Louis' widow Maria, on the basis of the Habsburg-Jagellon agreement of 1515. A simple acceptance of Ferdinand as king on the basis of hereditary right was out of the question. However, with the aid of some pro-Habsburg nobles, Maria succeeded in assembling a rump diet at Bratislava (Pozsony, Pressburg) which elected Ferdinand king on December 17, 1526. His claim was strengthened when the diet of Croatia also elected him king on January 1, 1527, although the Slavonian estates declared for Zápolyai.

Thus, in the moment of its supreme humiliation Hungary was saddled with two kings and faced the inevitable prospect of civil war between their respective partisans. This was not long in coming. In July 1527 Ferdinand invaded Hungary at the head of a strong army. By August he had seized Buda, and on November 3 was crowned king—by the same bishop who had crowned Zápolyai the previous year. By early 1528 the resistance of Zápolyai's forces had collapsed, and Zápolyai fled to Poland. For the moment, at least, Ferdinand appeared to have secured Hungary.

CENTRAL ADMINISTRATION   Ferdinand I (1526–1564) has been overshadowed by his brother Charles V and is regarded as a minor figure in European history. Yet he left a considerable mark on it. He was the true founder of the Austrian Habsburg empire. Although he was not a brilliant man, he was firm in character and tenacious in purpose. Like his brother, Ferdinand was a believer in royal absolutism. Although he lived up to the letter of his promises to the Bohemian and Hungarian estates, he set out from the beginning to transform the personal union of his Austrian *Erblande*, Bohemia, and Hungary into a real union.

Ferdinand welded his possessions into a real union by creating a set of central offices in Vienna for their administration as well as that of the German empire: the Privy Council (Hofrat) to advise him on all domestic and foreign affairs, the Chancellery (Hofkanzlei) to handle paper work, the Treasury (Hofkammer), and the War Office (Hofkriegsrat). He also created a Bohemian and a Hungarian Chancellery to handle the special affairs of the two kingdoms. He staffed all these offices with bureaucrats who were paid by him and loyal to him. Although invariably great noblemen, they were drawn from all of his possessions as well as his brother's possessions and, consequently, were held together not by loyalty to any particular country but by loyalty to the dynasty. From then until its collapse in 1918, the Habsburg empire rested on the twin pillars of the Habsburg bureaucracy and army.

SUCCESSION   In 1549, following an abortive rebellion in Bohemia,[1] Ferdinand obliged the Bohemian estates to "accept"

[1] See p. 43.

his son Maximilian in advance as his successor. In 1562 Maximilian was crowned king of Bohemia, and in 1563 he was also accepted and crowned king of Hungary. This established a precedent for "accepting" the Habsburgs as kings in Bohemia and Hungary during the lifetime of their predecessors and prevented conflicts over succession. Although still elective monarchies in principle, Bohemia and Hungary had become hereditary Habsburg possessions in fact. When Ferdinand I died, Maximilian II (1564–1576) succeeded him in Bohemia, Hungary, and Germany, without the slightest demur on the part of their estates.

Paradoxically, while securing the unity of his possessions as far as Bohemia and Hungary were concerned, Ferdinand I jeopardized it by partitioning the Habsburg *Erblande* in Austria among his three sons. Maximilian II received Austria "above and below the Enns River" (that is, Upper and Lower Austria); Charles received Inner Austria (Styria, Carinthia, Carniola, Gorizia, Internal Istria, and Trieste); and Ferdinand, the Tyrol and Anterior Austria (Voralberg and the scattered Habsburg possessions in southern Germany known as the *Vorlande*). Three Austrian Habsburg lines were thus established. However, in the seventeenth century the number of male Habsburgs, previously so abundant, abruptly declined. In 1619 the Viennese line and in 1665 the Tyrolese line became extinct, and the unity of the Habsburg *Erblande* was reestablished.

Struggle for Hungary

FIRST SIEGE OF VIENNA From his exile in Poland Zápolyai appealed to European monarchs for support against Ferdinand. When his appeal went unheeded, he turned to Sultan Suleiman, who agreed to intervene in Hungary. On May 10, 1529, Suleiman set out from Istanbul at the head of his army, but because of an unusually rainy summer he did not reach Buda until September 3. The Habsburg garrison surrendered, and Zápolyai was duly installed as king. The Turks then moved on to Vienna, which they reached on September 27, and besieged it. However, it was too late in the season to press the siege to a successful conclusion. On October 16, after several costly and unsuccessful assaults against the walls of the city and after devastating the countryside of Lower Austria, Suleiman raised the siege and returned to Istanbul. All of Catholic Europe, which had watched with bated breath this bold Turkish foray into the heart of Europe, sighed with relief.

If Suleiman had been able to take and hold Vienna, Bohemia and Germany would have been threatened next. But, at that time the Ottoman armies were organized only for summer campaigning—from St. George's Day (April 23) to St. Demetrius' Day (October 26) by Christian reckoning—when their horses could graze in the fields. Vienna lay over a hundred days' march from Istanbul, the starting point of Suleiman's campaigns. Thus, Bohemia and Germany were then beyond the radius of effective Turkish action.

PARTITION OF HUNGARY Fighting in Hungary continued until 1533, when a truce was arranged under which Ferdinand and Zápolyai retained the portions of Hungary that their forces held at the time and both agreed to pay tribute for them to the sultan. The twofold division of Hungary presently became a threefold one.

In 1539 Zápolyai, who was then aged, widowed, and childless, secretly agreed with Ferdinand that on his (Zápolyai's) death Hungary should be reunited. However, he remarried shortly after the pact, and in 1540, soon after his death, his widow bore a son, János Zsigmond (John Sigismund), whom the east Hungarian nobles acclaimed as king. When Ferdinand claimed Zápolyai's part of Hungary, Suleiman intervened, ostensibly to protect the claim of the infant king, but actually to forward his own cause. In 1541 the Turks occupied Buda for the third time, and this time they kept it for themselves. János Zsigmond was installed in Transylvania as tributary prince under Ottoman protection.

Ferdinand resisted the partition until the outbreak of the Schmalkaldic War in Germany and difficulties in Bohemia forced him to yield. In 1547 his envoy in Istanbul concluded a truce that recognized the partition. Moreover, Ferdinand agreed to pay an annual tribute of 30,000 gold ducats to the sultan, thus recognizing him, by implication, as his suzerain in Hungary. Suleiman recognized him as de facto king in Hungary but in practice treated him and János Zsigmond as tributary princes on an equal footing.

Hungary was thus divided into three parts: in the center was Turkish Hungary, which consisted of a wedge of territory with a base in the south stretching from Croatia to Transylvania and an apex in the north reaching into central Slovakia; in the east was the principality of Transylvania, which comprised also a band of Hungarian territory known as the "Parts" *(Partes);* and in the west and north was Habsburg, or Royal, Hungary, which consisted of Croatia (without Slavonia), a narrow band of territory along the Austrian border (present Burgenland), and northern Hungary (Slovakia).

STALEMATE IN HUNGARY   Ferdinand I waged war with Suleiman from 1551 to 1562 to evict the Turks from Hungary as did Maximilian II (1564–1566), but they were unable to dislodge the Turks. In 1566 Suleiman, who was by then aged and infirm, took personal command of his troops. He died while besieging the fortress of Sziget in southwestern Hungary. Although his troops took the fortress, which was heroically defended to the last breath by the Croat noble Nicholas Zrinski (Zrinyi), they, too, were unable to dislodge the Habsburg forces from Hungary. An Ottoman-Habsburg stalemate had developed in Hungary. Despite frequent conflicts, it lasted until the end of the seventeenth century. The Turks held Buda for 145 years. During this time the lines of division in Hungary sometimes shifted, but the balance of forces remained essentially the same.

The three parts of Hungary were not hermetically closed to one another. Their boundaries were not precisely defined lines; rather, they consisted of broad bands of no man's land with chains of fortresses on both sides. The boundaries were quite porous. Population and some trade moved across them. Still the division disrupted and retarded the political, economic, and cultural development of Hungary for at least two centuries. Border warfare was endemic. Whether in time of war or formal peace, raiders from both sides crossed the no man's land to plunder each other's territory. Particularly vexing to the people were the slave raids of the Turkish irregulars *(akinji)*, who annually carried off thousands of men, women, and children to sell them in the slave markets of the Near East. Even Turkish Hungary was not free of this vexation, for the *akinji* did not look too closely on which side of the boundary they caught their prey.

Modern nationalist Hungarian historians are wont to portray Hungary in the sixteenth and seventeenth centuries as the "shield of Christendom" against the Infidel Turk. Actually, it took the combined resources of the Habsburg empire to contain Turkish expansion. Habsburg Hungary was too small and impoverished to provide for its defense. Its defense depended largely on regular Habsburg forces, which were composed mainly of German mercenaries. The money necessary for their upkeep was provided principally by the lands of the Bohemian crown, which were the wealthiest among the Habsburg possessions. The Bohemian historian Anton Gindely (1829-1892) estimated that about 95 percent of the revenue voted by the diets of the lands of the Bohemian crown from 1526 to 1627 was taken out of the country by the Habsburgs. A large part of this was used for the defense of Hungary.

An important role in the defense of the Habsburg empire against the Turks was played by the famous "Military Frontier" *(Vojna Krajina)* in Croatia. It was organized during Ferdinand's reign by removing border districts from the jurisdiction of the diet of Croatia and placing them under the War Office in Vienna. The land in the districts belonged to the crown. The "frontiersmen" *(graničari, Grenzer)* were partly native Croats and partly Serb refugees *(uskoci)* from the Ottoman empire. They were free of serfdom and were given the use of the crown lands. In return, they owed lifelong and hereditary military service along the turbulent Turkish border. Fighting under German officers, they became famous for their military prowess and for their loyalty to the Habsburgs. Money for the upkeep of the Military Frontier was provided by the provinces of Inner Austria, the lands most exposed to Turkish attacks.

TURKISH HUNGARY   Suleiman organized his share of Hungary into four (later five) districts *(pashaliks)* under a *beglerbeg* (regional governor) at Buda. The Turks dispossessed the land-owners in Hungary, as they had done in Serbia and Bulgaria in the fourteenth century. The nobles were either killed or taken into captivity, unless they managed to flee to other parts of Hungary. The sultan kept one-fifth of the confiscated land for the use of the Ottoman state and distributed the rest among the Turkish feudal soldiers *(spahis)*. The peasants, in principle, were not disturbed. In fact, they were freed from serfdom, which was unknown in the Ottoman empire[2] at the time. Nevertheless, they suffered because of Turkish Hungary's location as an exposed outpost of the empire in Europe.

Southern Hungary, which had experienced the first impact of the Turkish invasions, was largely depopulated. Subsequently, seminomadic Serb herdsmen (mistakenly called Vlahs, like the Rumanians) migrated into the area from the Balkans. Even further north, where the indigenous Magyar population survived, the peasants, owing to the prevailing insecurity of life, were forced to abandon farming for herding. Village life was insecure, and the peasant population tended to be concentrated in relatively large "village towns." Much of the fertile land in Turkish Hungary, which previously had produced surpluses of grain, was used for grazing only or reverted to wilderness. This had an adverse effect on the economies of Royal Hungary and Transylvania, which were the less fertile parts of the country.

TRANSYLVANIA   In 1542, after the Turks broke up Hungary and isolated Transylvania, representatives of the three privileged classes in Transylvania—the Magyar nobles, the Saxon (German) townsmen, and the Szekel frontiersmen—met at Turda (Torda). They reaffirmed their old feudal "Union of Three Nations" and formed a diet. Subsequently, representa-

---

[2] It was not until the late seventeenth and the eighteenth centuries, with the progressive decay of the Ottoman empire, that the feudal estates *(timars)* were transformed into hereditary estates *(chifliks)* and the Balkan peasants were reduced to a form of bondage.

tives of the nobility in the adjoining Hungarian Parts were admitted to the diet. The Rumanians, who constituted a majority of the Transylvanian population, were not recognized as a nation and admitted to the diet, for they belonged overwhelmingly to the peasant class and could not, therefore, by contemporary definition, constitute a "nation."

Because of the balance of Ottoman and Habsburg forces in Hungary, Transylvania enjoyed a precarious independence during most of the period of partition. In some ways its position resembled that of modern Switzerland. It was a sort of neutral buffer between Turkey, Austria, and Poland. Before Mohács the Transylvanian princes were appointed by the Hungarian kings and were merely administrative and military officials. After Mohács they were elected by the diet, and by playing off the Turks against the Habsburgs, they were able to act the part of sovereign rulers. It was a very dangerous game, however, calling for diplomatic and military skills of the highest order, which not all of them had.

As an Ottoman protectorate, Transylvania suffered less from Turkish marauding than did Royal Hungary. The Saxon towns were able to trade with the Ottoman empire as well as the Habsburg empire, Germany, and Poland, and enjoyed a moderate prosperity. Since class, religion, and language coincided in Transylvania, social differences were sharply drawn; the lot of the despised Rumanian peasants was particularly hard.

ROYAL HUNGARY   Although at times the smallest segment of the country, Habsburg Hungary was the carrier of the idea of the Hungarian state. Ferdinand I lived up to the letter of his coronation promise to respect the feudal constitution of Hungary. The diet continued to meet, and the feudal offices of the kingdom were maintained. However, gradually the powers of the king increased and the importance of Hungarian institutions declined.

The creation of imperial offices in Vienna for the administration of all Habsburg possessions diminished the importance of the Hungarian feudal offices. As early as 1531 the Hungarian offices were removed from exposed Buda to Bratislava (Pozsony, Pressburg), near the Austrian border. Here they were safer from the Turks but under closer supervision of the court. After the partition of Hungary, the diet met and coronations were held in Bratislava. The highest official of Hungary was the palatine. He held the most important administrative, judicial, and military functions in the country and represented the estates vis-à-vis the king. In 1534, on the death of the incumbent palatine, Ferdinand I failed to appoint a successor. Instead, he appointed a *locumtenens regni* (viceroy), who represented the king vis-à-vis the estates. Although a palatine was later appointed, the importance of his office had diminished. The importance of Royal Hungary was also limited by the autonomy of Croatia, which had its own diet and administration under the *ban* (an official corresponding to the palatine in Hungary). From the middle of the sixteenth century the Croat diet sent a delegation to the Hungarian diet to assure some coordination between Royal Hungary and Croatia.

Another factor that strengthened the king's position was the decline of the old Hungarian nobility. Many of them had perished at Mohács, and others were impoverished by the loss of their estates in Turkish Hungary. Their place was taken by new magnates who had won distinction in Habsburg service. Ferdinand I began the practice of conferring hereditary aristocratic titles (for example, baron, count) on loyal magnates.[3] This tended to formalize the distinction between magnates and gentry, which had grown since the partition because the loss of the most fertile Hungarian lands to the Turks put a premium on large estates that could produce surpluses of food. Later, in 1608, the diet, which had until then sat as a single house, was divided into the "House of Magnates" *(Tabula Magnatum)* and the "House of Nobles" *(Tabula Nobilium)*. In the former sat all the magnates, royal officials, and high dignitaries of the Church. In the latter sat the deputies of the gentry, elected in

---

[3] Before Mohács the Hungarian nobility, like the Polish, bore no hereditary aristocratic titles. The *Tripartitum* recognized no distinction between large and small nobles (magnates and gentry).

the counties, and representatives of the royal towns as well as canons of the Church.

Ferdinand I was disappointed by his repeated failure to reunite Hungary, and toward the end of his rule he neglected the country. The defense of Royal Hungary cost more than it yielded in revenue. During the era of partition the Habsburgs tended to value it principally as a buffer between their more valuable possessions in Austria and in Bohemia and the Turks.

Protestant Reformation and Catholic Counter-Reformation

IMPACT The formation of the Habsburg empire coincided with the spread of the Protestant Reformation. Whether emanating from Wittenberg or Geneva, the Protestant Reformation gained a wide following in Austria, Bohemia, and Hungary, where by the middle of the sixteenth century probably a majority of the peoples had accepted the Lutheran, the Calvinist, or the more radical Anabaptist and Unitarian doctrines. The Protestant revolt had caught the Catholic Church unprepared, but by the middle of the sixteenth century the Church reformed its ranks. At the Council of Trent (1545–1564) it redefined its doctrines and under Jesuit guidance launched the Catholic Counter-Reformation. The two movements went hand in hand with the Renaissance movement in the Habsburg empire. Unlike the Italian Renaissance, the Northern Renaissance had religious roots. It reached a climax in the sixteenth century, when the Italian Renaissance had already faded, and was inextricably intertwined with the religious currents of the day.

Initially, the Reformation and Counter-Reformation had a stimulating influence on the cultures of the peoples of the Habsburg empire. The Protestants translated the Bible into vernaculars and used vernaculars in their church services. Both Protestants and Catholics used vernaculars in their polemical writings in an effort to gain as wide an audience as possible for their respective points of view. The growth of native religious literature gave the intellectual life of Austria, Bohemia, and

Hungary a broader base than it had had when the language of church and intellectual intercourse was Latin only. Ultimately, however, the Reformation and Counter-Reformation had a deadening effect on the cultural development of these lands. They caused an excessive concentration on religious subjects and neglect of secular matters, exacted a rigid adherence to religious orthodoxy, whether Protestant or Catholic, engendered a spirit of religious and intellectual intolerance, and provoked civil and religious wars, which interacted with international wars and kept the empire in a state of constant turmoil until the Peace of Westphalia.

AUSTRIA Luther's doctrines gained supporters among all classes in the Austrian duchies as early as the 1520s. Ferdinand I, who was a loyal son of the Catholic Church, was much alarmed. When the "Peasant War" (1524–1526) spread from Germany to Austria, he savagely suppressed it. When Luther's sympathizers tried to take over the University of Vienna, he prevented it, whereupon the Lutheran professors and students departed for German universities. But, Ferdinand was unable to stem the rising tide of the religious revolt, because the Catholic Church was in a state of complete disarray and was unable to defend itself. Therefore, at the Council of Trent Ferdinand urged a compromise with the Protestants. It was not until the arrival of the Jesuits in Vienna in the 1550s that the Catholic Church began to close its ranks and fight back. Among them was the great Dutch Jesuit (St.) Peter Canisius (1521–1597), whose simple, clear catechism became for the Catholics what Luther's catechism was for the Lutherans.

It was rumored that Maximilian II contemplated conversion, although probably for political rather than religious reasons. In the end, under the pressure of his family, he did not take the fateful step. However, he was an affable, charming, and easy-going man and showed tolerance toward the Protestants in Lower and Upper Austria. His brothers were less tolerant. Duke Charles stoutly fought the Protestants in Inner Austria, but he was forced to grant them freedom in a "religious pacification" in 1572. More successful was Duke Ferdinand of the Tyrol, among whose peasantry Protestantism never gained much of a following. Protestantism reached a high tide in Austria around 1570. By then most of the powerful Austrian feudal houses—the Starhembergs, Polheims, Dietrichsteins, Khevenhulers, Zinzendorffs, and others—as well as townsmen and peasants adhered to it.

SLOVENES AND CROATS The Lutheran doctrine also gained a large following among the Slovenes of Styria, Carinthia, and Carniola. From these provinces it spread to neighboring Croatia, where the foremost feudal family, the Zrinskis (Zrinyis), adopted it. Most energetic among the Slovene reformers was Primož Trubar (Primus Truber). He translated the New Testament and composed a catechism and hymnal in the Slovene language; this marked the first use of that tongue for literary purposes. Štefan Konzul and Antun Dalmatin, Croat reformers, translated the Bible into the Croat language. Both Slovene and Croat religious literature was printed at Urach near Tübingen in Germany, where a printing press with the Cyrillic alphabet was set up to diffuse the Protestant doctrines among the Southern Slavs.

HUNGARY The Turkish invasion in 1526 coincided with and facilitated the spread of the Protestant Reformation in Hungary. The death of two archbishops and five bishops at Mohács disorganized the Catholic Church and left it defenseless. Luther's doctrines found early adherents among the German townsmen in northern Hungary (Slovakia) and Transylvania. Partly under the influence of the Germans and partly under the influence of Protestant preachers from Bohemia, many Slovaks embraced Luther's doctrines. Among the Magyars, Mátyás (Matthias) Biró was an early convert to them, but after returning from a long exile in Geneva Biró introduced Calvin's doctrines in Hungary.

　　Until the middle of the sixteenth century there was no clear-cut division between the Lutherans and Calvinists in Hungary. In 1549, however, five royal towns in northern Hun-

gary adopted the *Confessio Pentapolitana,* which was based
on the Lutheran Confession of Augsburg. Other German towns
and the Slovaks followed suit. The Magyars, on the other hand,
generally accepted a Calvinist confession of faith drafted by
Mátyás Biró and Peter Melius and adopted at a synod in Debrecen in 1567. Debrecen became the Hungarian Geneva and
Calvinism a Magyar national faith.

In 1541 a Magyar preacher, János Sylvester, published
the New Testament and in 1590 another preacher, Kálman
Károli, the whole Bible in the Magyar language, which previously had scarcely been used for literary purposes. The
Slovaks, owing to their linguistic proximity to the Czechs, were
able to draw on the rich Czech religious literature. They accepted the Czech Bible of Kralice and used the Czech language
for literary and liturgical purposes. In turn, they made an
important contribution to Czech Protestant literature with the
publication in 1638 of the *Cithara Sanctorum (Harp of the
Saints).* Known better as the *Tranoscius Hymnal,* it was a collection of about four hundred hymns—some original compo-
sitions, others partly translated from German, and still others
adapted from old Hussite hymns by Jiří (George) Tranovský,
a Silesian preacher who had found refuge in Slovakia during
the Thirty Years' War.

TRANSYLVANIA The principality of Transylvania was the first
European country to adopt complete religious freedom. Because
of the precarious balance between nationalities in Transylvania
and their identification with different faiths—the Saxon townsmen with Lutheranism, the Magyar nobles and Szekel frontiersmen with Calvinism, and the Rumanian peasants with Greek
Orthodoxy—the Transylvanian diet found it expedient to
recognize in successive decrees all "established" denominations
in the principality.

In 1550 the diet recognized the Catholics and Protestansts,
whose numbers at the time were roughly equal. In 1564 after
the Protestants had formally divided into Lutherans and Calvinists, the diet recognized both as equal. Finally, in 1572 the
Unitarians were also recognized as "established" and on equal

footing with the Catholics and Protestants. Just as in politics for the Rumanians, so also in religion, the Orthodox Church, which was the church of the Rumanians, was granted only "tolerance" but not equality with the "established" faiths.

BOHEMIA   The lands of the Bohemian crown were well prepared for the Protestant Reformation by the Hussite upheaval in the fifteenth century. Unlike the Hussite movement, which appealed principally to the Czechs, the Lutheran movement appealed to the Germans of Bohemia as well as to the Czechs. Luther's defense of John Hus in his famous debate with the Catholic theologian Johann Eck at Leipzig in 1519 naturally gave great satisfaction to the Czechs. His defense of Hus and his later encouragement of the Bohemian Protestants created a climate of cordiality between the Czech and German Protestants, which had never existed before between the Czechs and Germans and which was to disappear forever during the subsequent period of Counter-Reformation.

A century after its emergence, the Utraquist Church of Bohemia was already in decline. Based on the vague Compacts of Basel, it now differed from its parent Catholic Church only in the symbolic matter of allowing the lay to partake of the Eucharist "in both species" (the cup and the wafer). In competition with the new doctrines of Luther and Calvin, it began to disintegrate. Like the Church of England at the time, it divided into a conservative wing that leaned toward Catholicism and a radical wing (the neo-Utraquists) that leaned toward Protestantism. Sometimes behind the facade of the Utraquist Church and sometimes openly, Lutheranism and Calvinism spread in Bohemia. Even the Anabaptists gained a modest following.

The Unity of Czech Brethren likewise grew in numbers and influence. Beginning in the fifteenth century as a sectarian movement with appeal only to the humblest elements of the Bohemian society, it now attracted many townsmen and noblemen as well as the foremost Czech intellectual leaders. In fact, the movement became the center of a remarkable Czech literary efflorescence in the sixteenth century. Its leader Jan Blahoslav composed the first Czech grammar and standardized the Czech literary language. A committee of Czech Brethren was responsible for the magnificent Czech translation of the Bible (the "Bible of Kralice"), which remains for the Czech and Slovak Protestants to this day what the King James version of the Bible is for English-speaking Protestants. Schools of the Czech Brethren were the best of their kind not only in Bohemia but also in Poland, to which many Czech Brethren emigrated after 1547 to escape a renewal of official harassment.

Ferdinand I viewed the spread of Protestantism in Bohemia with alarm, but he was hampered in his efforts to halt it by his imperfect control of the country and his coronation pledge to respect the Utraquist Church. Protestantism could not be stamped out as long as the nobles and towns retained their feudal privileges. He scored an important success in 1547 when, by quickly moving troops into Bohemia, he nipped in the bud a movement to form a Bohemian Protestant army to go to the aid of the Schmalkaldic League in Germany.[4] He took the occasion to assert his authority. The leaders of the movement were arrested, four of them executed, and the property of all was confiscated. The towns involved in the movement were fined and placed under appointed "royal mayors." The bans against the Czech Brethren and other sectarians were renewed and harshly enforced. Two years later the Bohemian estates were obliged to accept Maximilian II in advance as their king.[5]

Ferdinand I sought by all means to strengthen the demoralized and disorganized Catholic Church in Bohemia. In 1556 the Jesuits were introduced there. The Clementinum, their college in Prague, soon became the arsenal of the Counter-Reformation in that land. In 1561 Ferdinand obtained from Pope Pius IV the appointment of an archbishop to the archiepiscopal see of Prague, which had been unoccupied since the outbreak of the Hussite wars 140 years earlier. Meanwhile, the Bohemian diet endlessly discussed the doctrinal confusion

[4] See p. 9.
[5] See pp. 30–31.

in the Utraquist Church, but Ferdinand opposed and Maximilian evaded a solution. In 1575, after long debates between leaders and factions, the diet submitted to Maximilian the "Bohemian Confession" *(Confessio Bohemica)*, which was based largely on the Lutheran Confession of Augsburg and was designed to create a national Bohemian Protestant Church. Maximilian refused to approve it, contenting himself with giving the neo-Utraquists a verbal assurance of freedom of worship and allowing them to elect fifteen "defenders" *(defensores)* of their faith. This was, at best, a policy of salutary neglect, which might be reversed by a less tolerant sovereign.

Rudolf II and Matthias I

RUDOLF II   The accession of Emperor Rudolf II (1576–1612), who had been accepted by the estates of Bohemia, Hungary, Lower and Upper Austria, and Germany during Maximilian's lifetime, marked the beginning of the militant Counter-Reformation in the Habsburg empire. Harassment of the Protestants, previously sporadic and camouflaged, now became systematic and open.

Educated in Spain at the court of Philip II, Rudolf was a zealous Catholic. Like several of his Spanish relatives, he was mentally unbalanced and eccentric, and toward the end of his reign he was incompetent to rule. His only claim to distinction was his early interest in the Scientific Revolution that was then beginning in Europe. He took a keen, though amateur, interest in the sciences, failing to distinguish, for instance, between chemistry and alchemy and astronomy and astrology. It was at his court in Prague that Tyho de Brahe and Johann Kepler accomplished their pioneer work in astronomy, while casting horoscopes for him.

Rudolf transferred the Habsburg court to Prague. During his long reign the Hradčany castle in Prague rather than the Hofburg in Vienna was the focal point of Habsburg policy. Thanks in part to his patronage, the Gothic core of the "Old Town" of Prague began to be surrounded by churches and palaces built in the new baroque style, which came to symbolize Spanish influence during the Counter-Reformation.

HUNGARY, TRANSYLVANIA, AND THE TURKS   In 1586 the Jesuits were brought to Royal Hungary to launch the Counter-Reformation. However, as long as Transylvania and Turkish Hungary remained havens of religious freedom, the Protestant cause in Hungary was safe. In their part of Hungary the Turks granted the Christians complete religious freedom. They were quite indifferent to the Christians' religious quarrels, regarding all Christians as misguided and contemptible *rayah* (cattle). However, since the Habsburgs were champions of the Catholic cause, the Turks were inclined to protect the Protestant cause.

After the death of János Zsigmond the diet in Transylvania elected a Magyar magnate, István (Stephen) Báthori (1570–1581), prince. Báthori, who was an able soldier and statesman, was elected king of Poland in 1575. Although a Catholic himself, he respected the religious rights of the Protestants. To balance Habsburg pressure on Transylvania and Muscovite pressure on Poland, he pursued a pro-Turkish policy, but he was by no means a Turkish puppet. This policy was pursued also by his brother and successor as Transylvanian prince, Krystóf (Christopher) Báthori (1581–1586). But István's son, Zsigmond (Sigismund) Báthori (1586–1602), shifted to a pro-Habsburg policy, which had disastrous results for Transylvania.

In 1593 what had begun as border warfare between Hungary and Turkey flared up into full-scale war. With Zsigmond Báthori's approval, Transylvania was occupied by Habsburg forces under the ruthless general Giorgio Basta, who inaugurated a reign of terror against the Protestants. During the period of confusion that followed the country was briefly occupied by the Wallachian prince Michael the Brave.[6] Zsigmond's incom-

---

[6] Since Prince Michael had previously occupied Moldavia, his occupation of Transylvania united the Rumanians for the first time in recorded history under a Rumanian leader. Although he scarcely acted as an agent of Rumanian nationalism, he has been acclaimed by modern Rumanian nationalist historians as a national hero.

petence and Basta's excesses provoked a reaction and produced a leader—István (Stephen) Bocskay, a Calvinist Magyar nobleman. Bocskay drove the Habsburg forces not only out of Transylvania but also out of northern Hungary. In addition, he raided Moravia. In 1606, in the Treaty of Vienna, Bocskay forced the Habsburgs to recognize him as prince of Transylvania and to guarantee the religious freedom of the Protestants in Royal Hungary. Later in the same year, at Zsitva Torok, he mediated a peace between the Turks and the Habsburgs which left the balance of their forces in Hungary unchanged.

Although the Peace of Zsitva Torok (1606) did not alter the situation in Hungary much, it did mark an important turning point in Habsburg-Ottoman relations. The sultan recognized the emperor as equal and, in return for a lump sum, freed him from the humiliating obligation of paying annual tribute for his share of Hungary. The peace treaty, the first to be signed between the two powers outside of Istanbul, revealed Turkey's growing decline. For the next half-century the Turks remained inactive on the Hungarian border.

Bocskay's hopes for civil and religious peace in Transylvania and Hungary failed to materialize. He died, or was murdered, shortly after the Peace of Zsitva Torok. Another Báthori became prince of Transylvania, and conflicts between the Catholics and Protestants continued. The Protestants found a champion in Gábor (Gabriel) Bethlen, another Magyar Calvinist nobleman, who with Turkish assistance became prince of Transylvania (1613–1629).

CROATIA AND INNER AUSTRIA The Counter-Reformation scored the greatest success in Croatia. In 1572 and 1573 Croatia was swept by a great peasant revolt, for which the Protestants were blamed. Thereafter the Protestant cause in Croatia declined rapidly. In 1609 the diet outlawed Protestantism, which disappeared from the country without leaving the slightest trace.

In 1573 the peasant revolt spread from Croatia to the Slovene peasants of Inner Austria. There, too, it tended to weaken the Protestant cause. Frightened by the revolt of their Slav peasants, the German Protestant nobles lessened their resistance to the Habsburgs and the Counter-Reformation. The University of Graz, founded by the Jesuits in 1584, provided an arsenal for the Catholic cause. The accession of Archduke Ferdinand (the future Emperior Ferdinand II)[7] in 1590 marked the beginning of the end of the Protestant cause in Inner Austria.

BROTHERS' WAR Rudolf's hostility to the Protestants and his increasingly erratic policies brought his possessions to the verge of civil and religious war. In 1606 his relatives recognized his brother Matthias as head of the Habsburg family, and they raised an army to force Rudolf to abdicate. Hungary, Upper and Lower Austria, and Moravia defected to Matthias' camp. Bohemia, Silesia, and the Lusatias remained loyal to Rudolf. In 1608 the two factions made peace. Rudolf retained the loyal provinces and the imperial crown, and Matthias took the rest. The division of the Habsburg possessions, however, was only temporary. Since Rudolf was childless, the Bohemian, Silesian, and Lusatian estates recognized Matthias' right to succession.

In 1609, in return for their loyalty, the Bohemian Protestants extorted from Rudolf the famous Letter of Majesty, which granted freedom of worship to nobles and their serfs as well as to townsmen who professed the Bohemian Confession. At the same time the Catholic and Protestant estates signed an agreement guaranteeing each other freedom of worship everywhere, even on their own property.

Rudolf, deeply embittered by his defeat, was never reconciled to the division of his possessions and the concessions to the Protestants in Bohemia and Hungary. He spent the rest of his years plotting against Matthias. Armed conflict did break out again between the brothers, but it was ended shortly by Rudolf's death in 1612. Matthias I (1613–1619) then reunited the Habsburg possessions and secured the imperial crown.

The conflict had increased the tensions between the Protestants and the Catholics to the breaking point. In Germany the Protestants formed the Protestant Union under Elector Palatine Frederick (1608). The Catholics replied by forming the Catholic League under Duke Maximilian of Bavaria (1609). On all sides

[7] See p. 51.

The Defenestration of Prague, May 22, 1618, which precipitated the outbreak of the Thirty Years' War. *(New York Public Library)*

there were signs that a struggle to the bitter end was imminent. The conflagration was set off in Bohemia.

DEFENESTRATION OF PRAGUE   Emperor Matthias I returned the imperial capital to Vienna. Being childless, he chose as his successor Archduke Ferdinand, the ruler of Inner Austria. Matthias confirmed Rudolf's Letter of Majesty in Bohemia. Ferdinand, who was elected and crowned king of Bohemia in 1617, likewise confirmed it, but the guarantee was systematically violated or evaded by his representatives at Prague, the Catholic Bohemian noblemen Jaroslav Martinic and Vilém (William) Slavata. The agreement between the Catholic and Protestant estates was likewise not lived up to. It was an infringement of this agreement that produced the explosion.

In 1617 the archbishop of Prague ordered the destruction of a Protestant church built on his property at Hroby (Klostergrab). At about the same time the abbot of Břevnov closed a Protestant church on the monastery's property at Brunov (Braunau). On May 23, 1618, after a meeting of the Protestant defenders of the faith at Prague, a delegation led by Count Heinrich Thurn made its way to the Hradčany castle to protest to Ferdinand's representatives against these actions. Their conference with Martinic and Slavata became stormy. The royal representatives were abused as "Jesuit scum" and then seized and "defenestrated" (thrown out of the window of the council chamber), together with their scribe Philip Fabricius. The three men fell some fifty feet below onto a pile of garbage in the moat and escaped unhurt. A rather pointless act of violence, the "Defenestration of Prague," is generally regarded as the starting point of the Thirty Years' War.

Thirty Years' War, 1618–1648

BOHEMIAN REVOLT   In European history great wars often begin over obscure local issues in obscure parts of the continent and then spread like wildfire, engulfing one country after another. Each combatant enters the conflict for aims of his own, and the nature of the war changes. When the conflagration has burned itself out, the original belligerents may have disappeared and the original issues may be forgotten. The Thirty Years' War is a good case in point. It began over obscure issues in Bohemia, became a great contest between Catholic and Protestant Europe, and ended up primarily as a political conflict between the Habsburgs and France.

After the Defenestration of Prague the Protestant estates of Bohemia chose thirty directors, who took over the government of the country. They formed a Protestant army, which was placed under the command of Count Thurn. Silesia and the Lusatias sent troops to strengthen it. The Protestant Union in Germany also sent troops, under Count Ernst von Mansfeld, to its aid. In an outburst of religious intolerance the directors expelled the Jesuits. The archbishop of Prague and other Catholic prelates and nobles fled the country. The whole of Bohemia seemed to go Protestant, but the Protestant triumph proved short-lived.

The acts of the Protestant directors constituted a revolution, albeit an aristocratic one. Unlike the Hussite revolution two centuries before, the Bohemian Protestant revolt in 1618 had no nationalist or social overtones. It was a revolt of the privileged estates, both Czech and German, to preserve their religious freedom and corporate privileges. They made no attempt to enlist the support of the peasant masses, who stood by passively throughout the conflict. Unlike the situation during the Hussite wars, German-speaking Silesia and Lusatia eagerly supported Bohemia, while Czech-speaking Moravia hung back.

FERDINAND II The news of the Bohemian revolt produced consternation in Vienna. The aged Emperor Matthias I was irresolute. His intimate adviser, the archbishop of Vienna, Cardinal Melchior Khlesl, though the leader of the Counter-Reformation party in Austria, counseled conciliation. On the other hand, Matthias' heir presumptive Ferdinand advised repression. Before Matthias made a decision one way or the other, he died on March 20, 1619, and Ferdinand succeeded him.

Ferdinand II (1619–1637) was a man of little talent but of strong convictions and firm character. He had been educated by the Jesuits at their famous college at Ingolstadt in Bavaria. In his devotion to Catholicism and in his conviction that he was an instrument of God he resembled his uncle Philip II of Spain. He equated Protestantism with rebellion. He had shown his metal when, as a youth only twenty years old, he succeeded his father in 1590 as ruler of Inner Austria. At the time the provinces were almost wholly Protestant. Thirty years later when he left them to become head of the Habsburg family, they were almost wholly Catholic. During that period he had closed the Protestant churches, expelled the Protestant pastors, and given the Protestant nobles and townsmen the choice of adopting Catholicism or emigrating—without taking their property. The peasants were not given this choice; they were converted forcibly. On succeeding Matthias, Ferdinand proposed to apply the same policies to all Habsburg possessions.

The situation was tense. The Bohemians were in rebellion, and the Austrian estates, which were for the most part Protestant, threatened to join them. However, by his courage and the timely arrival of a few troops, Ferdinand managed to cow the Austrian estates. In June 1619, when Thurn and the Bohemian army arrived before Vienna, they did not dare join the Bohemian rebels. Thurn was forced to retire to Bohemia. By his firmness Ferdinand managed to split the German Protestant princes; the elector of Saxony, who was a Lutheran, disassociated himself from the Protestant cause. In August 1619 Ferdinand was elected German emperor. At the same time the Bohemian diet declared him deposed and elected in his place Elector Palatine Frederick, who was the leader of the Protestant Union and son-in-law of King James I of England.

END OF BOHEMIA'S INDEPENDENCE   In electingFrederick I (1619–1620) the Bohemian estates hoped to secure the help of the German Protestants and of England. Their choice, however, proved unfortunate. Frederick had little talent as a statesman and none as a soldier. A strict Calvinist, he alienated the Lutherans in

Germany as well as those in Bohemia. German Protestant help proved negligible, and none came from England. The only ally Bohemia secured was the Transylvanian prince Gábor Bethlen. Ferdinand I, on the other hand, obtained the support of Maximilian of Bavaria, the head of the Catholic League in Germany, and of his Spanish cousin Philip III.

In November 1619 Bethlen and Thurn converged on Vienna, but the cold, lack of supplies, and a timely diversion in Bethlen's rear[8] forced them to retreat from the imperial capital. In 1620 the army of the Catholic League under Baron Tilly (Jan Tserklaes) and the imperial army under Karl Bouquoy linked their forces in Austria. The Protestant estates, which had imprudently shown their colors during Bethlen's and Thurn's advance, were suppressed.

From Austria the Catholic armies invaded Bohemia and advanced toward Prague. On November 8, 1620, the Bohemian army, consisting of poorly paid and disaffected mercenaries, supported only by a Transylvanian contingent, made a stand on the White Mountain, an elevated plain near Prague. In the ensuing battle it was completely defeated and routed. On receipt of the news of defeat, Frederick (the "Winter King") panicked and fled to Silesia. No attempt was made to defend Prague. The Bohemian revolt had collapsed.

The Battle on the White Mountain, though a mere skirmish compared to the pitched battles in the Hussite wars, determined the fate of Bohemia for centuries. The imperial commissioners, Prince Karl Liechtenstein and Cardinal Franz Dietrichstein, moved quickly to consolidate Ferdinand's victory. The ringleaders of the revolt who had not fled abroad were arrested. In 1621 forty-five of them were condemned to death, twenty-one of whom were actually executed in the Old Town Square of Prague. The property of all rebels (680 in all) was confiscated. The Letter of Majesty was revoked, and Protestants in Bohemia suffered the same fate as those in Austria. The Mora-

---

[8] With the cooperation of King Sigismund III Vasa of Poland, who was married to a Habsburg princess and an ardent Catholic, Habsburg agents recruited a band of Ukrainian Cossacks who invaded and pillaged Transylvania.

vian Protestants were punished less harshly. The Silesian and Lusatian Protestants escaped punishment altogether, for by agreement with Ferdinand their lands were occupied by the troops of the Saxon elector. Although constitutional changes affecting Bohemia's sovereignty did not take place until 1627, the Czechs rightly regard the Battle on the White Mountain as marking the end of Bohemia's independence.

The Hungarian Protestants escaped, for the moment, the fate of the Austrian and Bohemian Protestants because Ferdinand was too preoccupied with the affairs of Germany to attend to them. In 1621 he concluded peace with Bethlen at Mikulov (Nikolsburg). Under its terms Bethlen renounced the crown of Hungary, to which the Hungarian estates had elected him, and Ferdinand recognized him as prince of Transylvania. In regard to the Hungarian Protestants, the Peace of Mikulov confirmed the terms of the Peace of Vienna with Bocskay in 1606.

SPREAD OF THE WAR   The suppression of the Bohemian revolt and peace with Bethlen did not end the conflict, for it had already spread to Germany. In 1620 the Spaniards moved from the Netherlands and overran the Palatinate. Frederick was deprived of his possession, and his electoral vote was transferred to Maximilian of Bavaria. The Protestant Union was dissolved, but as fast as Ferdinand and his allies suppressed the foci of Protestant resistance, new ones arose. In 1622 the Spaniards moved up from Milan to occupy the Valtelline and establish a direct link with the Austrian Habsburgs, whereupon France entered the war, though for the moment only against the Spanish Habsburgs. In 1624 when Ferdinand and Maximilian had almost defeated the Protestants in northern Germany, King Christian IV of Denmark intervened to rescue them.

At this juncture Ferdinand found an able general in Albrecht of Wallenstein (Waldstein) (1583–1634), a Bohemian nobleman who was born into a Protestant family but was converted to Catholicism. In 1624 Ferdinand made him duke of Friedland and commissioned him to raise an army. Wallenstein paid his mercenaries, who were drawn from the four corners of Europe, by allowing them to pillage the lands they overran. Wallenstein's army proved as great a scourge in Bohemia and Germany as the Turks had been in Hungary.

By 1629 Wallenstein and Tilly had conquered most of northern Germany and mainland Denmark. Christian IV, who had fled to the islands off Denmark, was forced to conclude peace and withdraw from the conflict. Victory over the Protestant princes and the uniting of Germany in an absolute monarchy appeared to be within Ferdinand's grasp. On March 29, 1629, as the first step toward consolidating his victory, he issued the famous Edict of Restitution. It provided that the ecclesiastical states that had been secularized since the Peace of Augsburg in 1555 were to be restored to the Catholic Church and that only Lutherans (not the Calvinists) were to enjoy freedom of worship. Wallenstein, who had counseled against the edict and had incurred the wrath of the Catholic "bitter-enders," was dismissed.

SWEDISH AND FRENCH INTERVENTION Wallenstien's conquest of northern Germany had alarmed Gustavus II Adolphus (1594–1632), the Protestant king of Sweden, who had been engaged for some time in the conquest of the southern coast of the Baltic Sea from Russia and Poland, in an effort to transform that sea into a Swedish "lake." The prospect of a Habsburg victory in Germany also alarmed Cardinal Richelieu (1585–1642), who had been in charge of French policy since 1624. French diplomacy, therefore, extricated Gustavus Adolphus from war with Poland (Truce of Altmark, 1629) in order that he might intervene in Germany. In 1630 the Swedes landed in Germany and advanced toward the Danube and Rhine rivers, while the troops of the Saxon elector, who allied himself with the Swedes, overran Bohemia. Ferdinand was forced to recall Wallenstein. Gustavus Adolphus roundly defeated him in the climactic battle of Lützen (1632), but he himself perished in the fray. His chancellor, Axel Oxenstjerna (1583–1654), acting for the minor Queen Christina (1632–1654), continued his policies, but the king's death had deprived the Protestant cause of its best champion. An impasse developed. The enigmatic Wallenstein secretly negotiated with France, Sweden, and the German

Albrecht Wallenstein, 1583–1634. Painting after Sir Anthony Van Dyck.
(The Granger Collection)

Protestant princes. Word of his treasonous activity eventually reached the court in Vienna. In 1634 he was dismissed by Ferdinand again. He was assassinated by his own Irish officers while trying to pass to the enemy.[9]

In 1635, by ceding the Lusatias to the elector of Saxony in the Peace of Prague, Ferdinand managed to bring the elector over to his side. Thereupon Richelieu determined to intervene directly in Germany to rescue the faltering Protestant cause. Two years later Ferdinand died, still vainly pursuing the *ignis fatuus* of German religious and political unity. His son, Emperor Ferdinand III (1637–1657), was anxious to end the war that was turning Germany and his own possessions into a wasteland.

PEACE OF WESTPHALIA   As early as 1641 Ferdinand III opened negotiations with the German Protestant princes. In 1643 he did so with Sweden, and in 1644, despite Spanish objections, with France. Richelieu died in 1642, but his policies were ably continued by his assistant and successor, Cardinal Mazarin (1602–1661). The peace negotiations, which were conducted at Münster and Osnabrück, dragged on for seven years because of the large number of parties and the complexity of the issues involved. Despite Ferdinand's objections, Mazarin insisted that the German princes and even the prince of Transylvania be represented in the peace negotiations. In 1648 a series of treaties known collectively as the Peace of Westphalia were signed, and the terrible Thirty Years' War came to an end.

The Peace of Westphalia marked a great victory for French policy. It guaranteed the sovereignty (*Landeshoheit*) of the German states. France, as one of the signatory powers, became a guarantor of their sovereignty and thus of German disunity and weakness. The independence of the Swiss Union and the United Provinces (the Netherlands), long existing in fact, was likewise internationally recognized.

---

[9] Wallenstein's enigmatic character and aims long intrigued German writers. Among other works, they inspired Schiller's great dramatic Wallenstein trilogy (1798–1799).

The religious issue in Germany was resolved by an elaborate compromise. The Peace of Westphalia guaranteed the religious freedom of German Catholics and Protestants (both Lutheran and Calvinist). In the German diet Catholic and Protestant princes were carefully balanced and organized into the *Corpus Catholicorum* and *Corpus Evangelicorum*. When religious issues were raised, both corporations had the right to invoke the "right to sit apart" (*jus eiundi in partes*), that is, religious problems were not to be settled by majority of the diet but by conference and agreement between the two corporations. This guaranteed a permanent impasse in the diet and thus its impotence.

The Habsburgs had failed to impose Catholicism and absolutism in Germany. They retained the dubious honor of presiding over the Holy Roman Empire, but from the Peace of Westphalia to its final doom in 1806 the empire was nothing but a ghost.

CHAPTER THREE

Consolidation and Expansion
1648–1739

Aftermath of the Thirty Years' War

SOCIAL AND ECONOMIC TRANSFORMATION Reminiscent of the Turkish wars and the devastation they wrought in Hungary, the Thirty Years' War caused much destruction, depopulation, and impoverishment in Germany, in Bohemia, and, to a lesser extent, in Austria.[1] The economic, social, and cultural depression resulting from the Thirty Years' War combined with certain broad and long-range trends in Europe to leave the lands of the Habsburg empire lagging behind the countries of Western Europe.

[1] The Cossack, Swedish, and Russian wars (the "deluge" of Poland, 1648–1667) had very similar results in Poland-Lithuania. Consequently, the social, economic, and cultural trends in the second half of the seventeenth century and the first half of the eighteenth century were much the same in the whole of East Central Europe.

Already in the Middle Ages significant social, economic, and cultural differences existed between the countries of Western Europe and the lands of Austria, Bohemia, and Hungary, but both regions operated on the same feudal-agrarian principle, and neither had an inherent advantage over the other. At the outset of modern times, however, overseas discoveries, the diversion of Eastern trade around Africa from the Mediterranean to the Atlantic seaboard, the Turkish wars, and other factors disrupted the old European trade routes and trade patterns, and the center of European economic gravity shifted from the Mediterranean to the Atlantic. The economy of Western Europe became transformed along capitalist lines. Its middle class, which controlled the new sources of wealth, began to jostle with the old landed nobility for position and demanded a share of political power. A similar development did not occur in the lands of the Habsburg empire or in eastern Germany and Poland-Lithuania. In Germany, Bohemia, and Hungary the influx of American gold and silver and the ensuing "price revolution" (inflation), among other things, made mining unprofitable, and once-flourishing mining towns declined. The growth of large cities in Western Europe did, however, create markets for the farm products of the lands of East Central Europe.

The changes combined to give the feudal-agrarian character of the lands of the Habsburg empire and those of eastern Germany and Poland-Lithuania a new lease on life. Landed estates in the area tended to grow larger and more profitable. Often they became self-sufficient economic units, producing nearly everything they consumed and selling their surplus farm products to distant rather than local markets. At the same time differences between large and small landowners tended to increase. While the former were generally in an improved position, the latter were often caught in an economic squeeze and forced off the land. Furthermore, townsmen were often forced to supplement their income by farming. This tended to disrupt the normal exchange of services between town and country; that is, the exchange of manufactures for farm products. Deprived of trade and their proper economic function, the towns stagnated. There were, of course, exceptions. Vienna, for instance, continued to prosper because of imperial patronage. On the whole, however, in the sixteenth and seventeenth centuries towns in the Habsburg empire, and in East Central Europe generally, tended to decline, while those in Western Europe experienced great expansion.

The natural social concomitant of this economic development is fairly obvious: In East Central Europe the nobles remained the dominant social class; the townsmen sank into insignificance; and the peasants were reduced to a bondage that scarcely differed from slavery.[2] Small nobles (knights) in Austria and Bohemia, having lost contact with the land, eventually disappeared as a distinct class. In Hungary the gentry were better entrenched. Although often impoverished, they stubbornly clung to their land and status and survived. Paradoxically, this development occured at the same time during which in Western Europe the nobility declined; the townsmen (bourgeoisie) rose to influence; and peasant serfdom disintegrated.

DECLINE OF CULTURE   The period following the Thirty Years' War was marked by a cultural decline among the peoples of the Habsburg empire. Even though Leibnitz (1646–1716) and a few other creative minds appeared on the German scene at this time, German culture too stagnated. Polish culture also entered a period of decadence. Undoubtedly, the fact that religion ceased to inspire European culture generally had something to do with the decline. In Western Europe science took the place of religion as a source of intellectual inspiration. In East Central Europe, however, the Scientific Revolution found few votaries, despite the fact that it had been initiated by the pioneering work in astronomy of Copernicus at Torun and of Tyho de Brahe and Kepler at Prague.

With the triumph of the Counter-Reformation in the

---

[2] The post-World II Marxist historians of East Central Europe who have examined this social transformation carefully, often refer to the deterioration of the peasant status in the fifteenth century as the "second serfdom" in order to distinguish it from the earlier medieval serfdom that had largely disintegrated by the fourteenth century.

Habsburg empire, the polemics between the Catholics and Protestants (and, to a lesser extent, the Orthodox), which had provided a stimulus to the national cultures of its peoples, ceased. The flood of catechisms, missals, hymnals, postils, hagiographies, and other religious literature that had been put out in an effort to win souls ran dry. Latin recovered its position as the language of intellectual intercourse. The indigenous languages of the Habsburg peoples fell into disuse for literary purposes. German remained the language of trade and, to some extent, of the Habsburg bureaucracy. However, Czech, Magyar, and a fortiori the Southern Slav tongues, Rumanian, Ukrainian (Ruthenian), and Slovak, reverted to or remained languages of the kitchen and the nursery. For about a century, until reawakened by the European enlightened movement, the national cultures of the Habsburg peoples remained in a state of torpor.

SUBJECTION OF BOHEMIA   While the Habsburgs failed to impose Catholicism and absolutism in Germany, they succeeded in doing so in their own possessions. With the decline in the importance of the Holy Roman Empire, the Habsburg central administration gradually ceased to concern itself much with German affairs and concentrated on the affairs of the Habsburg possessions. The Privy Council was gradually transformed from a primarily "imperial" to a primarily "Austrian" institution. Although the Habsburg possessions still did not constitute a legal entity, they became a de facto state and the principal power in East Central Europe.

The first to feel the heavy hand of Habsburg centralism was Bohemia. Although Ferdinand's victory in the Battle on the White Mountain gave him an opportunity to introduce royal absolutism in Bohemia, he moved cautiously, awaiting the outcome of the conflict with the Protestant princes in Germany. It was not until 1627 that he promulgated the famous "Renewal Ordinance" (*Vernewerte Landesordnung*) that altered the Bohemian constitution. The kingdom of Bohemia became a hereditary Habsburg possession, like the Austrian *Erblande*. Henceforth the advance "acceptance" of kings in Bohemia became superflous and coronation merely a symbolic ceremony. The diets of the lands of the Bohemian crown were deprived of initiative and the right to attach conditions to money bills; they could discuss only measures submitted to them for discussion. The king reserved to himself the right to appoint all royal officials. The German language was put on an equal footing with Czech. The autonomy of the three estates (lords, knights, and townsmen) was severely curtailed. The Catholic clergy were restored to the status of an estate and given precedence over the other estates. The lands of the Bohemian crown were reduced to the status of provinces, equal with each other and with the Austrian duchies. Only the Bohemian Chancellery in Vienna, through which the court transmitted orders to the Bohemian provinces, remained as a reminder of the former sovereignty, unity, and independence of the Bohemian kingdom.

The Thirty Years' War, too, had tragic economic and social consequences for Bohemia. During the course of hostilities the Catholic and Protestant armies had swept across the Bohemian lands inflicting frightful destruction. The country was impoverished, depopulated, and diminished by the loss of the Lusatias to Saxony in 1635. It is estimated that the Bohemian population declined from about 3 million in 1618 to about 800,000 by 1654. Many towns and innumerable villages were abandoned and left in ruins.

RECATHOLICIZATION AND GERMANIZATION OF BOHEMIA   After the Battle on the White Mountain the Jesuits were recalled to Bohemia, and the University of Prague was entrusted to them. Progressive steps were taken against the Protestants. First the Czech Brethren and Calvinist pastors were expelled and then the Lutheran ministers (1622–1624). But it was not until the Protestant cause in Germany appeared to have collapsed that the Counter-Reformation was fully launched, and what the Czechs call the period of "Darkness" (temno) in their history descended on Bohemia.

In 1627 the Catholic faith was made the only legal religion in the country. As a result of this drastic measure, mass emigration of Protestant nobles and townsmen took place. Protestant peasants were compelled to stay and adopt Catholicism. Most of the Bohemian religious refugees found haven in Germany, Poland, Hungary, and Holland. They had been the most active and best-educated elements in Bohemia. Many of them served in German Protestant armies or in the Swedish army. Others made valuable contributions to the culture and commercial enterprise of the countries in which they found refuge. The most illustrious among them was the last bishop of the Czech Brethren, Jan Amos Komenský (Comenius) (1598–1670), who was a pioneer of modern pedagogy and prolific writer of grammars, encyclopedias, and textbooks. His *Orbis Pictus* (World in Pictures) was the first children's picture book. While sojourning in England, he was invited to go to Massachusetts and become head of the newly founded Harvard College. He declined the invitation but a group of Czech (Moravian) Brethren did make their way to the New World and settled in Pennsylvania.

Many Bohemian Protestants, however, did not emigrate, but remained at home, outwardly converted to Catholicism, and waited for the storm to blow over. They hoped that the Swedish and Protestant armies would liberate them. To ferret out such secret Protestants, a virtual inquisition was organized. Zealous priests interrogated suspects, searched their homes, and destroyed suspect literature. Since during the preceding two centuries the larger part of Czech literature had been produced by Hussite and Protestant writers, the destruction of such literature was a disaster for Czech culture.

The Protestant princes failed to liberate Bohemia or — despite the pleas of Comenius and other émigrés — to insert in the treaties of Westphalia some provision for the protection of Bohemian Protestants. In 1781 when Emperor Joseph II lifted the ban on the Protestants, only a handful of Czechs and virtually none of the Germans in Bohemia availed themselves of the new freedom to profess Protestantism again. The great majority of the Czechs remained Catholic. However, the identification of the triumph of the Counter-Reformation with their national disaster, the memory of which was revived by nineteenth-century Czech nationalist historians, had made the Czechs perhaps the least fervent of Europe's Catholics.

As a result of the triumph of the Counter-Reformation Bohemia was largely germanized. Confiscation of Protestant property placed at Ferdinand's disposal a vast fund of land and wealth, which he distributed among Wallenstein's captains and other nobles who had served him loyally. The flight of the Protestant nobles and townsmen made it possible to buy valuable property for a pittance. Fortune hunters flocked from the four corners of the far-flung Habsburg possessions to Bohemia to get in on the bonanza. About 60 percent of the land changed hands. Germans (with family names Lichtenstein, Schwarzenberg, Thurn-Taxis), Netherlanders (Buquoy), Spaniards (Colloredo), Portugese (Silvatarouca), Italians (Piccolomini), and even Scots (MacNeven) and Irish (Taaffe) amassed vast properties in Bohemia. The estates of the Schwarzenbergs eventually amounted to 495,000 acres (the Schwarzenberg kingdom, as it came to be known). Bohemia became a land of great lords and large estates. Small landowners (the knights) virtually disappeared. The new "carpetbagger" nobility of Bohemia speedily became "Bohemian" but never "Czech" in sentiment; in language and culture it became German. Even the few remaining old Czech Catholic noble families (the Martinics, Lobkovics, Czernins, Kounics, Kolovrats) were soon germanized. The new nobles of Bohemia never developed a solidarity with the Czech people among whom, and off whom, they lived, but were loyal to the Habsburg dynasty, to which they owed their fortunes.

Since the Bohemian towns were already heavily germanized, the Czech people were reduced to a nation of peasants—at a time when peasants did not count in the European social scheme. A casual foreign traveler in Bohemia at the beginning of the eighteenth century would have thought himself to be in a German land. Until they effected a national revival in the nineteenth century, the Czechs were one of Europe's "submerged" nationalities.

AUSTRIA The germanization of Bohemia was an unfortunate but unintentional by-product of the Counter-Reformation.

Ferdinand II dealt as harshly with the Protestants in Lower and Upper Austria as he had in Inner Austria and later in Bohemia. In 1623 the University of Vienna was handed over to the Jesuits. In the same year a new university was established at Salzburg to act as the focal point of the Counter-Reformation in Upper Austria. By decrees in 1625 and 1628 Protestantism was banned in Lower and Upper Austria. Protestant nobles and townsmen had the same choice of conversion or emigration as in Bohemia, and their property too was given to alien fortune hunters, many of whom were, in fact, the same men who received estates in Bohemia. In the following generations the Austrian and Bohemian nobility often intermarried and were largely merged into a supranational Habsburg aristocracy. Since they were German-speaking, they were accepted in Austria while they remained aliens in Bohemia.

The triumph of the Counter-Reformation was even greater in Austria than in Bohemia; by the beginning of the eighteenth century Protestantism in Austria had practically vanished. Yet, this did not have the same unhappy consequences for the national existence of the German Austrians as it did for the Czech Bohemians. Consequently, the Austrians were not alienated from the Church. On the contrary, Austrian Catholics have been among the most devout and ultramontane in Europe.

HUNGARY Ferdinand II was unable to apply coercive measures against the Protestants in Hungary, owing to the agreements with Bocskay in 1606 and Bethlen in 1621. However, as a result of efforts of the Catholic Church itself, the Counter Reformation made much progress in Hungary during his rule. Its success was due principally to the brilliant leadership of Cardinal Peter Pázmány (1570–1637), who was first adviser to the Hungarian archbishop-primate of Esztergom and then (1616–1637) his successor. Although Pázmány was born into a Calvinist family, he was educated and converted to Catholicism by the Jesuits, whose order he joined in 1587.

Pázmány brought to the tasks of the Counter-Reformation the erudition of a Jesuit and the fervor of a neophyte. In the spirit of the decrees of the Council of Trent, he tightened the discipline and improved the educational standards of the

Hungarian clergy, both of which had declined since Mohács. He elevated the higher school in Trnava (Nagyszombat) in Slovakia, where the archbishops resided during the Turkish occupation of Esztergom, to a university. For the higher education of the Hungarian seminarists he established colleges in Vienna (the Pazmaneum) and Rome. He wrote a prolific polemical literature against the Protestants and engaged in personal missionary effort among them. In the Jesuit tradition of trying to influence the influential, he concentrated his efforts on winning back to Catholicism the Protestant magnates. His efforts were remarkably successful; most of the higher nobility returned without coercion to the fold of the Catholic Church. By the time of the Peace of Westphalia Hungarian Protestantism was in full retreat.

TRANSYLVANIA Meanwhile, Transylvania remained a haven of religious freedom. The Turkish inactivity after the Peace of Zsitva Torok and the Habsburg preoccupation with the Thirty Years' War permitted Gábor Bethlen (1613–1629) and his successor, György (George) I Rákóczi (1629–1648), to conduct themselves as independent sovereigns. At Alba Iulia (Gyulyafehérvár, Karlsburg), his capital, Bethlen maintained an elaborate court and patronized the arts and sciences. Showing a sense of social justice unusual for a Magyar magnate, he introduced reforms that alleviated the conditions among the Rumanian peasant serfs. Rákóczi was less solicitous of their welfare, but inadvertently he, too, rendered the Rumanians a service. A Calvinist, like Bethlen, he encouraged Calvinist proselyting among the Rumanian Orthodox. A press was established at Alba Iulia which published the New Testament and religious literature in Rumanian. The Rumanian language was introduced into the liturgy of the Orthodox Church in Transylvania, but Church Slavic or Greek was still used in Wallachia and Moldavia. This tended to alienate the Rumanians of Transylvania from their kinsmen and coreligionists across the Carpathian Mountains, but it had the unexpected—and by the Magyar Calvinists undesired—effect of stimulating a Rumanian cultural revival in Transylvania in the eighteenth century.

Since the Transylvanian princes were thorns in the side of the Habsburgs, French diplomacy naturally supported them. In 1644 when Ferdinand III opened peace negotiations with France, Rákóczi moved his troops into Hungary to assure that his interests were not forgotten in the negotiations. Ferdinand III found it prudent to confirm the concessions to Bocskay and Bethlen in the Treaty of Linz (1644) with Rákóczi. On French insistence, Rákóczi's envoy signed also the treaties of Westphalia (1648). However, the Peace of Westphalia proved the swan song of Transylvanian independence, for it freed the Habsburgs to exert an influence in the east again.

Struggle for the Mastery of Europe

BALANCE OF POWER   Unlike Ferdinand III, his Spanish relative Philip IV refused to accept the Peace of Westphalia. The Franco-Spanish conflict continued. It was not until 1659 that defiant Spain was brought to heel by France, along with England, which under Charles I (1625–1649) had aided the French Protestants at La Rochelle but under Oliver Cromwell (1653–1658) allied itself to France against Spain. The Peace of the Pyrenees (1659) marked the end of Spain as a first-rate European power and, together with the Peace of Westphalia, the ascendancy of France in European affairs.

Two years after the conclusion of the Peace of the Pyrenees Mazarin died. The youthful Louis XIV (1643–1715) assumed personal rule in France. He continued the historical French policy of trying to put the eastern frontier of France on the "natural" line of the Alps and the Rhine. The rivalry between the House of Austria and the House of France continued to be the central theme of European international relations. Louis supported every enemy of the Habsburgs and every element of dissension in their camp. At the same time, the Ottoman empire under the energetic Köprülü grand viziers (Mehmet, 1656–1661, and Ahmed, 1661–1678) showed a resurgence of aggressiveness in Europe.

The Thirty Years' War was the last European war that was motivated, initially at least, by religious causes. Henceforth,

European international relations were determined primarily by political (dynastic) and economic considerations. The Peace of Westphalia marked the onset of classical European diplomacy, which was consciously based on the concept of the balance of power. This concept reflected the growing secular and "scientific" spirit of the Europeans and their mechanistic concept of the universe and human affairs. In the peace treaties of Westphalia the first conscious effort was made to systematize and conventionalize international relations under a body of rules loosely called the "law of nations" *(jus gentium)*. Warfare was no less prevalent than before, but it became better regulated—at least, in Western Europe. The Turkish wars remained, as before, barbarous. Mercenary armies, such as those of Wallenstein that had been organized for specific campaigns and then disbanded, increasingly gave way to standing armies that were fed, clothed, and paid out of royal treasuries. In 1650 a standing Habsburg army was organized by General Raimondo Montecuccoli (1609–1681), a veteran of the Thirty Years' War.

LEOPOLD I Ferdinand III's successor was his second son Leopold I (1657–1705), who had originally been prepared for a career in the Catholic Church. With his hooked nose, cold eyes, and hanging "Habsburg lip," and with his vindictiveness toward foes and ingratitude toward supporters, Leopold was a typical Habsburg. He was a man of little talent but of firm convictions. Like his contemporary and rival Louis XIV, he was sustained in his acts by a firm belief in the divine right and inspiration of monarchs. Establishment of royal absolutism and Catholicism was his aim. Although the efforts of his minister Prince Eusebius Lobkovic to improve the efficiency of his government by creating a cabinet with a prime minister failed, Leopold greatly strengthened Habsburg authority at home and abroad.

An intolerant Catholic, he pressed the Counter Reformation relentlessly even though by the opening of his reign the Protestants no longer constituted a serious threat to the dynasty. From his earlier priestly training he retained a fondness for the company of priests, who swarmed to his court. The dominant cultural influence at court was Italian. The baroque style that had entered the empire from Italy reached its flowering during his reign in the "high" baroque architecture of Fischer von Gerlach (1656–1723). Gerlach built an addition to the Hofburg and designed, though his death prevented him from executing it, the palace of Schönbrunn—the Habsburg answer to the palace of Versailles. Gerlach's numerous palaces and churches have left a permanent mark on the architecture of the Inner City of Vienna.

The Peace of Westphalia brought the Habsburg empire only a short respite from war. Leopold's long reign was filled with wars in the west and the east. Leopold was no soldier himself, but he was fortunate in finding remarkable military commanders. Never before or since did the empire enjoy a greater martial reputation.

END OF TRANSYLVANIA'S INDEPENDENCE   The revival of Ottoman activity in Central Europe was soon felt in Transylvania and Hungary. Prince György II Rákóczi (1648–1660) incurred both Turkish and Habsburg displeasure by intervening in Poland in the First Northern War.[3] The sultan decided to replace him with a more compliant prince. In 1660 the Turks invaded Transylvania and crushed Rákóczi's army at Cluj (Klausenberg, Kolosvár). Rákóczi died from wounds suffered in the battle. His death marked the end of Transylvania's independence.

The Turks and the Habsburgs supported rival candidates for his succession. In the ensuing struggle the Habsburg candidate was killed. The Turkish candidate, Mihály (Michael) Apafy (1662–1690), gained the throne, but he was a mere Turkish puppet. During the conflict Transylvania was devastated, and its modest prosperity came to and end.

WAR IN HUNGARY   In 1663 border warfare between Hungary and Turkey erupted into a full-scale war. The sultan declared

---

[3] The First Northern War (1655–1660) resulted when King Charles X Gustavus (1654–1660) of Sweden attacked Poland. Tsar Alexis of Russia, the Great Elector Frederick William of Brandenburg, and Rákóczi joined in the attack. The courts in Vienna, Istanbul, and Paris became alarmed lest Poland be destroyed. French diplomacy mediated the Peace of Oliva (1660). Although Poland survived the Deluge, it never fully recovered from it.

war on Leopold I and invaded Hungary. The Turkish aggressiveness in Hungary, after almost sixty years of inactivity, caused a sensation and prodded somewhat of a revival of the crusading spirit in Catholic Europe. The diet of Germany met in a permanent session at Regensburg[4] and declared war on Turkey. Several of the German princes heeded the call to arms and went to the rescue of Leopold I. Even Louis XIV, anxious to make a good impression in Germany, yielded to the instances of the pope and sent an expeditionary corps to Hungary. He also permitted his South German satellites (the League of the Rhine) to go to Leopold's aid.

Although initially the Turks scored several notable victories, on August 1, 1664, after the arrival of French and German reinforcements, the imperial commander, Raimondo Montecuccoli, decisively defeated them at St. Gotthard on the Raba (Raab) River. Ahmed Köprülü at once sued for peace. Fearful of the growing influence of Louis XIV in Germany, Leopold I was anxious to wind up the war in Hungary. Therefore, in the Truce of Vasvár (1664) he not only recognized Apafy as prince of Transylvania, but also allowed the Turks to keep the Hungarian fortresses they had conquered and even paid them a "gift" of 20,000 ducats. Louis XIV apologized to the outraged sultan for the help he had given to Leopold I and reverted to the traditional French Turcophile policy.

WESSELÉNYI CONSPIRACY The humiliating Truce of Vasvár, coming after the great victory at St. Gotthard, outraged the Hungarian nobility. The Palatine Ferenc (Francis) Wesselényi, the Croat ban Peter Zrinyi, the scion of the Transylvanian princes Ferenc I Rákóczi, and other magnates entered a conspiracy to depose Leopold I and proclaim Royal Hungary independent. The conspirators secretly negotiated with the

---

[4] The diet of Regensburg became known as the "perpetual diet," because it was not adjourned until the dissolution of the empire in 1806. The representatives of the German princes in the diet were simply replaced as they retired or died. The diet thus became a permanent congress of diplomats—a sort of German United Nations assembly—ineffectual and useless, except perhaps as a forum of German opinion.

Turks and France, but they were slow to act. In 1670, after six years of plotting, they were betrayed. The court at Vienna moved swiftly to crush the conspiracy.

Wesselényi died of natural causes. Peter Zrinyi and another Croat magnate, Ferenc Frankopan, who went to Vienna to plead for mercy for the conspirators, were summarily executed. Severe repression followed, and it was turned into a witch hunt against the Protestants. The conspiracy had not been a Protestant one; its leaders had been Catholics and its aims political. In Habsburg eyes, however, Protestantism and rebellion were synonymous. The archbishop-primate, György Szelepcsényi, and his adviser and later successor, Leopold Kollonics, prevailed on Leopold I to seize the opportunity to crush Protestantism in Hungary.

In 1670 a special commission was established at Bratislava to investigate and punish the conspirators. It interrogated, tried, and passed sentences on over 2000 persons, among whom were about 450 Protestant ministers. Some were condemned to death, while others were sentenced to prison or lost their property. Zealous Catholic inquisitors were given a free hand to move against the Protestants. During 1671 and 1672, accompanied by imperial soldiers, they went from town to town in northern Hungary, seizing Protestant ministers and prominent laymen and closing Protestant churches. The unfortunates were given a choice of apostasy or being sent to Habsburg galleys at Naples. In 1673 the feudal constitution of Hungary was suspended and the country placed under a directorate with dictatorial powers. German was given an equal status with Latin as the official language, and officials were ordered to learn "Slavic" but not Magyar. Hungary appeared to go the way of Bohemia after the Battle on the White Mountain fifty years before.

THÖKÖLY INSURRECTION Hungary, however, was not as helpless as Bohemia. The Turks were still in the country, and France was always ready to assist anti-Habsburg rebels. In 1672 Louis XIV launched the second of his aggressive wars, the Dutch War (1672–1678), into which Leopold I was drawn. In the same year guerrilla warfare broke out in northern Hungary. The insurrectionists called themselves *kuruc*, like Dósza's peasant "crusaders" in 1514.[5] The Habsburg troops stationed in Hungary were derisively called *labanc* by the Hungarians (from *láb*, the Magyar word for foot). The insurrection found a leader in a young Protestant magnate in northeastern Hungary, Imre (Emerich) Thököly (1656–1705), whose father had been implicated in the Wesselényi conspiracy. During the persecution of the conspirators, Imre Thököly had been obliged to flee to Poland and then to Transylvania. In 1678 he returned from exile and placed himself at the head of the *kuruc* insurrection, which had political as well as social and religious overtones. In the next two years the rebels overran most of northern Hungary.

Leopold I tried to appease the rebels by restoring the Hungarian constitution and summoning the diet to Sopron in 1681. It enacted limited freedom for the Protestants. However, Thököly rejected these concessions as insufficient. He hoped to realize the aim of the Wesselényi conspiracy: the overthrow of the Habsburgs. Apparently, he hoped to become king of Hungary himself. In 1682 he married Ilona (Hellen) Zrinyi, daughter of the executed Peter Zrinyi and widow of Ferenc I Rákóczi, and opened negotiations with the Turks and the French. Ottoman policy was then directed by Ahmed Köprülü's brother-in-law, the Grand Vizier Kara Mustafa (1678–1683), a very ambitious statesman. Kara Mustafa proposed to do what Suleiman the Magnificent himself had failed to do, namely, to expel the Habsburgs from Hungary and to capture Vienna. In 1682 the sultan recognized Thököly as "king of Upper Hungary," and in the following year he declared war on Leopold I.

SECOND SIEGE OF VIENNA Early in 1683, after wintering in an advance camp at Edirne (Adrianople), the Ottoman army under Sultan Mehmet IV and Kara Mustafa moved up to Belgrade. The sultan remained there while Kara Mustafa and the army moved on to Vienna, which they reached on July 14. Unlike the situation in 1529, it was early enough in the season to press

[5] See p. 25.

the siege to a successful conclusion. They were joined there by Thököly and the Hungarians.

Although Leopold I was well enough informed about the Turkish moves, he was preoccupied with the French threat and chose to ignore the information. In May he had succeeded in detaching from the French side and bringing over to his own King Jan (John) III Sobieski (1674–1696) of Poland, who had won renown (and the Polish crown) by fighting and defeating the Turks in the Ukraine. However, Leopold made no preparation to parry the Turkish thrust to Vienna. When the Turks advanced, he fled to Passau to seek help in Germany, and the imperial army under Duke Charles of Lorraine retreated toward Bratislava, there to await reinforcements and an opportune moment to relieve Vienna.

The defense of the capital was entrusted to a small garrison of some 13,000 men under Count Rudiger von Starhemberg and his adjutant, the Bohemian noble Zdeněk Kaplíř of Sulevic. The siege wore on through the summer. By the end of August the walls of the city had been seriously damaged by the constant Turkish bombardment and mining. The garrison, stoutly supported by the Viennese citizenry under the courageous Mayor Andreas Liebenberg and the students of the University of Vienna, was worn out by the struggle and decimated by an epidemic of dysentery. Starhemberg succeeded in smuggling out messages to the emperor, pleading for relief ever more urgently. Daily, the story goes, he mounted the tower of the Cathedral of St. Stephen to survey the besieging force and to look for the arrival of a relieving army. The Turks carried out several attacks, but Kara Mustafa delayed the grand assault in the hope that the city would offer to capitulate and pay ransom for sparing its citizens. In such an event the indemnity would go to him, whereas if the city were taken by storm, the soldiers would be free to plunder it. The delay proved fatal to the Turks.

On September 11, after much bickering and delay, a relieving army of imperial, German, and Polish troops under Duke Charles of Lorraine and Jan Sobieski approached Vienna and encamped on the Kahlenberg, an Alpine escarpment west of the city. On the morning of September 12 the Christian and

Turkish armies clashed. The battle of Vienna was a debacle for the Turks. Leaving his baggage behind, Kara Mustafa fled with the defeated army in a head-long rout toward Hungary. On his return to Belgrade, he tried to blame the defeat on Thököly, who fled with him to Turkey. Sultan Mehmet had Thököly imprisoned, but he ordered Kara Mustafa executed for incompetence. The Turkish defeat at Vienna began the long Ottoman retreat from Europe, which did not end until the conclusion of the Balkan wars in 1913.

Triumph in Hungary

CONQUEST OF HUNGARY   Unlike his actions after his victory at St. Gotthard, Leopold I, on the insistence of his advisers, decided to follow up his victory at Vienna by pressing the war with the Turks to a victorious conclusion. On the initiative of Pope Innocent XI, Leopold's defensive alliance with Jan Sobieski was converted into an offensive alliance styled the Holy League, with the ultimate objective of driving the Turks out of Europe. Shortly after the battle of Vienna a campaign was mounted to drive the Turks out of Hungary. The Poles accompanied the expedition as far as Parkan and then returned home to fight the Turks in the Ukraine. In 1684 Venice and in 1686 Muscovite Russian joined the Holy League, thus forcing the Turks to disperse their forces on several fronts.

In 1686, after a hard-fought siege, Buda, which the Turks held for 145 years, fell to the Habsburg forces. In the following year the imperial army under Duke Charles of Lorraine routed the Turks at Harsány, near the field of Mohács where the Hungarians had gone down in 1526. By the end of 1687 all of Hungary, except its southeastern corner, was freed of the Turks.

The Turkish debacle at Vienna also spelled disaster for the Thököly rebellion. Habsburg forces under the brutal General Antonio Caraffa occupied northern and eastern Hungary without encountering any, or little, resistance. Only Thököly's wife Ilona upheld her family's (Zrinyis') tradition of *beau geste* resistance against hopeless odds[6] by holding out in the fortress

[6] See above p. 33.

of Mukachevo (Munkács) in Ruthenia until 1688. Although Caraffa encountered little resistance, he wreaked vengeance on the rebels, especially the Protestants. Hard on his heels, the Jesuits arrived to press the cause of the Counter-Reformation in Hungary.

SETTLEMENT IN HUNGARY After the conquest of Hungary Leopold's advisers urged him to deal as sternly with the country as his grandfather, Ferdinand II, had dealt with Bohemia after the Battle on the White Mountain. Archbishop Kollonics worked out a radical proposal for reform, "the Organization of the Kingdom of Hungary" *(Einrichtungswerk Königreiches Ungarn)*, which would have broken the power of the rebellious Hungarian nobility and transformed the country from a feudal into a modern bureaucratic state. It envisioned, among other things, the abolition of county autonomy and the replacement of elected noble officials with paid bureaucrats, reform of the *Tripartitum*, introduction of Austrian laws, taxation of the nobility, and legal equality for the serfs. This was too radical a proposal for the day. Leopold was no reformer. He appreciated the role of the nobles as unpaid policemen over the serfs. Not for another century, until Joseph II, was the Habsburg court prepared to dispense with the nobles and extend the bureaucracy down to the local level.

Leopold I contented himself with reducing the Hungarian estates to obedience. He was prepared to confirm the feudal Hungarian constitution, subject only to certain reservations. In 1687 he summoned the diet at Bratislava and obliged it to abolish the principle of elective monarchy and to proclaim the Habsburg dynasty (including the Spanish branch) hereditary in Hungary in the male line. The diet was also obliged to repudiate the *jus resistendi* (article 31 of the famous Golden Bull of King Andrew II of 1222), which the Wesselényi comspirators had invoked to plot the overthrow of the Habsburgs.

As for the Protestants, the diet confirmed the limited freedom granted them by the diet of Sopron in 1681. However, in 1691 Leopold issued an "explanation" *(Explanatio Leopoldina)* of the act, which defined the Protestant rights as narrowly as possible. The Lutheranism and Calvinism were reduced to "tolerated" religions, and their adherents were permitted to worship only in "inarticulated" places, that is, in the towns and villages where they were established at the time. If they moved to noninarticulated towns, they were deprived of the solace of their church. Other Protestant denominations were banned. Lutheran and Calvinist churches had to be inconspicuous in appearance (for example, no belfry on their buildings) and located at the outskirts of towns rather than in the center. Conversion of Protestants to Catholicism was encouraged, but Catholic apostasy was forbidden. The serfs were deprived of the right to determine their religion; if their masters were Catholic, they could oblige their serfs to adopt Catholicism, but Protestant nobles could not oblige Catholic serfs to adopt Protestantism.

The Counter-Reformation, however, aimed against the Greek Orthodox as well as the Protestants. As early as 1642 the Orthodox Ruthenian bishop of Mukachevo, Vasil Tarashevich, had been induced to accept communion with the Catholic Church on the basis of the Four Articles of the Council of Florence.[7] However, the union lapsed during the Thököly uprising. The Ruthenian Greek Catholic (Uniat) Church was not definitely established until 1689.

The conquest of Turkish Hungary created special problems, which were to last long into the eighteenth century. The area was underpopulated. Moreover, the departure of the Turkish landowning class left vast tracts of land without owners. In 1690 a "Commission for the newly acquired territory" *(Neo-acquisita Commissio)* was established to verify the title deeds

---

[7] In 1439, at the Council of Florence, the Byzantine emperor John VII and the patriarch of Constantinople, hard pressed by the Turks, accepted the principles for the reunion of the Eastern and Western churches: (1) supremacy of the popes, (2) the Catholic *filioque* clause in the Nicene Crede, (3) the existence of Purgatory, and (4) use of unleavened bread in the Eucharist. Otherwise the Eastern Orthodox Church was to retain its customary practices, such as use of Greek, Slavic, or vernaculars in liturgy and the marriage of priests. Although the Greek Orthodox Church subsequently repudiated the Union of Florence, its Four Articles later became the basis for the formation of the Greek Catholic (Uniat) Church in Poland and the Habsburg empire.

to the property in the area. In principle, those who owned property in the area before the Turkish conquest were to receive it back. However, after a century and a half of Turkish rule it was often impossible for descendants of former owners of property in the area to prove their claims. This left a vast fund of land in the hands of the Habsburg court, from which it rewarded the loyal pro-Habsburg Catholic nobility of Hungary. The Catholic Church was likewise given vast tracts of land. Many fortune hunters among Habsburg military commanders also acquired property in the area, although there was nothing like the rush of carpetbaggers into Bohemia after 1620. Most of the great magnate families of modern Hungary—the Eszterházys, Pálffys, Károlyis, Andrássys, and others—acquired their wealth and noble titles at this time, but they were mostly indigenous to Hungary.

Thanks to Leopold's relative moderation, Hungary escaped the fate Bohemia had suffered in being inundated with foreigners and integrated with Austria under a single administration; it retained its nobility and feudal autonomy. The triumph of the Counter-Reformation in Hungary was likewise more limited than in Austria and Bohemia. Although severely hampered, the Protestants survived in Hungary, alone among the Habsburg possessions, in more than token numbers.[8]

TRANSYLVANIA In 1687, at the approach of the ferocious Caraffa, Prince Mihály Apafy and the Transylvanian diet hastened to renounce their allegiance to the sultan and submit to Leopold. The emperor confirmed the prince and the religious freedom and political autonomy of the three privileged "nations" of Transylvania. However, in 1690 when Apafy died, Leopold would not permit the diet to elect his son as his successor. The Turks then made a desperate attempt to save their hold on Transylvania by appointing Thököly prince and sending him into the principality with a large army. They were soon driven out, and Transylvania was definitely brought under Habsburg control.

[8] About 19 per cent in 1910, including Transylvania and Croatia.

Nominally, Transylvania was reunited with Hungary. To permit real integration of Transylvania and Hungary would have strengthened the rebellious Hungarian nobility. The Habsburg court was too skilled at the game of divide and rule to permit that. In the *Diploma Leopoldina* (1691) the political autonomy and religious freedom of the three "nations" of Transylvania were confirmed. A governor's office *(Gubernium)* was created at Alba Iulia and later transferred to Cluj (Koloszvár, Klausenburg). The young Apafy was induced to renounce his claim to the principality, and a Transylvanian Chancellery was created in Vienna. Except during Joseph II's rule and the Revolution of 1848, Transylvania was governed as a separate unit until the Austro-Hungarian Compromise of 1867.

Since the *Diploma Leopoldina* guaranteed the freedom and equality of the Transylvanian Protestants (including the Unitarians), the Jesuits, who had come to Transylvania with the Habsburg army to press the cause of the Counter-Reformation, concentrated on the conversion of the Orthodox Rumanians. During 1697 and 1698 they induced the metropolitan of Alba Iulia and most of the Orthodox clergy to accept the Four Articles of the Council of Florence and form the Greek Catholic (Uniat) Church of Transylvania. In 1699 Leopold recognized it and granted it equality with the Catholic and Protestant churches. To be put on a footing of equality with the despised Rumanian peasants deeply shocked the Magyars, Szekels, and Saxons. In the diet the Protestants and Catholics united in protesting Leopold's decision. It was not until Leopold threatened to use force that the diet brought itself to recognize the Greek Catholic Church. Even then its equality remained largely theoretical.

Communion with the Roman Catholics alienated the Greek Catholic Rumanians to some extent from their Orthodox kinsmen in Transylvania and the Danubian principalities. On the other hand, it exposed them to more enlightened Western influences. In the eighteenth century the Greek Catholic Church became the cradle of the Rumanian cultural and national revival.

Failure in the Balkans

INVASION OF THE BALKANS   With the conquest of Hungary largely completed, the imperial army in 1688 under Duke Charles of Lorraine and Margrave Ludwig (Louis) of Baden crossed the Sava River and invaded the Balkans. It took Belgrade, which the Turks had held for 166 years, and then fanned out into Wallachia, Bulgaria, Serbia, and Bosnia. As the army advanced, the Orthodox Serbs and Bulgarian Catholics[9] rose against the Turks. Their actions aided the imperial army in its rapid advance into the Balkans. In 1689 the army took Vidin in Bulgaria and Nish and Pristina in southern Serbia. One column under General Enea Piccolomini fought its way into Macedonia. Hopes ran high in Vienna that the Holy League's aim of driving the Turks out of Europe might soon be realized.

However, the outbreak of the War of the League of Augsburg in 1689[10] forced Leopold to recall most of his army from the Balkans for service in Western Europe. At the same time Sultan Mehmet appointed as grand vizier another energetic Köprülü, Mustafa (1689–1691). He reorganized the Ottoman army, infused it with new fighting spirit, and launched a counteroffensive. While one army with Thököly invaded Transylvania, other Turkish armies began to push the reduced imperial forces out of Serbia, Bosnia, and Macedonia.

ORIGINS OF HABSBURG BALKAN POLICY   The court in Vienna cast about for a way to save as much as possible of the Balkan conquests. Leopold's northern allies, Poland and Russia, could be of little assistance in the Balkans. Russia's performance in the war had been particularly disappointing. The Russians, then under the regency of Sofia (1682–1689), acting for her two minor brothers, the cotsars Peter I (1682–1725) and Ivan V (1682–1696),

[9] In the seventeenth century many Bulgarians, disaffected by the ruthless exploitation by Greek clergy, entered into communion with the Catholic Church. The bishop of the Bulgarian Uniat Church, Peter Parchevich (1656–1674), secretly visited Poland, Vienna, and Venice, seeking help for his coreligionists.

[10] See pp. 85–86.

had launched two unsuccessful attacks against the Crimean Tartars and then lapsed into inactivity. The Venetians under Francesco Morosini were more active and successful in the western Balkans. However, Venice was primarily a naval power and could not relieve Austria of much of the burden of land fighting. In these circumstances the court looked to the Balkan Christians as natural allies against the Turks.

In 1689 Vienna sent a Serb notable, Djordje (George) Branković, who was a descendant and namesake of the last despot of Serbia before the Turkish conquest,[11] to Serbia and Bosnia to rouse the Serbs to active opposition. But once there, Branković began to play for his own hand; he hoped that the Serbs might free themselves by their own efforts and he become their prince. An independent Serb state was not what Vienna had in mind. On instructions from Vienna, Ludwig of Baden invited Branković to his camp and arrested him. He was interned until his death in Bohemia.

Vienna also sought to engage the services of the Serbian patriarch Arsenije III Crnojević. Piccolomini negotiated with him at his residence at Peć (Ipek) in Macedonia. Arsenije, who was also in touch with the Venetians, under Morosini, committed himself to support the Habsburg forces in the Balkans. As a result of negotiations with him, on April 6, 1690, Leopold issued a proclamation addressed to all the Christian peoples of the Balkans, but meant primarily for the Serbs, appealing to them to rise and support the imperial forces. However, by then the Turks had recovered the initiative and were driving the imperial army out of the Balkans. Arsenije found it prudent to withdraw with the imperial army northward. In the fall of 1690 the patriarch, some 36,000 Serb fighting men, and their families, numbering in total about 200,000 persons, crossed the Sava River into southern Hungary.

SERB PRIVILEGE   Before departing from Serbia the Serbs held a conclave at Belgrade. They selected a delegation under Bishop Isaia Djaković to go to Vienna to petition the emperor to grant

[11] See p. 11.

them protection and refuge and guarantee their religious and political rights. Leopold was very reluctant to grant their demands, but he needed the Serb fighters against the Turks. Moreover, he hoped that he would eventually reconquer Serbia and that the Serbs would then return home. Thus, on August 20, 1691, he signed the famous Serb Privilege which was inspired by the Ottoman millet system[12] under which the Serbs lived in Serbia.

The Privilege recognized and guaranteed the freedom and autonomy of the Serbian Orthodox Church and Archbishop (Metropolitan) Arsenije Crnojević[13] as its head. The metropolitan was granted extensive powers over church members and property. Arsenije's successors were to be freely elected by a church synod. The jurisdiction of the Serb metropolitans in Hungary was also extended over the remainder of the Orthodox Rumanians in Transylvania—an unfortunate decision because the Serbs had little understanding for the special needs and aspirations of the Rumanians. Leopold, as well as his successors, steadfastly refused to grant the demand that the Serbs be recognized as a self-governing political entity, authorized to elect their military and political leader *(vojvoda),* and allowed to live in a defined autonomous area *(Vojvodina)* with a status similar to that of Croatia or Transylvania.

Leopold's assumption that the Serbs would return to Serbia never materialized. Instead, the *Prečani*[14]—as the Serbs of Hungary came to be called by their kinsmen in Serbia—settled permanently in Slavonia (a Croat province) and in Banja and Bačka in Hungary proper. Partly, they were incorporated in the Military Frontier, which presently extended from Croatia along

[12] The Ottoman millet system grouped the peoples of the Ottoman empire, regardless of where in the empire they lived, into self-governing religious communities under their respective ecclesiastical heads, for example, the Orthodox patriarch of Constantinople, the Armenian Catholicos, the Grand Rabbi, etc.
[13] Arsenije Crnojević was obliged to resign as patriarch of Peć and content himself with the dignity of metropolitan of Karlovci, the Danubian town where he took up residence.
[14] From the Serbocroat word *preko,* meaning across; that is, across the Sava and the Danube rivers, which formed the boundary between the Ottoman and Habsburg empires.

the Sava, Tisza, and Maros rivers all the way to Transylvania, where it linked with the old Transylvanian military frontier. As military frontiersmen *(graničari, Grenzer)*, together with the old Serb and Croat frontiersmen, the Prečani took on the brunt of fighting the Turks. In addition, they saw service on western battlefields, wherever the Habsburg armies fought. Outside the Military Frontier they were subject to the manorial jurisdiction of Hungarian and Croat landowners. Their relations with the Hungarian authorities became very stormy. The guarantee of Serb religious freedom was not always respected, and the Jesuits never tired of schemes to bring the Serbs into communion with the Roman Catholic Church, like the Ruthenians and Rumanians. These efforts were always stoutly resisted.

Although often ill-treated, the Prečani were exposed to more enlightened influences in the Habsburg empire than their kinsmen in the benighted Ottoman empire, and in the eighteenth century their communities became the centers of the Serbian national and cultural revival.

Peace of Karlovci   To counter the Habsburg policy of appealing to the Balkan Christians, Mustafa Köprülü adopted a shrewd policy. The Bulgarian Uniats, who were isolated from the Habsburg empire, were ruthlessly exterminated. However, toward the Serbs, who could find refuge in the Habsburg empire, he adopted a conciliatory attitude. There were no reprisals against them. Arsenije III Crnojević was replaced by a new, pro-Turkish patriarch, who called for the Prečani to return home. Indeed, many of them, disillusioned by the treatment given them in Hungary, did that. The Turks thus successfully checked the new Habsburg Balkan policy. Nevertheless, when they tried to recover their positions in Transylvania and Hungary, they met with failure. In 1691 when the Ottoman army ventured north of the Sava River into Hungary, it was met by Ludwig of Baden at Slany Kamen (Salankemen) and crushed. Mustafa Köprülü himself perished in the rout. An impasse developed between the Turkish and imperial forces, which lasted until after the end of the War of the League of Augsburg when troops from the west were sent to Hungary.

Leopold entrusted the command of the army in Hungary to Prince Eugene of Savoy (1663–1736), who was destined to become the most famous soldier in Habsburg history as well as a statesman of distinction. Like most celebrated Austrian generals, Eugene, who was a member of a side line of the House of Savoy, was not an Austrian. He was born and brought up in Paris. Originally, he hoped to enter the service of Louis XIV, but Louis refused him a commission — a refusal the king later had cause to regret. Instead, Eugene entered Leopold's service in the army sent to relieve Vienna in 1683. He fought in the battle of Vienna and in Hungary and then in the War of the League of Augsburg. In 1697 he was put in command of the imperial army in Hungary and in the same year justified Leopold's confidence in him by surprising the Ottoman army as it crossed the Tisza River at Senta (Zenta) and completely annihilating it.

The chances that the Holy League could bring the war with Turkey to a successful conclusion then appeared good. In 1695 Tsar Peter I assumed personal conduct of Russian policy and reactivated Russia's part in the war. He assaulted the fortress of Azov at the mouth of the Don River and captured it in 1696. In the following year he set out on his famous first tour of Europe, the diplomatic purpose of which was to seek support for the war with Turkey. At the same time Morosini, in a last flash of Venetian martial glory, conquered the Peloponnese and advanced into Attica. However, once again events in the west frustrated success in the east. The events leading to the War of the Spanish Succession[15] led England and Holland to offer mediation between the Ottoman empire and the Holy League. They wished to disengage the Habsburg empire from the war with Turkey in order that it might take part in the coming struggle in the west with France. Habsburg interests in the west always took precedence over their interest in the east. Leopold was ready for peace with Turkey. And so were Poland and Venice. When Peter I arrive in Vienna in 1698 to press for continued war with Turkey, he was coldly rebuffed.

In November 1698 a peace conference opened at Karlovci

[15] See p. 87.

Prince Eugene of Savoy crushes the Turks at Senta, 1697. *(New York Public Library)*

(Karlóca, Karlowitz) on the Danube River. Lord Paget, the English envoy who was chairman of the conference, sought to arrange peace between Austria and Turkey and prevent it between Russia and Turkey in order to free Austria's hands and keep those of Turkey busy during the coming struggle with France. On January 26, 1699, peace was concluded on the basis of *uti possidetis* (that is, each belligerent keeps that which it has conquered). Thus, Austria retained all of Hungary (except the Banat of Temesvar), Slavonia, and Transylvania; Poland kept Podolia with the fortress of Kamieniec; and Venice retained the Peloponnese, the coastal towns of Albania, and the remaining part of Turkish Dalmatia but restored Athens to the Turks. Russia was unceremoniously left to fend for itself. All Russia managed to get was a truce.[16] Peter I was outraged by what he regarded as Austrian and English treachery at the Karlovci conference. They took "no more notice of him than a dog" he raged to the English ambassador, and he vowed that "In my lifetime I shall never forget what they have done to me."[17] Indeed, until his death Austro-Russian relations remained strained.

The Peace of Karlovci constitutes an important milestone in the history of East Central Europe as well as the Near East. It marked the opening of the perennial "(Near) Eastern" question. The Ottoman empire had ceased to be a military threat to Europe, but it became a permanent diplomatic problem to it. From the Peace of Karlovci to the Peace of Sèvres (1920) the Near Eastern question was a frequent concern to the European diplomatic chancelleries.

Compromise in the West and in Hungary

LEAGUE OF AUGSBURG   Louis XIV watched Leopold's success against the Turks at Vienna in 1683 and in Hungary afterward with a jaundiced eye. In 1688 he launched the third of his aggressive wars, which forced Leopold to fight on two fronts. However,

---

[16] Russia and Turkey did not conclude peace until a year later, by the Treaty of Constantinople (1700).

[17] B. H. Sumner, *Peter the Great and the Ottoman Empire* (Oxford, Eng. 1949), p. 20.

Louis' aggressiveness and haughty disregard of European opinion began to be counterproductive; the European balance of power began to operate against France. In the first two of his wars Louis had benefited from the sympathy of the German Protestant princes and in England from that of the Stuart kings Charles II (1660–1685) and James II (1685–1688), who had spent their exile during Cromwell's dictatorship in France. England had joined in the Dutch War (1672–1678) against Holland. However, Louis' revocation of the Edict of Nantes in 1685 and persecution of the French Protestants caused apprehension among the German Protestant princes. Tales of woe spread by Huguenot refugees inflamed Protestant opinion not only on the Continent but in England too.

In 1686 Leopold I, the kings of Spain and Sweden, and the electors of Bavaria, Saxony, and the Palatinate formed the League of Augsburg against France. The "Great Elector" of Brandenburg, Frederick William (1640–1688), who had pursued a pro-French policy before the revocation of the Edict of Nantes, concluded a secret alliance with Leopold. Finally, the fall of James II and the arrival of William and Mary to power in England (the Glorious Revolution) in 1689 led to a change in English policy. William III of Orange, stadholder of Holland (1672–1702) and king of England (1689–1702), was a bitter foe of Louis XIV. In 1689 England and Holland joined the League of Augsburg.

The entry of maritime England and Holland into the War of the League of Augsburg (1688–1697) projected it overseas into the colonies, where it was known as King William's War. The century-long Anglo-French duel for colonial supremacy began. Henceforth, great European wars usually had a colonial counterpart. While French and Habsburg armies clashed on the Rhine and in Italy, English and French armies fought in North America and later in India and their navies fought on the high seas. European wars thus tended to become miniature world wars.

The War of the League of Augsburg and its colonial counterpart proved inconclusive. With certain exceptions, the peace treaties of Ryswick (1697) marked a return to the status quo ante.

SPANISH SUCCESSION   Hardly were the treaties of Ryswick signed when reports of the imminent death of King Charles II (1665–1700) of Spain, long ailing and childless, started diplomatic sparring over Spanish succession. The reports proved false; the unhappy king hung on to life for another three years, but the unsavory haggling over his heritage never stopped.

The mothers and wives of both Leopold I and Louis XIV were Spanish infantas. Both, consequently, aspired to the Spanish succession. The accession of Leopold I to the Spanish throne would have linked the possessions of the Spanish and Austrian Habsburgs, as was the case under Charles V in the sixteenth century. This would have presented a danger to France. On the other hand, the linking of Spain and France and their large overseas possessions under Louis XIV would have presented a threat to England and Holland. Both possibilities would have upset the European balance of power. Realizing that the European powers would resist his accession to the Spanish throne, Leopold renounced his Spanish claim in favor of the younger of his two sons, Archduke Charles. For similar reasons Louis renounced his Spanish claim in favor of his grandson, Duke Philip of Anjou. This still left the Spanish succession in doubt. A Habsburg-Bourbon conflict appeared inevitable. The prospect was averted briefly when a third claimant appeared. Elector Maximilian Emmanuel of Bavaria, who was married to a Spanish princess, offered the candidacy of his son Joseph Ferdinand. However, Joseph Ferdinand died in 1699. Intricate negotiations were conducted to resolve the problem. It would be superfluous to review them here; suffice it to say that they failed.

On November 1, 1700, Charles II died. In May 1701 the War of the Spanish Succession (1701–1713) broke out. Like the War of the League of Augsburg, it had a colonial counterpart — Queen Anne's War.

Austria was joined in a Grand Alliance by England, Holland, Brandenburg and sundry other German states, and later Portugal. France was joined by Bavaria, other South German states, and the duke of Savoy, who however later defected to the other side.

Fighting took place in Spain, Italy, Germany, the Netherlands, and the colonies and on the high seas. In the Spanish Netherlands (Belgium) the duke of Marlborough (John Churchill) defeated the Spanish and French and advanced into Germany, where he linked up with Prince Eugene of Savoy. When the French and the Bavarians tried to march down the Danube valley toward Vienna, where they hoped to link up with Hungarian rebels, they were intercepted by Marlborough and Eugene and decisively defeated in the twin battles of Blenheim and Hochstädt (August 13, 1704). The French, however, gained an upper hand in Spain, where the conflict became a civil war between the partisans of Archduke Charles (styled King Charles II) and Philip of Anjou (styled King Philip V).

PEACE OF UTRECHT   In 1705 the long reign of Leopold I came to an end. His son Joseph I (1705–1711) was a very different man. He was freer of clerical influence and Catholic intolerance. Educated as a German, he gave his court a German style. Later historians tried to draw a parallel between him and his enlightened namesake and eventual successor Joseph II. However, it is difficult to say what would have been the character of his reign, for he died suddenly of small pox after only six years of rule.

Joseph I left no male heir. The Austrian succession, consequently, devolved on his younger brother Charles (styled Charles VI, 1711–1740, as Holy Roman emperor). Not unnaturally, this unforeseen reunion of the Spanish and Austrian possessions cooled the desire of Charles' allies to support his claim in Spain. A year before, the Whigs, who had been the most hawkish about the war, fell from power in England, and the Tories came to office determined to end the war. The death of Joseph I facilitated the efforts of the Tory foreign secretary Henry St. John to arrange peace. The treaties of Utrecht, Rastadt, and Baden (1713–1714) are usually grouped together under the name of the Peace of Utrecht. They provided for a compromise. Philip V was recognized in Spain and the colonies, but the Spanish possessions in the Netherlands (Belgium) and Italy (Milan and Naples) went to Charles VI, while Sicily, the remaining Spanish possession in Italy, went to the duke of Savoy as a reward for foresaking Louis XIV and joining the allies. England took Gibraltar and Minorca and in the colonies Newfoundland, Hudson Bay, Acadia, and St. Kitts. From Spain the English obtained *Asiento*, or assent to trade under strict limitations with Spanish colonies. The electors of Bavaria and Cologne, who had lost their possessions after Blenheim and Hochstädt, were restored.

RÁKÓCZI INSURRECTION   Hungary had been seething with unrest since the Peace of Karlovci. Despite his promise to respect the Hungarian constitution, Leopold had failed to convoke the diet since 1687. The country was ruled in a dictatorial way by military commanders and treated as occupied enemy territory. The highhandedness of the Habsburg authorities, the pillaging by Habsburg mercenaries, and the terrible social and economic conditions prevailing in the country after two generations of foreign wars and internal rebellion provoked another Hungarian uprising against the Habsburgs.

In 1703 a peasant uprising broke out in northeastern Hungary. Gradually the Ruthenian and Slovak peasants were joined by impoverished German townsmen and the gentry. The magnates, against whom the rebellion was originally directed, held aloof from it until 1704 when Ferenc II Rákóczi placed himself at its head and transformed it from a social rebellion into a national Hungarian uprising against the Habsburgs. Ferenc II Rákóczi (1676–1735) was a son of Ferenc I Rákóczi and Ilona Zrinyi and stepson of Thököly. As a child he had been seized from his mother after the fall of Mukachevo[18] and on Leopold's orders placed with Jesuits in Bohemia to be educated. Unlike his Calvinist forebears, he was a Catholic. But family tradition outweighed the influence of his Catholic education.

The time seemed propitious for launching the rebellion. Habsburg garrisons in Hungary had been reduced by the recall of troops for service in the War of the Spanish Succession. In the first flash of rebellion most of Hungary went over to Rákóczi.

[18] See pp. 74–75.

The Transylvanian diet hastened to elect him prince. Louis XIV offered him subsidies and sent French officers to advise him. The rebels spoke hopefully of meeting the French in the streets of Vienna. However, the battles of Blenheim and Hochstädt put an end to this dream. Without foreign assistance the Hungarian uprising was doomed.

From the beginning of the War of the Spanish Succession, French diplomacy had sought eastern allies. However, Poland, Russia, and Denmark, on the one hand, and Sweden under Charles XII (1697–1718), the redoubtable Lion of the North, on the other, had just begun the bitter Great Northern War (1700–1721). Turkey was disinclined to pull chestnuts out of the fire for France by attacking Austria so soon after the Peace of Karlovci. The Turks were more inclined to use the distraction of Europe to settle accounts with either Russia or Venice, the two weaker members of the late Holy League. Projects of intervention were endlessly discussed in the sultan's divan (council of state). Peter's spectacular victory over Charles XII at Poltava in 1709 tipped the scales in favor of fighting Russia first. Peter responded to the sultan's declaration of war in November 1710 by issuing, in imitation of Leopold's proclamation of 1690, a manifesto to the Balkan Christians — a harbinger of Austro-Russian rivalry in the Balkans. He also toyed with the idea of helping Rákóczi, but his campaign in Moldavia came to an abrupt end when a superior Ottoman army surrounded his army at Staneliste on the Pruth River. He considered himself fortunate to have escaped personal capture by concluding a humiliating truce (July 21, 1711) under which he retroceded Azov to the sultan and lost all the other advantages gained in the Peace of Constantinople in 1700.

PEACE OF SZATMÁR   Joseph I did not have the same dislike for the Hungarians as his father Leopold had. In 1706 he offered to pardon the rebels if they laid down their arms. The offer was spurned, and the diet at Onod in 1707 declared him deposed. In imitation of Poland it set up an aristocratic republic with Rákóczi as ruling prince. But the republic was short-lived, for the imperial army gradually pressed the rebels eastward and recovered control of most of Hungary. A proud man, Rákóczi refused to entertain peace and declined an amnesty, preferring exile. His departure into exile in 1710[19] opened the way to negotiations between Joseph I and the rebels. After Joseph's death they were continued by Charles VI and ended in the conclusion of peace at Satu Mare (Szatmár) on April 29, 1711.

In the total picture of contemporary European war and diplomacy the Rákóczi uprising was but an episode. Nonetheless, it had important consequences for the internal development of the Habsburg empire. The Peace of Szatmár was in a sense the first Austro-Hungarian compromise; it laid the basis of Austro-Hungarian dualism. Technically, it returned to the settlement of 1687. The Hungarian estates accepted Charles VI as hereditary king, and he solemnly confirmed the Hungarian constitution; that is, in return for the unconditional acceptance of the Habsburg dynasty he gave the Hungarian nobility a free hand to run the internal affairs of Hungary as they best saw fit. The difference was that this time both sides were determined to keep the bargain.[20] Hungary definitely escaped the fate of Bohemia of being reduced to a series of provinces and integrated with the provinces of Austria (and Bohemia) into a single state.

The Last Habsburg

CHARACTER OF CHARLES' REIGN   Charles VI (1711–1740), who was the last male Habsburg, had been groomed to be king of Spain. His Spanish experience was reflected in his tastes and policies. He preferred Spanish counselors to German. Spanish

[19] Like Thököly, Rákóczi ended his days in Turkish exile. Despite his failure, or perhaps because of it, he is surrounded in nationalist Magyar historiography with a romantic aura of a national martyr. J. Bihári composed the stirring Rákóczi March in his honor (1809), which Berlioz used in the Damnation of Faust and Liszt in the Hungarian Rapsody No. 15. The march was supposedly inspired by an old kuruc song, and was officially forbidden in Hungary as seditious until 1867. In 1906 Rákóczi's remains were brought home from Turkey and reinterred in Hungary amidst an outburst of Hungarian patriotism.

[20] During the Turkish Austrian war of 1717–1718 when Rákóczi from his Turkish exile issued an appeal to the Hungarians to rise, there was no response.

etiquette was restored at the court in Vienna after a lapse under Joseph I, whose education and tastes were German. The baroque style continued in vogue, reaching its "late" stage. The Jesuits continued in high favor at Charles' court. Counter-Reformation measures were maintained in force. The remnants of the Protestants in Austria and Bohemia were relentlessly harried out of existence. In Hungary the Protestants were protected by the Peace of Szatmár, but Charles effectively barred them from holding public office by supplementing the *Explanatio Leopoldina* with the *Carolina Resolutio* (1731), which required all Hungarian public officials to take a Catholic oath.

To fill the spiritual and cultural void wrought in the lives of the Habsburg peoples by the Counter-Reformation, the Jesuits promoted ostentatious public worship, processions (especially the Feast of Corpus Christi), pilgrimages to local shrines, and veneration of local saints. St. Leopold the Margrave was worshipped in Lower Austria, St. Florian in Upper Austria, and St. Noburga in the Tyrol. In Hungary the cult of the "Marian kingdom" *(Regnum Marianum)* was promoted. In Bohemia the cult of St. Venceslas was deemed to be too Czech and was discouraged. Instead, to make the Czechs forget their Hussite and Protestant past, the Jesuits assiduously promoted the cult of St. John of Nepomuk, an obscure fourteenth-century saint who had supposedly suffered a martyr's death for refusing to betray the secret of the confessional to King Venceslas (Václav) IV (1378–1419). The Czechs regard Charles' reign as marking the nadir of their national existence. However, Bohemia experienced an economic revival,[21] which later assured a Czech cultural and national revival.

PRAGMATIC SANCTION   Having lost the contest for the Spanish succession, Charles VI sought to protect his Austrian possessions from partitioning, such as had befallen the Spanish Habsburg possessions. In 1713 he promulgated the famous Pragmatic Sanction, declaring his possessions to be indivisible and hereditary in both the male and female lines of the House of Austria.

[21] See p. 94.

The succession was to go to his eldest son or (if he had no sons) to his eldest daughter or (if he had no daughters) to the eldest daughter of Joseph I.

The Pragmatic Sanction was originally only an Habsburg "house" (dynastic) rule. However, after his only son died in infancy, leaving his daughters as his sole heirs, Charles pressured and cajoled, one by one, the diets of his various possessions to enact it as their internal law. The Pragmatic Sanction became the first fundamental law common to all Habsburg possessions and their first legal tie. Its unifying character was weakened in Hungary, though, because the Hungarian diet exacted from Charles confirmation of the Hungarian constitution and autonomy as conditions of Hungarian approval.

Charles also endeavored to secure international confirmation of the Pragmatic Sanction by bargaining with the principal European monarchs. Eventually, in return for various concessions, most of them pledged to respect it — only to repudiate their pledges the minute he died.

MERCANTILISM   Charles' sojourn in Spain and his maritime experience in the Mediterranean awoke in him a mercantilist interest in trade and industry. His administration made efforts to develop foreign trade. Trieste and Rijeka (Fiume) were declared free ports, and their facilities were improved. Trieste was connected to Vienna by a new road constructed across the Alps through the Semmering. Chartered companies were established at Trieste for trade with the Ottoman empire and at Ostend in Belgium for overseas trade. However, the belated Austrian venture into overseas trade was not especially successful; the Ostend company was presently abolished to secure English approval for the Pragmatic Sanction. More important than the development of Austrain foreign trade was the revival of internal trade and the development of industry.

ECONOMIC REVIVAL   During the course of the eighteenth century the Habsburg empire experienced a gradual economic revival. The Turkish menace was over. Although wars with the Turks continued, they were now fought on Ottoman, not

Habsburg, territory. The empire continued to be involved in Western wars, but Western warfare became less destructive in the eighteenth century than before. At the same time, with the Habsburg triumph over the Protestants and the rebellious Hungarians, the empire experienced internal peace, which permitted its productive forces to reassert themselves.

Most remarkable was the economic recovery of Bohemia. During Charles' reign the foundations were laid for Bohemia's future large industries. Interestingly, the initiative to establish manufacturing in Bohemia was not taken by townsmen (the middle class) but rather by the nobility. The "carpetbagger" nobility of Bohemia was freer than, for instance, the Hungarian, of feudal inhibitions against engaging in trade and industry. The Martinics and Wallensteins established textile mills, the Countess Gallas the first cotton mill, and the Harrachs the first glass works. At the same time there was a great expansion of Bohemian peasant cottage industries. Bohemia made great strides toward establishing a balanced, industrial and agricultural, economy in the eighteenth century and toward becoming the industrial center of the empire in the nineteenth.

Hungary likewise experienced a recovery, although it proceeded along different lines.

COLONIZATION OF HUNGARY The Turkish wars and internal strife in the seventeenth century had left Hungary economically depressed and grossly underpopulated. Former Turkish Hungary was virtually void of population.[22] To fill the void, the Habsburg administration began a systematic colonization of the depopulated areas that continued throughout the eighteenth century. Although little noted by Western historians, this colonizing effort was comparable to the contemporary Russian colonization of Siberia and not much smaller than the Spanish, French, and English overseas colonization.

[22] Estimates of the Hungarian population after the Turkish withdrawal at the end of the seventeenth century vary from 2.5 million to 4 million. Even if the higher figure is accepted, a population of 4 million is very small for a country with an area of about 125,000 square miles.

The settlement of Serb refugees from the Ottoman empire in southern Hungary in 1691 has already been noted.[23] In the eighteenth century other Serb refugees followed. Slovaks and Ruthenes from northern Hungary, Rumanians from Transylvania, and Germans from Austria, Bohemia, southern Germany, and as far as Lorraine were also settled in the depopulated areas.

As a result, first, of the Turkish wars and then of colonization, the ethnographic picture of Hungary was completely scrambled. The Magyars were first pushed north and east into the Slovak, Ruthene, and Rumanian ethnic areas and then were drawn back into the central plain of Hungary. But interspersed with them in the plain were substantial islands of German, Slovak, Ruthene, Rumanian, Serb, and Croat colonists. Moreover, as the Magyars returned to the central plain, the Slovaks, Ruthenes, and Rumanians tended to advance their ethnographic limits behind them. In the narrow corridor along the Austrian border that had linked Habsburg-held Croatia and northern Hungary (Slovakia) during Hungary's partition, Croat and German settlers to a considerable extent had displaced the Magyars. The Banat, which Prince Eugene of Savoy conquered in 1718, became a virtual ethnographic museum, in which Serbs, Rumanians, Germans, Magyars, Slovaks, Ruthenes, and Bulgars intimately mingled. The net result of all this population movement was a decline of the Magyar and an increase of non-Magyar population in Hungary.[24]

[23] See p. 81.
[24] In the later nationalistic age when population statistics became political weapons, both Magyar and non-Magyar historians tried strenuously to assemble figures on the distribution of the nationalities in Hungary at various stages of its history. However, these figures are not very reliable. The first census in Hungary was taken in 1787 during the reign of Joseph II. It registered a population of 8.5 million (a remarkable increase since the beginning of the century), but it did not break the count down by nationality. C. A. Macartney, *The Habsburg Empire, 1790–1918* (New York, 1969), p. 81, without citing his source, gives the following "approximate figures" on Hungary's population (including Croatia, Transylvania, and the Military Frontier) in 1780: Magyars, 3,360,000; Germans, 945,000; Slovaks, 1,220,000; Ruthenes, 290,000; Rumanians, 1,565,000; Croats,

However, the population shifts did not always work to the Magyars' disadvantage. During the partition of Hungary most Magyar nobles fled from Turkish Hungary into Transylvania, Croatia, and northern Hungary (Slovakia, Ruthenia). So numerous were they that they largely magyarized the indigenous nobility in these areas. The transmutation of the old Croat magnate family of Zrinski into Zrinyi may be cited as an example. A great-grandson of the hero of Sziget,[25] Miklos Zrinyi (1616–1664), was a distinguished Magyar poet and writer and a Hungarian patriot. Within the social scheme of Hungary, in which only the noble counted, this was a great advantage. In northern Hungary the impoverished German towns were likewise partly magyarized and, to a smaller extent, slovakized. In the "Saxon" towns of Transylvania, however, the German element held out firmly.

Success and Failure in Foreign Policy

THE BALKANS The Peace of Utrecht permitted Charles VI to attend to Habsburg interests in the Balkans, where Turkey was showing a renewed aggressiveness. In 1714 the Turks declared war on Venice, and in the following year drove the Venetians out of the Peloponnesus peninsula and their remaining islands in the Aegean archipelago. In 1716 Charles VI made an alliance with Venice, and in the same year he prodded the Hungarian diet to provide a permanent Hungarian contingent to the imperial army.

Emboldened by their success against Venice, the Turks took the initiative and declared war on the Habsburg empire. In the summer of 1716 a large Ottoman army under the Grand Vizier Damad Ali invaded Hungary. At Petrovaradin (Pétervarda, Peterwardein) he was met by Prince Eugene of Savoy, by now a legendary commander. Although his force was in-

---

885,000; Serbs, 655,000; Jews, 90,000; gypsies, 135,000; others, 25,000. If these figures are correct (and non-Magyar sources would certainly dispute them), the Magyars constituted 41.2 percent of the population of Hungary in 1780.

[25] See p. 33.

ferior, Eugene completely annihilated the Ottoman army (August 5, 1716). Damad Ali himself perished in the fray. Eugene then moved into the Banat, the last Ottoman enclave in Hungary, and after a brief siege of Timişoara (Temesvár) conquered the province. Encouraged by these successes, the court at Vienna began to contemplate further action in the Balkans.

In 1717 Eugene crossed the Danube River and besieged Belgrade. A large Ottoman army moved up to relieve it. For a moment, caught between the garrison of Belgrade and the relieving force, Eugene was in a precarious position. However, he repeated the feats of Senta and Petrovaradin, crushed the relieving army, and forced Belgrade to capitulate. Then he overran northern Serbia, while another Austrian army overran western Wallachia. However, once again Habsburg dynastic interests in Western Europe obliged Charles VI to sacrifice their interests to the east.

The story of Karlovci was repeated. At Požarevac (Passarowitz) in Serbia, through English mediation, peace was restored between Turkey and Austria and Venice on the basis of *uti possidetis* (July 21, 1718). The Habsburgs retained their conquests in the Banat, northern Serbia, and western Wallachia (Oltenia) and the Turks their conquests from Venice in Greece.

At the time the Habsburg court regarded the Peace of Požarevac as only a temporary halt in Austrian expansion at the expense of the decaying Ottoman empire, but subsequent events proved it to have been the high watermark of Habsburg expansion in the Balkans.

ITALY Charles VI's involvement in war with the Ottoman empire inspired Cardinal Alberoni (1664–1752), the astute minister of Philip V of Spain and promoter of the king's second marriage to the ambitious Italian princess Elizabeth Farnese, to try to undo the peace settlement of Utrecht and recover the Spanish possessions in Italy. In 1717 Spanish troops landed in Sardinia and Sicily and seized them. But the other West European powers were determined to maintain the status quo of Utrecht. Alberoni's French rival, Cardinal Dubois (1656–1723), took the lead in promoting a quadruple alliance (France, England, Holland, and Austria) to safeguard it. Faced with a strong coalition, Philip V yielded. Under the Peace of The Hague (1720) Sicily was awarded to Charles VI, and the duke of Savoy was compensated with Sardinia. As the Peace of Požarevac in the Balkans, the Peace of The Hague constituted the apex of Habsburg influence in Italy.

WAR OF THE POLISH SUCCESSION   In 1733 the question of Polish succession precipitated another round in the old conflict between Austria and France. Austria and Russia, allies since 1726,[26] backed the candidacy of the deceased Polish king's son, Elector Augustus III of Saxony, while France backed that of Louis XV's father-in-law, Stanislaw Leszczyński, to the Polish throne. Leszczyński was elected by a narrow majority, but in 1734 he was driven from Poland by Russian and Saxon troops.[27] France, which was unable to bring him effective aid, attacked Russia's ally Austria. The conflict shifted from Poland to the Rhine and Italy. France was joined by Spain and Sardinia (the duke of Savoy). Eugene of Savoy, by then old and ailing, was sent to the Rhine, but he was unable to repeat his old victories over the French, and his lieutenant, General Mercy, was beaten by the Spaniards in Italy. In 1735 a Russian corps was sent to the Rhine (for the first time in history) to assist the Austrians, but it arrived too late; a preliminary peace had been signed in Vienna.

Negotiations for a definite peace were spun out until 1738. The problem was what to do with the dispossessed and needy relatives of the principal combatants: Leszczyński, father-in-law of Louis XV; Duke Francis of Lorraine, son-in-law of

[26] The Austro-Russian alliance was engineered during the reign of Empress Catherine I (1725–1727) by Count Andrey Osterman, one of the numerous Germans brought into Russian service by Peter the Great. It lasted until 1762 when Catherine II allowed it to lapse.

[27] For Leszczynski it was the second exile. He had been king of Poland once before, 1704–1709, during the Great Northern War, when he was backed by Charles XII of Sweden, until driven from Poland by Peter the Great after the Battle of Poltava.

Charles VI; and Don Carlos, son of Philip V and Elizabeth Farnese. In the end, the timely extinction of the Medici dynasty (1737) in Tuscany provided the key to solve the problem. The final Peace of Vienna (November 18, 1738) provided for a perfectly symetrical adjustment of the Bourbon and Habsburg claims that was typical of the mechanistic concept of the balance of power in eighteenth-century Europe. Leszczyński renounced Poland and was compensated for it with Lorraine, with the provision that after his death the duchy was to go to Louis XV; Francis renounced Lorraine and was compensated with Tuscany, with the provision that it was to be a secundogeniture, that is, was to be ruled by a collateral Habsburg line; Charles VI renounced the Kingdom of Two Sicilies (Naples and Sicily), which was awarded to Don Carlos as a secundogeniture with the provision that it was never to be united to Spain. The powers confirmed the Pragmatic Sanction.

The Peace of Vienna marked a setback for Charles VI in Italy. Almost simultaneously he suffered a setback in the Balkans.

TURKISH WAR   In 1736 war erupted between Russia and Turkey. Unlike Peter's campaign in 1711, the new Russian campaign against the Turks was successful. The Russians overran and devastated the Crimean khanate and in 1737 captured Ochakov, the Turkish fortress guarding the entry to the mouth of the Dnieper River.

The court at Vienna was disquieted by the Russian successes and offered Austrian mediation. In 1737 when this failed, Charles joined Empress Anna (1730–1740) in war against Turkey. Eugene of Savoy died in 1736 and his lieutenants—Seckendorff, Königsegg, and Wallis—proved less brilliant. Initially, the imperial army overran Vidin on the Bulgarian side of the Danube River, Niš in southern Serbia, and parts of Bosnia, but then its luck ran out. In 1738 the Ottoman army, which had been reorganized by a French adventurer and renegade, Claude de Bonneval (Ahmet Pasha), drove the Austrians not only out of their new conquests but also those of 1718. The Serbian patriarch Arsenije IV Jovanović and Serb insurrectionists, who helped the Austrians, found it prudent to withdraw with them north of the Sava and the Danube rivers into southern Hungary.

PEACE OF BELGRADE   In 1739, despite fresh Russian successes in Moldavia, Charles VI, by then old, ailing, and fearful for the safety of his possessions after his death, decided to accept French mediation and conclude peace. Empress Anna reluctantly followed suit. Under the Peace of Belgrade (September 18, 1739) Austria retroceded northern Serbia (including Belgrade) and western Wallachia (Oltenia) to Turkey but retained the Banat. Russia received nothing for its expensive victories except Azov and then had to promise to raze its fortifications.

The Peace of Belgrade marked a severe setback for the Habsburg Balkan policy. At the time, the court at Vienna did not regard it as irremediable. The Ottoman-Habsburg conflict had gone on for 200 years; what was lost in one war could be recovered in the next. Events, however, were to prove that the days of Austrian southeastern expansion were over. The Ottoman-Austrian boundary was fixed on the Sava and the Danube rivers and remained there for 140 years, until the Congress of Berlin (1878).

The course of the war had shown Russia to be the stronger of the two allies. This was in striking contrast to the Austrian and Russian roles in the previous Turkish wars. Henceforth, the Serbs and other Balkan Christians began to look to Russia rather than Austria for liberation. By failing to concentrate on eastern expansion for the sake of their western dynastic ambitions, by constantly shifting their attention and strength from one to the other, the Habsburgs had failed in both the east and the west—or, at best, scored only limited successes in both. If they had been willing and able to concentrate on the liberation of the Balkan Christians from the Turkish rule, which they proudly claimed to be one of their missions, it is not inconceivable that the Habsburg empire might have replaced the Ottoman empire as the dominant power in the Balkans. The whole Danubian area, instead of only the mid-Danube basin, might have passed under Habsburg rule, which would have had an incalculable effect on European history.

CHAPTER FOUR

Reform
and Reaction
1740–1815

Maria Theresa

PERSONALITY   Maria Theresa (1740–1780) was the eldest daughter of Charles VI and the only woman who ever occupied the Habsburg throne. She succeeded her father in the Habsburg hereditary possessions in accordance with the Pragmatic Sanction. She could not succeed him in the Holy Roman Empire, the laws of which allowed only the election of males to the throne. At the time of her accession in October 1740, she was a young woman, twenty-three years old, married to Francis I, who was successively duke of Lorraine, duke of Tuscany, and Holy Roman emperor (1745–1765).[1] She was raised in an atmosphere of Catholic piety and throughout her life remained a devout Cath-

[1] The dynasty was henceforth named Habsburg-Lorraine.

olic. A devoted wife and mother (she bore sixteen children), Maria Theresa maintained an atmosphere of moral rectitude at her court, which contrasted with the libertine and frivolous atmosphere at most European courts of the period. In contrast to the Spanish pomp of her father's court, the style of her court was mainly German and somewhat bourgeois, which greatly endeared her to her Viennese subjects.

ENLIGHTENMENT By 1740 the spirit of European eighteenth-century enlightenment was beginning to permeate the empire. Enlightenment ideas first reached Vienna through Germany and Italy. Later, after the conclusion of the Franco-Austrian alliance in 1756 when contacts between Paris and Vienna multiplied, they came also from France. In the latter part of the eighteenth century Vienna became a center of enlightenment in its own right, radiating its spirit not only throughout the empire but beyond it into the Balkans. Maria Theresa was personally unaffected by enlightened rationalism. She professed a distaste for the doctrines of the enlightened *philosophes*. However, she was pragmatic rather than doctrinaire in approach; her policies were rational, realistic, and practical. A devout Catholic, she maintained the Counter-Reformation measures against the non-Catholics in force. However, she was not unaware of the excesses of the Counter-Reformation Church and was determined to control it. She insisted that papal decrees and encyclicals be subject to royal review and approval (*placetum regium*) before they were promulgated in the empire.

ADVISERS Maria Theresa was an able, courageous, and energetic statesman. She chose able and frequently enlightened counselors, but she kept the power of decision firmly in her own hands. Her husband Francis I was formally her coruler, but he was not given a large voice in the affairs of state. Her intimate adviser in foreign affairs was a Moravian noble, Count (later Prince) Václav (Wenzl) Kaunic (1711-1794), who was regarded as the most astute diplomat of his time. First he was Maria Theresa's envoy to the court of Versailles and then for over forty years (1753-1794) minister of foreign affairs. Her most influential adviser in domestic affairs was a Silesian nobleman, Count Friedrich Wilhelm Haugwitz. After his death in 1765, which coincided with that of Francis I, Maria Theresa made her son Joseph her coruler. Joseph II also succeeded his father as Holy Roman emperor (1765–1790). However, as in the case of his father, Maria Theresa did not allow Joseph II much initiative in the affairs of state except in foreign policy and military affairs, for which he had no talent.

War of the Austrian Succession

PRUSSIAN CHALLENGE Charles VI's fears for the safety of his possessions after his death proved well warranted. Maria Theresa was immediately confronted with a hostile European coalition, which disregarded the Pragmatic Sanction and claimed various of her possessions. The principal challenge came from Prussia, a newcomer among European powers, with which Austrian relations had been good despite occasional friction.

Like Austria, Prussia was not a natural historical unit; it was largely the creation of the Hohenzollern dynasty. Its foundations were laid during the latter part of the Thirty Years' War by the Great Elector Frederick William (1640-1688) of Brandenburg. He transformed his scattered possessions—the duchy of Cleves astride the lower Rhine, the electorate of Brandenburg between the Elbe and the Oder rivers, and the duchy of (East) Prussia east of the Vistula River—into a single state by laying down certain principles and policies, to which he and his successors adhered with rare consistency. If the Hohenzollerns were to play the role of important sovereigns, they had to husband their meager resources but be ready to defend their possessions and to take advantage of any opportunity for aggrandizing them that might arise. Caution and calculation, thrift and efficiency, discipline and order were the principal characteristics of Hohenzollern policy, and the army was the chief instrument. Frederick William inherited from his father 230 soldiers and left his son a well-organized standing army of 24,000 men.

Frederick I (1688–1713) secured an honor that added to Hohenzollern prestige and helped to unify their domains. For joining Leopold I in the War of the Spanish Succession, the emperor awarded him the right to use the royal title in the duchy of Prussia, which lay outside and was not part of the Holy Roman Empire (until 1657 it had been a fief of the king of Poland.) On January 18, 1701, amidst much ceremony, Frederick crowned himself "king in Prussia" at Königsberg in Prussia (not at Berlin in Brandenburg). The powers recognized him as king in the Peace of Utrecht. In time king *in* Prussia became king *of* Prussia. Although he continued to reside at Berlin, all of the Hohenzollern domains came to be known as Prussia, just as all the Habsburg possessions were known as Austria.

King Frederick William I (1713–1740) was a faithful continuator of his father's and grandfather's policies. To retain everything he had inherited and to "make something extra" *(ein Plus machen)* were his aims. After the Great Northern War, he eschewed all foreign adventures and concentrated on internal consolidation, above all on building up his army. A simple, coarse, and parsimonious man, with a love of the minutiae of military life, the "Sergeant King" drilled his troops until the Prussian army became a model of military discipline and precision for other armies of Europe. When he died in 1740, Prussia had an area of only about 31,000 square miles and a population of about 2.2 million—a pigmy among the European powers. Austria had then an area of about 210,000 square miles (exclusive of Belgium and the Italian possessions) and a population of perhaps 14 million. The Habsburg statesmen scarcely thought of Prussia as a serious rival in Germany. However, Frederick William had left his son a well-filled treasury and an excellent army of 83,000 men. Frederick II (1740–1786) lost no time in putting both to use.

SILESIAN WARS When Charles VI died, despite his father's pledge to respect the Pragmatic Sanction, Frederick II raised a legally questionable claim to Silesia, economically the best-developed province of the Bohemian crown. Maria Theresa refused to relinquish Silesia, whereupon, on December 16, 1740, Frederick invaded it. The electors of Saxony and Bavaria and the kings of France and Spain joined him in the scramble for parts of the Austrian heritage. Russia, Austria's ally since 1726, had trouble over succession at the time and remained neutral. Only England, Holland, and Piedmont-Sardinia (duke of Savoy) supported Maria Theresa and formed the "Pragmatic Alliance" (so named because the allies respected the Pragmatic Sanction). The hostilities spread to the Rhine, Italy, and the colonies. Each belligerent pursued its own objectives. In Silesia and Bohemia it was the first contest between the Habsburgs and the Hohenzollerns for German leadership; on the Rhine it was a repetition of the War of the Spanish Succession; in Italy it was a repetition of the War of the Polish Succession; and in the colonies it was another round in the Franco-British struggle for colonial supremacy (King George's War). While Frederick invaded Bohemia, Elector Charles Albert of Bavaria, with French support, invaded Upper Austria. Maria Theresa's position appeared desperate. But the empress proved to be a plucky adversary.

In September 1741, bearing her infant son Joseph in her arms, she made a dramatic appearance before the Hungarian diet at Bratislava to appeal for Hungarian support. According to the reports of the famous scene, the chivalrous Hungarian estates, moved by her plight, rose to their feet and voted by acclamation to give their "life and blood for our king, Maria Theresa."[2] They promised to provide the money to raise the Hungarian contingent in the Habsburg army to 20,000 men and call out the nobles' *insurrectio* (feudal levy). Actually, a good bit of hard bargaining preceded the scene. Maria Theresa was obliged to swear to respect the Hungarian constitution in return for Hungary's aid.

Frederick II showed as little regard for the interests of his allies as he had shown for the rights of his adversary. In 1741 he concluded a secret truce with Maria Theresa which permitted her to divert troops from Bohemia to block the Franco-Bavarian advance toward Vienna. The Bavarians and the French supported by the Saxons then invaded Bohemia and captured Prague (November 1741). The compliant Bo-

[2] The Hungarian constitution provided only for male succession. Consequently, the Hungarian estates ignored Maria Theresa's sex, and acclaimed her as their "king." The laws of nature had been ignored, but the laws of Hungary upheld.

Maria Theresa and the infant Joseph before the diet of Bratislava (Pressburg), 1741. *(New York Public Library)*

hemian estates elected, and the archbishop of Prague crowned, Charles Albert of Bavaria king of Bohemia. In January 1742 he was also elected Holy Roman emperor as Charles VII (1742—1745).

To see the Wittelsbachs of Bavaria replace the Habsburgs of Austria as the leading German dynasty was more than Frederick had bargained for. He accepted English mediation, and in June 1742 concluded a preliminary peace with Maria Theresa. It was confirmed by the definite Peace of Berlin on July 28, 1742. Under its terms Maria Theresa ceded to Frederick the Bohemian county of Glatz (Kladsko) and the Bohemian province of Silesia, except the duchies of Teschen (Těšín), Troppau (Opava), and Jägerndorff (Krnov). Henceforth, the three duchies were known as Austrian (or Bohemian) Silesia to distinguish the area from Prussian Silesia. Freed on the Prussian side, the Austrians turned on the Bavarians and the French, drove them from Upper Austria and Bohemia, overran Bavaria, and advanced toward the Rhine. Saxony joined Austria. This spectacular reversal of Maria Theresa's fortunes disquieted Frederick. In 1744 he reentered the war against Austria,[3] invaded Bohemia, and captured Prague, but he was soon driven from Bohemia. The Bavarians and the French in the meanwhile retook Munich. The death of Charles VII in January 1745 led to a reconciliation between Maria Theresa and Charles' son, Elector Maximilian Joseph. By the Treaty of Füssen (April 22, 1745) she restored to him his possessions and he renounced the Bavarian pretensions to her possessions. In addition, he agreed to support the election of her husband Francis to the imperial throne. The election and crowning of Francis I as Holy Roman emperor in October 1745 restored that empty dignity to the House of Austria.

PEACE OF AIX-LA-CHAPELLE On May 11, 1745, the French under Marshal Maurice de Saxe defeated the Pragmatic Allies (the English, Austrians, and Dutch) under the duke of Cumberland

[3] The War of the Austrian Succession is better known in Austrian history as the First (1740–1742) and Second (1744–1745) Silesian wars.

at Fontenoy in Belgium, and on July 25 the French landed the Young Pretender Charles Stuart in Scotland to foment a rebellion. The British were forced to withdraw their troops from the Continent to attend to the Scottish rebellion, and the hostilities in the Netherlands came to a halt. In these circumstances Frederick, on the one side, and Maria Theresa and Elector Augustus III of Saxony, on the other, signed the Peace of Dresden (December 25, 1745), which reaffirmed the terms of the Peace of Berlin as far as Silesia was concerned. Under its terms Frederick recognized Francis I as emperor and Saxony was restored but had to pay Frederick a war indemnity.

The war dragged on over Italian and colonial issues until October 1748 when the Peace of Aix-la-Chapelle (Aachen) was concluded. It provided for a return to the status quo ante in the colonies and a new division of Bourbon and Habsburg spheres in Italy. The Spanish Bourbons installed a second collateral line in Parma and Piacenza. The Habsburgs retained Milan and Tuscany but relinquished a part of Milan (west of the Ticino) to the duke of Savoy (Piedmont-Sardinia). The French Bourbons (Louis XV) got nothing for their efforts, whether in Europe or the colonies, except a depleted exchequer. The treaties of Füssen, Dresden, and Aix-la-Chapelle, referred to by the general name of the Peace of Aix-la-Chapelle, provided for an inconclusive peace, which augured ill for its permanence.

Seven Years' War

DIPLOMATIC REVOLUTION In 1755 conflict broke out again between the French and the British in the American colonies, and it led to the resumption of war in Europe. This, incidentally, showed the growing importance of the colonies in European history. Previously, colonial wars were a side show of European wars. Now, the French and Indian War (1755-1763) in the American colonies precipitated the Seven Years' War (1756-1763) in Europe.

Maria Theresa was deeply humiliated by the outcome of the War of the Austrian Succession. She was determined to recover Silesia and Austrian leadership in Germany. Her determination to settle accounts with Frederick II, whom she loathed, was directly or indirectly the mainspring of most of her reforms. As early as 1742 foreign affairs, until then handled by the Privy Council, were transferred to the newly created Secret State Chancellery *(Geheime Haus-Hof-und Staatskanzlei)*, which was the Austrian foreign office. It was entrusted also with the handling of the affairs of Belgium and the Italian provinces, which did not form, properly speaking, a part of the Habsburg empire.

Kaunic, who was appointed foreign minister with the personal title of state chancellor in 1753, sought to refurbish Austria's alliances with Britain and Russia. On September 8, 1755, with his encouragement, Britain and Russia concluded a convention at St. Petersburg. Under its terms Russia undertook to provide troops in return for a British subsidy in the event of an attack by France and its allies in Europe. However, on January 16, 1756, King George II (1727–1760), fearing for the security of Hannover, the home of his dynasty in Germany, concluded a treaty of neutrality with Frederick II at Westminster.

The Treaty of Westminster wrecked Kaunic's carefully prepared plans. Since it bound Britain to neutrality in the event of a renewal of the Austro-Prussian conflict, the British alliance lost its *raison d'être* for Austria. Kaunic, therefore, proposed to seek a rapprochement with France. He was well acquainted with the thinking at the court of Versailles, at which he had served as Maria Theresa's ambassador until 1753. The cynicism of Frederick II and his utter faithlessness during the War of the Austrian Succession had revealed to the French court his true value as an ally, and his success in the war had caused it to wonder whether Prussia might not be a greater threat to French interests in Germany than Austria. Under these circumstances, Kaunic succeeded in securing, through Madame de Pompadour, a defensive alliance between Maria Theresa and Louis XV. Under the Treaty of Versailles (May 1, 1756) the ancient foes, the House of Austria and the House of France, that had fought each other in nearly every European conflict during the previous two centuries and a half, were reconciled and pledged each other aid in the event of a European war. So sensational did this reversal of alliances appear to contemporary Europeans that it became known as the "Diplomatic Revolution" in 1756. A month after signing the Treaty of Versailles France formally opened the Seven Years' War by declaring war on Britain.

THIRD SILESIAN WAR Frederick II regarded the Treaty of Versailles as a threat to Prussia. It had long been a Hohenzollern maxim that if war appeared inevitable, Prussia must strike first in order to overwhelm its enemies before they could mobilize their superior manpower and resources. Faithful to this maxim, Frederick II struck with lightening speed across Saxony at Austria (August 1756). Before long he had reason to regret his rash initiative.

The outbreak of war between Prussia and Austria put Russia in the anomalous position of being allied to two enemies, Austria and Britain. Forced to choose between them, Empress Elizabeth (1741—1762), who had reason to dislike Frederick II, decided in favor of Austria. In December 1756 Russia and a little later Sweden joined the Franco-Austrian alliance. Elector Augustus III of Saxony, whose territory Frederick had violated, also declared war on Prussia. On January 11, 1757, Russia concluded a special treaty with Austria under which both parties agreed to provide 80,000 troops against Prussia and not conclude a separate peace until Austria recovered Silesia and Saxony was restored. Austria also agreed to provide Russia a subsidy.

Prussia thus faced a formidable coalition, while its only ally, Britain, was not inclined to fight on the Continent. William Pitt the Elder (1708–1778), who had just become prime minister, agreed to provide Prussia with subsidies but not troops because he was determined to use all of Britain's strength for a final reckoning with France in the colonies. Fortunately for Prussia, the allies produced no great generals, while Frederick II proved a commander of genius. It was for his feats in the Seven Years' War that he won the accolade the Great. Exploiting Prussia's advantage of "inner lines," he shuttled his troops backward and forward, lashing out at each member of the coalition as they converged on Prussia in an uncoordinated fashion from all directions. He defeated each in turn. Nevertheless, Maria Theresa and Elizabeth were determined to crush and dismember Prussia. Despite great incompetence on the part of their generals, the sheer Austrian and Russian numbers prevailed over Frederick's generalship. In August 1759 the combined Russian and Austrian armies inflicted a crushing defeat on the Prussians at Kunersdorff. In October 1760 the Russians followed up the victory by raiding and burning Berlin.

At the same time French resistance in the colonies collapsed with the fall of Montreal, and George II died. His successor, George III (1760–1820), was born in England and was less concerned with Hannover. There was no reason for Britain to continue the war. In October 1761 Pitt, who believed that "America had been conquered in Germany," was forced out of office, and the subsidies to Prussia were discontinued. Prussia appeared doomed. Its treasury was empty, and much of the country ravaged. Frederick despaired of victory and considered suicide, but the timely death of Empress Elizabeth in January 1762 saved him.

PEACE OF HUBERTUSBURG   Elizabeth's successor, Peter III, was a great admirer of Frederick the Great, and he at once took steps to withdraw from the anti-Prussian coalition. On May 5, 1762, he concluded a separate peace with Frederick and restored to Prussia all the territories occupied by the Russian troops. Sweden followed suit. On June 16, 1762, Peter III signed an alliance with Frederick directed against Austria. His brusque reversal of Russia's alliances and other erratic policies provoked a palace revolution, led by his own wife Catherine. On June 28 he was overthrown and shortly afterward slain. Catherine II (1762–1796), who succeeded him, at first repudiated the alliance with Prussia, but later she quietly renewed it.

France, beaten in the colonies and in financial difficulties, had neither the reason nor the means to continue the war. Austria and Saxony were left alone to face Prussia. Frederick recovered the initiative. After a series of victorious engagements, he forced Maria Theresa and Augustus III to sign the Peace of Hubertusburg (February 15, 1763), confirming the treaties of Berlin (1742) and Dresden (1745). At the same time (February 10) France signed the Peace of Paris, recognizing the loss of its colonial empire.

The loss of Silesia represented a serious economic setback to the Habsburg empire. The loss of its largely German population also represented a setback to the German element in the empire, for it assured the Czechs a majority — and ultimately control — in the remaining Bohemian provinces.

Maria Theresa's Reforms

FISCAL POLICY   The original motive of Maria Theresa's reforms was to strengthen the empire for the struggle against Prussia. The army had to be reorganized and expanded. This cost money. In order to raise money, the fiscal system of the empire was reformed, which led, in turn, to comprehensive social, economic, and administrative reforms. The reforms applied, it should be noted, principally to the Austrian and Bohemian provinces; Hungary, owing to Maria Theresa's promise in 1741 to respect the Hungarian constitution, was largely exempt from them. The situation in the Italian provinces, Belgium, and Polish Galicia (acquired in 1772)[4] was likewise different and will not be considered here.

In 1748 Count Haugwitz obtained from the Austrian and Bohemian diets a pledge to raise a stipulated sum of money in taxes over the following ten years (the Decennial Recess) to augment the armed forces. The principal source of revenue in the empire was the land tax. Land was broadly divided into "rustical" and "dominical." In principle, the rustical lands were the villein holdings or that part of the lord's manor cultivated by the serfs for their own sustenance, and the dominical land was the demesne or that part of the estate cultivated for the lord's own needs. However, land owned outright by the peasants also came under the category of rustical land, and dominical land

[4] See below p. 125.

rented to the peasants remained in the category of dominical land. Until the Decennial Recess when the nobles consented to the taxation of the dominical land, at about half the rates assessed for the rustical land, the latter alone was taxed. In order to prevent tax evasion, it was important for the government to have a complete and accurate survey of the rustical land. Maria Theresa ordered a survey of it, which was completed by 1748 (the First Theresan Cadaster) and revised by 1756 (the Second Theresan Cadaster).[5] In principle, one-third of the peasants' income was to go for taxes, manorial dues, and the tithe to the Catholic Church (paid also by the Protestants to the Catholic Church). However, the Second Theresan Cadaster stipulated that in the Bohemian provinces, which were the most taxed of the Habsburg dominions, 42 percent of the peasants' income should go for taxes, dues, and the tithe. However, according to one source,[6] actually, because of high assessments, about 73 percent of the Bohemian peasants' income was taken by the state, the landlords, and the Church.

THE MILITARY   The funds provided by the Decennial Recess enabled the Habsburg military leaders to increase the imperial army to 108,000 men. To improve the technical quality of officers, a military academy was organized at Wiener Neustadt. A general staff was created. In 1773, to assure a steady supply of recruits for the army, "general conscription" (draft) was instituted. In 1771, in preparation for the first draft of recruits, the first "conscription" (census) was taken (except in the Tyrol and Hungary). The educated classes and townsmen were exempted from the obligation of military service; thus the burden fell heavily on the peasantry.

The army, however, failed to justify the care lavished on it. It did not recover Silesia and humble Prussia in the Seven Years' War, largely because Maria Theresa was unable to find good generals. Archduke Charles of Lorraine (1712–1780),

[5] The two cadasters constitute precious sources of information on the socioeconomic conditions in the empire.

[6] Robert J. Kerner, *Bohemia in the Eighteenth Century* (New York, 1932), p. 45.

Francis I's brother, who commanded Austrian armies in the Silesian wars, failed to live up to the fame of his grandfather and his namesake in Leopold's time. Gideon Laudon (1717–1790), a Scot in Maria Theresa's service, who won distinction in the Seven Years' War, was at best a competent professional but not an inspired commander. The fault was perhaps that the high command was reserved to members of the dynasty and high nobility, who by the end of the eighteenth century had become increasingly idle, frivolous, exclusive, and socially parasitic.

SOCIAL REFORMS In 1742 Maria Theresa considered emancipating the peasants to enlist their support in the war with Prussia. However, with her keen sense of political realities, she discarded the idea as premature. Nevertheless, she was determined to protect the peasants from abuse by the nobles, not so much because of any eighteenth-century humanitarianism or a sense of social justice as because she realized that exploitation of the peasants by the nobles impaired their taxpaying capacity. Royal commissions were appointed to investigate peasant abuses, and pressure was applied to the nobles to redress them. In 1775 a violent peasant jacquerie broke out in Bohemia, which provoked the usual hysterical cries of "Hussite plot" in Vienna even though its motives were purely social. The revolt was bloodily suppressed by the army, but in August 1775 Maria Theresa issued a patent (decree) defining the peasants' duties to their noble masters. No machinery was provided to enforce it. However, the patent at least provided a standard to which the peasants could refer to protect themselves against noble abuse.

ECONOMIC PROGRAM Guided by a continuous desire to augment her revenue, Maria Theresa and her advisers took a keen interest in the economic development of the empire. In harmony with the physiocratic doctrines then fashionable in Europe, they placed an emphasis on agriculture. Nonetheless, trade and industry were not neglected. Some restrictions placed on trade and industry by the guilds were removed. As elsewhere in Europe, the government claimed a monopoly of the sale of tobacco. In 1775 a simplified and uniform tariff was adopted in the lands of the Habsburg empire. Hungary was excluded from it, not as a concession to Hungarian particularism, for it was detrimental to the Hungarian economy, but to protect Austrian and Bohemian agriculture from the competition of the Hungarian, which was not as heavily taxed. Even without Hungary, however, the Austrian tariff area was at the time the largest single-tariff area in Europe outside the Russian empire. Internal trade was stimulated by the construction of roads, the adoption of uniform weights and measures (those of Lower Austria), and the reform of the currency. In 1762 the municipal bank of Vienna was authorized to issue banknotes, which at first bore interest. In 1771 a stock exchange was opened in Vienna, which testified to the development of a capitalist economy in the empire.

Considerable attention was given to the development of external trade. An Oriental Academy was founded in Vienna to train consular officials for service, principally in the Ottoman empire in which several new Austrian consulates were opened. In 1775 a new East India company was established at Trieste to develop overseas trade. It attempted to open trading posts in India, but it was not much more successful than the earlier Ostend company.

CENTRALIZATION AND BUREAUCRATIZATION Maria Theresa made long strides toward the centralization and bureaucratization of the empire's administration. In Bohemia she was partly motivated by the feckless defection of the Bohemian estates during the Bavarian-French invasion in 1741. Although she refrained from taking reprisals against the estates, she was determined to tie Bohemia firmly to Austria. In 1749 she revoked Bohemia's constitutional charter, the Renewal Ordinance of 1627,[7] and abolished the separate Bohemian Chancellery in Vienna that had been the last vestige of Bohemia's separate statehood. At the same time the Austrian Chancellery was abolished, and the functions of the two chancelleries were merged.

[7] See p. 61.

Their judicial functions were transferred to a newly created common "Supreme Court" *(Oberste Justizstelle)*, while their administrative and fiscal functions were entrusted to another new common agency, the "Directory of Public and Fiscal Affairs" *(Directorium in publicis and cameralibus)*. In 1762, out of deference to the protests of the Bohemian estates, the Directory was slightly reorganized and renamed Joint Bohemian and Austrian Chancellery.

The term Kingdom of Bohemia continued to be used in official nomenclature, but it lost all practical meaning. The Bohemian provinces (Bohemia, Moravia, and Silesia) continued as administrative units on an equal footing with one another and the Austrian provinces (Upper Austria, Lower Austria, Styria, and so forth). Their provincial diets still met, but the sphere of local self-government was steadily circumscribed. In each of the three Bohemian provinces the king's lieutenants, who had been chosen from the local nobility, were replaced with governors, who were usually Bohemian nobles but were appointed and paid by Vienna. The councils of lieutenancy were replaced with governors' offices *(gubernia)*. Since the assessment and collection of taxes were in the hands of local noble officials, who were not paid and were often indolent and inefficient, Maria Theresa sought to improve tax collection by extending the imperial bureaucracy downward to the county level and to replace elected noble county officials with paid bureaucrats.

GERMANIZATION An incidental by-product of the centralization and bureaucratization of Bohemia's administration was its germanization. This did not indicate any conscious German nationalism on the part of Maria Theresa, but only bureaucratic convenience and the cultural disparity existing in the eighteenth century between the Germans and the Czechs. Habsburg bureaucrats were a heterogeneous lot, held together by a common loyalty to the dynasty. For the sake of administrative efficiency and uniformity they had to use a common tongue. Latin had proved too cumbersome and already in the seventeenth century had been gradually replaced in official usage by German, the language of the most numerous and evolved nationality in the empire. In the second half of the eighteenth century under the stimulus of European enlightenment the Germans effected a remarkable cultural revival. Thanks to Goethe and other luminaries of the German enlightenment, German became a true *langue de civilisation,* almost on a par with French. The Czechs were to effect a remarkable cultural revival too, but it did not come until the nineteenth century. In the meantime, Czech remained a vernacular, a folk idiom, scarcely used for literary purposes.

At the opening of the diets of Bohemia and Moravia a few ceremonial phrases were still uttered in Czech. However, this was not an expression of conscious Czech nationalism either but, like the use of Norman French phrases in English coronations, a mark of respect for Bohemia's feudal past. On the part of the German-speaking Bohemian nobility it also revealed a desire to preserve their feudal rights against Habsburg bureaucratic encroachment by identifying themselves with Bohemia's feudal past.

EDUCATIONAL REFORMS   The influence of enlightenment on Maria Theresa's policies was best shown in her educational reforms. While her hated rival, Catherine II, who was hailed by Voltaire as the Semiramis of the North, paid eloquent lip service to enlightened principles but did little about education, Maria Theresa deplored enlightenment but created a comprehensive secular educational system in her empire. Until her reign education was regarded as a matter of the churches and towns only. She made it a matter of concern to the state. In 1773 when Pope Clement XIV abolished the Jesuit Order, Maria Theresa seized its vast property and used it to create a school fund. In the following year she issued a law, prepared by an enlightened Silesian churchman and educator, Prior Johann Felbiger, which provided for the establishment of primary schools in every parish. In towns "main" schools and in the provincial capitals "normal" schools for the training of teachers were established.

The *gymnasia* (classical high schools), which passed from the control of the Jesuits to that of the Piarists, remained bastions of old-style classical training. The universities, however, were taken over by the state, their curricula revised (history, geography, natural sciences, and courses in administration for the training of the growing ranks of the imperial bureacracy were added), and lay teachers were increasingly appointed to their teaching staffs. Owing principally to the efforts of Gerhard van Swieten, a Flemish physician and adviser on higher education, medical schools were greatly improved. The medical school of the University of Vienna became an important center of medical training and research—a position which it maintained until the twentieth century. An incidental by-product of the reform and secularization of the schools was their germanization. Latin was a dead language, incapable of expressing the whole range of new thought engendered by enlightenment. It was also a symbol of medieval scholasticism and as such despised by the enlightened *philosophes.* Increasingly, it gave way to German as the language of instruction in Austrian and Bohemian schools.

Altogether, the catalog of Maria Theresa's reforms was impressive, but it was under her son Joseph II that the reform of the empire really culminated.

Maria Theresa and Hungary

HUNGARIAN AUTONOMY Maria Theresa handled Hungary, unlike Bohemia, very gingerly. She lived up to the letter of her oath to uphold the Hungarian constitution. She had herself crowned "king" of Hungary, convoked the diet regularly, and interfered little in the internal affairs of the country—as long as Hungary paid its stipulated share of taxes, the principal one of which was the *contributio* (war tax) for the upkeep of the army, and sent recruits for the six Hungarian regiments that formed a part of the imperial army.

To allay potential Hungarian opposition, Maria Theresa used a mixture of conciliation and flattery. She treated the symbols of Hungarian statehood with great tact. In 1758, with Pope Clement XIII's permission, she assumed the title of Apostolic king, which according to Hungarian national tradition had been awarded to St. Stephen. Toward the great magnates she adopted a policy similar to Louis XIV's policy of "domesticating" the great nobles of France. She invited them to her court and bestowed honors and rewards on them. She encouraged them to send their sons to the Theresianum, an academy that she founded in Vienna for the education of noble youths (1746). For the sons of the gentry, she founded the Royal Hungarian Bodyguard (1764), to which each county was invited to send two youths. To honor those Hungarians who served her loyally, she created the Order of St. Stephen. After the dissolution of the Jesuit Order, by her famous patent *Ratio Educationis* (1777), she reformed and brought the Hungarian system of education under state control. The Peter Pázmány University was transferred from Trnava to Buda and enlarged by a medical school. Law schools were opened in Bratislava, Košice (Kassa), Györ, Zagreb, and Oradea Mare (Nagy Varad) and a mining school established at Baňská Štiavnica (Schemnitz, Selmec).

Maria Theresa's conciliatory policy eventually bore fruit. The Hungarian magnates were transformed at her court from a feudal nobility into a court aristocracy, and became genuinely attached to the dynasty. Previously rather rustic, they acquired in the cosmopolitan atmosphere of Vienna polish and sophistication, often preferring to speak German and French to their native Magyar. However, they were never alienated from Hungary to the extent that the Bohemian nobles were from Bohemia; they always remained first and foremost Hungarian noblemen. The enlightened atmosphere of Vienna had the opposite effect of stimulating the Hungarian national consciousness of some Hungarians in Vienna. In 1772 György Bessenyei (1747–1811), an officer in the Hungarian Bodyguard in Vienna, published a book in Magyar,[8] which had not been used for literary purposes (other than religious literature) for a century. The event is regarded as the opening of the Magyar cultural revival.

SOCIAL AND ECONOMIC DEVELOPMENT   Anti-Habsburg feeling survived primarily among the Hungarian gentry, who lived on

---

[8] It was a translation of Alexander Pope's *An Essay on Man.*

the land and were less affected by the new currents of thought. They jealously guarded their feudal self-government in the counties against Habsburg bureaucratic encroachment and were stout Hungarian patriots. Hungarian patriotism should not be confused with modern Magyar nationalism. It was a class and regional feeling *(Landespatriotismus)* rather than an ethnic one. Matej (Matthew) Bél (1684–1749), an enlightened Jack-of-all-intellectual-trades of Slovak origin, expressed it well when he characterized himself as *lingua Slavus, natione Hungarus, eruditione Germanus* (a Slav by language, Hungarian by nation, and German by education). The fact that Hungary was a multinational state did not yet cause internal division, as it was to do in the nineteenth century, because the medieval corporate concept of society still prevailed. In theory, the estates, regardless of nationality and religion, constituted the Hungarian political nation. In practice, it was the nobility and the clergy because the townsmen had long sunk into insignificance. Of course, the fact that most of the nobles were Magyars made Magyar more especially a nobleman's language. However, its importance was limited by the fact that Latin was still the official language of the country, as well as the language of intellectual intercourse, while German was the language of trade and commerce. A more important division of the population than language was religion. The Counter-Reformation had whittled the Protestants down to the hard core. In the eighteenth century the religious communities became stabilized and hermetically closed to one another.

That class and religion rather than nationality divided the population did not mean that Hungary's ethnic groups possessed no self-awareness. Class, religion, and nationality often coincided and fortified one another, especially in the non-Magyar periphery of Hungary. In Transylvania the coincidence of class, religion, and nationality was almost perfect and sharply divided the Magyar Calvinist or Catholic nobles from the Saxon Lutheran townsmen and the Rumanian Orthodox or Uniat peasants. Each group possessed a keen sense of national identity. This was also true of the Orthodox Serbs in southern Hungary and, to a smaller extent, the Uniat Ruthenes of northeastern Hungary. On the other hand, religion and class separated the older "Saxon" Germans of Transylvania and northern Hungary, who were predominantly townsmen and Lutherans, from the newer (eighteenth-century) "Swabian" German settlers in central and southern Hungary, who were predominantly Catholics and peasants; the two groups did not mix much. The militant Catholicism of the Croats constituted a strong barrier between them and the Orthodox Serbs, despite their linguistic proximity, but not between them and the Catholic Magyars. The Croat magnates were already magyarized in the seventeenth century, and in the eighteenth century many of the Croat gentry also accepted the Magyar language and outlook. The absence of clear class, religious, and ethnic divisions in northern Hungary muted somewhat the national self-awareness of the Slovaks, especially their Catholic majority. In the eighteenth century the remnants of the Slovak-speaking gentry tended to be assimilated by the more numerous and prosperous Magyar gentry.

Unlike Bohemia, Hungary remained predominantly an agrarian country in the eighteenth century. The soil of central and southern Hungary had been left largely uncultivated under the Turks. When it was put to the plow again, it proved extraordinarily fertile. The internal peace in the Habsburg empire in the eighteenth century enabled its population to grow rapidly, reaching about 21 million in 1787, of which the Hungarian population accounted for about 8.5 million and the Bohemian about 4.4 million. This growth provided a steady demand for Hungarian farm products. As a result, the income of the Hungarian large and medium landowners in general rose steadily. The great magnates and the high dignitaries of the Catholic Church enjoyed truly princely incomes. They also had a monopoly of high offices, and, as members of the upper house of the diet, they had a veto over legislation. Consequently, they felt no compelling reason to tamper with Hungary's antiquated social and economic system. Yet it was the gentry that defended the old order most passionately. Quite parochial, they were more likely to repeat the old boast, *extra Hungarian non est vita et si est, non est ita* (outside of Hungary there is no life,

and if there is, it is not as good), than the cosmopolitan magnates. They were very proud of their right to vote although
according to the time-honored Hungarian tradition their votes
were "weighed," not "counted" *(voces ponderantur, nec num-
erantur);* the vote of a substantial nobleman might "weigh"
more than the votes of a score of poor ones.

The incomes of the gentry greatly varied, for they were
a numerous[9] and far from homogeneous class. Some were prosperous, while others, especially in the poor mountainous districts of Transylvania and northern Hungary, were quite poor.
The poorest of them, known as "sandal noblemen" *(bocskoros
nemes)*[10] eked out a meager living by farming or in the service
of larger nobles. Yet they clung to their status, not only because
it was tax-exempt, but because it gave them the psychological
satisfaction of standing above the peasants, from whom they
did not socioeconomically differ much.

The status of the peasants also varied greatly, from free
landowning peasants in the newly acquired lands to landless
cottagers and hereditary domestics in noble households. On
the whole, their lot was a hard one and tended to get worse
during the course of the eighteenth century because of the
chronic labor shortage. The peasants alone bore the whole
burden of taxation and military service, although the latter
was less onerous in Hungary than in other parts of the empire;
the Hungarian contingent in the imperial army was small and
enlistment in it was, at least in theory, voluntary. Maria Theresa found the conditions of the peasants so appalling that despite her reluctance to antagonize the nobles, she published
the *Urbarium* in 1767, which defined the peasants' duties to
the landowners. It was published in all the languages of Hungary and provided the peasants with a standard to which to
appeal in defending themselves against noble abuse.

Hungarian industrial development, even artisanal pro-
duction, was stifled by the lack of capital, the shortage of skilled

---

[9] The nobles large and small numbered about 5 percent of the population, or
about 400,000 in the 1780s, of which only 108 were titled.
[10] They were known as sandal nobles because they could not afford to buy boots,
the usual noble footwear, and wore homemade sandals.

labor, and the exclusion of Hungary from the Austrian tariff area, which gave an economic dimension to the growing Austro-Hungarian dualism. Hungarian towns lagged in development behind their Austrian and Bohemian counterparts. Buda, the national capital, experienced a certain renaissance under Maria Theresa. She built the Royal Palace in Buda. More important was the growth of Buda's twin and rival, the city of Pest, on the flat eastern bank of the Danube River. By 1800 the population of Vienna exceeded 100,000, that of Prague was about 80,000, and the combined populations of Buda and Pest[11] amounted to about 55,000. Hungarian townsmen, still in the main German, played no important role in the political, social, or cultural life of the country. When a Hungarian middle class arose in the nineteenth century, it was recruited not from the townsmen but largely from the gentry that had been forced off the land.

Foreign Affairs

PARTITION OF POLAND The death of King Augustus III of Poland in October 1763, a few months after the conclusion of the Seven Years' War, added strain to Austria's tense relations with Prussia and Russia. As usual, the three powers felt compelled to meddle in the Polish royal election. In April 1764 Catherine II and Frederick II concluded a treaty of alliance directed against Austria and agreed to pursue a common policy in Poland and Sweden.[12] The first fruit of the alliance was to impose on Poland their candidate for the Polish crown, Stanislaw August Poniatowski, a Polish nobleman and Catherine's former lover, who became a helpless pawn in her hands. Using as a pretext Polish oppression of the Orthodox and Protestant minorities (the Dissidents), Catherine reduced Poland to a Russian protectorate. In 1767 her crass meddling provoked civil war in Poland. The anti-Russian party formed the armed Confederation of Bar to unseat the puppet King Stanislaw (1764–

---

[11] The two cities were not merged until 1873.

[12] The treaty bound Russia and Prussia to provide each other military and financial assistance in the event of war with Austria and financial assistance only in the event that one or the other were involved in a war with a power other than Austria.

1795), end the Russian influence, and suppress the "Dissidents."
Stanislaw was unable to put down the Confederation, whereupon Catherine sent Russian troops into Poland to do so.

Austria, France, and Turkey were greatly alarmed. In
1768 when the Russians, in hot pursuit of the confederates,
violated Ottoman territory, the sultan declared war on Russia.
In the ensuing Russo-Turkish War (1768–1774) the Russian
forces scored spectacular successes on land and sea. The Russian army occupied the Danubian principalities and (for the
first time in history) crossed the Danube River into Bulgaria
while the Russian Baltic fleet sailed to the Mediterranean and
destroyed the Ottoman fleet in the Chesme Bay. Consternation
reigned at the court in Vienna. In 1770 when the Polish confederates fled to the Spiš towns in northern Hungary, which
King Sigismund had pawned to Poland in 1415,[13] Maria Theresa ordered her troops to occupy the towns and she annexed
them. However, she was not prepared to intervene against
Russia for fear of war with Prussia. Frederick II was himself
disgruntled over Catherine's successes, which promised to bring
Russia great territorial gains while Prussia got nothing but a
depleted treasury, for under the treaty of 1764 Prussia was
obliged to provide Russia subsidies. Therefore, in the winter
of 1770–1771 he sent his brother, Prince Henry of Prussia, to
St. Petersburg to seek compensations. The outcome of Henry's
mission was the decision to partition Poland.

Sin likes company. Austria was offered compensation
in Poland, too. Joseph II and Kaunic advised acceptance, but
Maria Theresa was appalled at the idea of sharing in the spo-
liation of a friendly Catholic kingdom. However, the Russians
and Prussians brushed aside her scruples by pointing out that
she herself had begun the partition of Poland by annexing the
Spiš towns. In the end she yielded. So inexorable was the logic
of eighteenth-century diplomacy that Austria could not refuse
a share of Poland; if Russia and Prussia expanded at the expense
of Poland, Austria had to do so too in order to keep a balance
of power in the area. Once Maria Theresa decided to share in

[13] See p. 21.

the partition of Poland, her demands were anything but modest, which elicited a sneer from Frederick that the more she cried over Poland the more she took of it.

GALICIA AND BUKOVINA   On August 5, 1772, the three powers signed the Treaty of Partition in St. Petersburg. Austria's share was the second largest in area (55,595 square miles) and the largest in population (2.1 million). It contained the richest salt mines in Europe and much fertile soil. The territory was given an historically doubtful name, "Kingdom of Galicia and Lodomeria,"[14] and organized into an Austrian province *(Land)*, with a governor and a diet at Lviv (Lwów, Lvov, Lemberg) representing the estates (unknown in Poland) of clergy, upper and lower nobility, and townsmen. The socioeconomic structure of Poland resembled that of Hungary. The nobles of Galicia were Catholic Poles or polonized Ruthenes, the townmen mostly Jewish, and the peasants about half Catholic Poles and half Uniat Ruthenes. As in Hungary before the battle of Mohács (1526) no legal distinction existed between the wealthy and poor nobles; Polish nobles bore no titles. There was, therefore, a frantic scramble among the wealthy nobles to acquire Habsburg titles in order to qualify for admission to the estate of upper nobility. There was no Polish central (royal) administration in Galicia, only organs of local self-government. Therefore, an Austrian bureaucratic organization was introduced. Its centralizing and germanizing tendencies were much resented. Despite the fact that Austria was the only Catholic state among the partitioning powers, Austrian rule was the least popular among the Poles.[15]

Three years after the partition of Poland, Austria extorted from the reluctant sultan, as compensation for Austrian mediation of the Peace of Kuchuk-Kainardji (1774) between Russia

[14] The annexation was historically justified by resurrecting an old and vague Hungarian claim to the ancient Russian principalities of Galich (Galicia) and Vladimir (Lodomeria), which, in fact, had lain mostly to the northeast of the Austrian share of Poland.

[15] After about 1870 there was a reversal of Polish feeling; Austria became the most acceptable of the partitioning powers.

and Turkey, the cession of the northernmost districts of Moldavia that were known as Bukovina (the Land of the Beech Trees). Bukovina, which was very thinly populated by Orthodox Rumanian and Ruthene herdsmen and peasants, was administratively attached to Galicia until 1849.

The loss of Silesia with its largely German population and the acquisition of Galicia and Bukovina with their heterogeneous populations further alienated the Habsburg empire from Germany and underlined its multinational character.

BAVARIAN SUCCESSION In 1777 there appeared to be a chance to redress the balance in favor of the German element. In that year Elector Maximilian Joseph of Bavaria died childless, and Austria raised a claim to a part of his heritage. The Bavarian succession was to go to the Palatinate Wittelsbach. The first in line of succession was Elector Charles Theodore (1742–1799) of the Palatinate, who was also childless. Joseph II and Kaunic pressured him into renouncing Lower Bavaria, which Austrian troops immediately occupied. However, Frederick the Great objected to this extension of Habsburg influence in Germany. He insisted that Charles Theodore assume his full heritage, and he backed his insistence by sending his army into Bohemia.

The ensuing War of the Bavarian Succession (1778–1779) proved to be a classical example of eighteenth-century cabinet warfare. Facetiously called the "Potato War" *(Kartoffelkrieg)* by the Germans, it was attended by much maneuvering but little bloodshed. Maria Theresa, who had misgivings about the Bavarian venture all along, asked for French and Russian mediation. This should have provided balance in the negotiations since France was Austria's ally and Russia was Prussia's. However, France did not like the Austrian expansion in Bavaria any more than Prussia and failed to back Austria. Under the Peace of Teschen (Těšín) (May 13, 1779) Austria received only a token part of Bavaria, the Innviertel (the Inn quarter). However, Joseph II did not regard the Peace of Teschen as the last word on the matter.[16]

---

[16] See below p. 136.

RETURN TO THE RUSSIAN ALLIANCE   Joseph II was disappointed in the French alliance. At this juncture, for reasons of her own, Catherine II became interested in a return to the Austrian alliance. Her great gains in the war with Turkey had whetted her appetite for more. She accepted the famous "Greek project" that proposed to expel the Turks from Europe and resurrect the Byzantine empire under her grandson Constantine. To realize such an ambitious project, Austrian rather than Prussian support was essential. In 1780 she invited Joseph II to visit her in Russia. Maria Theresa disliked Catherine II, but Joseph II proved receptive to her overtures. During their conversations at Mogilev and St. Petersburg they agreed on the conclusion of an alliance but disagreed over protocol. As Holy Roman emperor, Joseph claimed precedence over the empress of Russia. He insisted on his prerogative to sign the treaty first, which Catherine would not admit. The alliance was not consummated until May 1781, by an exchange of letters, which saved face both ways. By that time Maria Theresa had died, and Joseph had become the sole ruler of the Habsburg possessions. The Greek project was put off until a later time.

The Revolutionary Emperor

CHARACTER   Joseph II (1780–1790) was a true son of enlightened rationalism and the most sincere of the enlightened despots of the eighteenth century. "I have made philosophy the legislator of my empire," he declared. "Its logical principles shall transform Austria." He was, however, not a philosopher or an original thinker, but primarily a man of action. His reforms, on which his fame is based, were not inspired by theoretical study but by personal observation of conditions in his empire and abroad. A very restless man, he undertook innumerable inspection tours of the Habsburg possessions, often traveling incognito under the name of Count Falkenstein, and accompanied by only a small retinue or a single valet, to acquaint himself at first hand with their conditions. He also visited Germany, Italy, France, Belgium, and Russia. He lived frugally and dressed simply; he was the first European monarch to dress habitually in a simple military uniform. Impatient of pomp and circumstance, he virtually dissolved the court. A prodigious worker himself, he was harsh and demanding toward his subordinates. Characteristically, he had little appreciation for the fine arts. Although he felt compelled to provide a modest pension to Mozart (1756-1791) because the composer brought fame to the empire, he had little liking for his music. The greatest monument that he built was the large barracklike General Hospital in Vienna.

The ideas of what came to be known after him as Josephinism derived mainly from the *philosophes* of the Austrian enlightenment: Paul Josef Riegger, Karl Anton Martini, and Josef Sonnenfels, professors at the University of Vienna. They shared the French *philosophes'* belief in human progress, but they looked primarily to enlightened absolute monarchs to realize it, not elected parliaments. They wanted a stronger monarchy, not a weaker one. They were not liberals but *étatists*.

Joseph shared their view that the state stood above all, even the emperor. He justified his absolutist rule not by divine right but by conspicuous service to the state. "The state," he declared long before the English Utilitarians, meant "the greatest good for the greatest number." The widespread misery of the peasants that he found on his inspection tours appalled him, and their ignorance, superstition, and bigotry repelled him. The idleness of the decadent Austrian nobility angered him, and their ineffectualness filled him with contempt. Yet his concern for the peasants did not spring from any deep-seated humanitarianism but from his realization that they carried on their shoulders most of the burdens of the state. Likewise, his dislike of the nobles was not inspired by any egalitarianism—indeed, he considered the nobility indispensable for the state—but by his ire over the fact that they did not *earn* their privileges by commensurate service to the state.

Possessed of complete confidence in his judgment, Joseph was convinced that he knew better than his subjects what was good for them and was determined to impose reforms on them, if necessary, against their wishes. He regarded the remnants of feudal self-government as an irritating anachronism and never convoked the diets of his possessions. Instead, he ruled the empire by imperial fiat, through an ever-increasing bureaucracy. To assure the efficiency of the bureaucracy and the loyalty and obedience of his subjects, he created a secret police, whose agents and spies watched and reported on the activities of the empire's officials and the thoughts of its subjects. Joseph granted virtual freedom of the press, but at the same time he was driven by the logic of his reform policy to try to control the thoughts of his subjects. Beginning with the idea of freeing his subjects from oppression, misery, and superstition, he ended up by creating the first modern police state in Europe.

Joseph II is known in history as the Revolutionary Emperor. Whether meant as an accolade or an epithet, it is well warranted. Given a different education, he would have made a good Jacobin or Bolshevik.

Joseph regarded his mother's pragmatic reforms as illogical half-measures. He was determined to reform the empire throroughly and according to logical principles. During the ten years of his rule there poured forth a torrent of over six thousand decrees from Vienna on matters portentous and petty that affected every phase of his subjects' lives.

CENTRALIZATION AND GERMANIZATION   Joseph's ideal was a perfectly uniform state. There could be no exceptions, such as Hungary. He was determined to wipe out the Austro-Hungarian dualism and integrate Hungary fully in the empire. He refused to have himself crowned king of Hungary or Bohemia and had the Hungarian and Bohemian crown jewels carted off to Vienna to be stored away as relics of the past. He failed to fill the office of the Hungarian palatine and to convoke the diet. He systematically bypassed the Hungarian central offices, which were dominated by the Hungarian magnates. However, the main obstacle to centralization was feudal self-government in the counties that were dominated by the gentry. Therefore, in 1785, he first abolished the autonomy of Transylvania and Croatia—thus giving an inadvertent boost to Hun-

garian centralism—and then redivided the whole country into
ten larger regions under royal commissioners. German replaced
Latin as the official language in Hungary and Galicia. In Bohemia, Czech, which still had theoretical parity with German,
was dropped altogether. At the same time German was made
the sole language of instruction in all secondary schools and
universities.

Under Maria Theresa germanization was incidental; under
Joseph it became conscious policy. However, it is impossible
to agree with those modern German and German-Austrian
historians who affirm that Joseph was a conscious German nationalist. His preferred personal language—like that of the
upper classes in the whole German world at the time—was
French. Nor is there any indication that he ever rose from a
dynastic to a German-national concept of his empire. His policy
of germanization simply reflected his rationalist conviction
that since the Germans were the most numerous and most advanced people of the empire, it was reasonable that their language should be the *lingua franca* of the whole empire.

Joseph showed the same rationalist and utilitarian approach in his educational policy. He assiduously continued
his mother's policy of fostering primary-school education. However, in secondary and higher-school education he stressed
trade-training. Many of the classical *gymnasia* were abolished,
and in the universities priority was given to medical schools
to train doctors and law schools to train judges, lawyers, and
bureaucrats.

LEGAL REFORMS The influence of Riegger's, Martini's, and
Sonnenfels' enlightened views was best shown in Joseph's legal
reforms. Maria Theresa's penal code of 1769 still reflected a
medieval approach to crime by sanctioning torture, mutilation,
and barbarous methods of execution and by providing for lib-
eral use of the death penalty for such crimes as witchcraft, blas-
phemy, forging of public documents, and many others.

As early as 1781 Joseph decreed a new court procedure
that required, among other things, that both judges and lawyers
have legal training. At the same time, in two separate patents,

the manorial courts that dispensed justice to the largest segment of the population—the peasants—were reformed. They, too, were required to engage legally trained judges, and the litigants could appeal their verdicts. In 1787 a new General Penal Code was issued that did away with torture and mutilation, dropped from the list of crimes witchcraft and heresy, and reserved the death penalty for only very serious crimes. Perhaps most importantly, it firmly established the principle of equal punishment for equal crimes for nobles and commoners alike. Revision and unification of the civil codes of the various Habsburg possessions had begun in 1753, but they were not completed until 1811. In the meantime, however, Joseph proclaimed several laws reflecting the new rationalist approach to civil law. A new marriage law (1783), for instance, advanced the then revolutionary concept that marriage was not only a church sacrament but also a civil contract.

RELIGIOUS TOLERANCE Joseph II was a practicing and, presumably, believing Catholic. However, he regarded religious intolerance as a survival of medieval bigotry and superstition. On October 13, 1781, he brought to an end the Catholic Counter-Reformation by issuing the famous Patent of Toleration, which accorded the Protestants and Greek Orthodox tolerance but not equality with the Catholics in the empire. Joseph's tolerance had its limits though. He suppressed pietist sects, which he regarded as irrational, and had obdurate sectarians deported to Transylvania. Still, when one considers the Habsburg tradition, the Patent of Toleration was a radical measure indeed. It deeply shocked the majority of his subjects. However, contrary to the dire predictions of Catholic dignitaries, no mass defections from the Catholic Church occurred. In Bohemia and Austria only about 107,000 persons availed themselves of the patent to profess Protestant faiths again.

In a number of separate patents Joseph freed the Jews from most of the civil disabilities under which they had suffered. They were freed from the obligation to wear a distinct dress and reside in ghettos and from the prohibition to engage in certain trades. In 1787 there were about 350,000 Jews in the

empire, out of which about 210,000 resided in the newly acquired
Galicia. As a result of Joseph's policy, Polish Jews were permitted to move out of the crowded ghettos of Galicia into other
parts of the empire. Vienna, Prague, and Budapest, which had
only small Jewish communities in the eighteenth century, became important centers of Jewish life in the nineteenth century.

The Roman Catholic Church remained the state church
of the empire. Joseph, however, took the Erastian view that it
should concern itself with spiritual matters only and be sub-
ordinated to the needs of the state. Catholic clergymen were
forbidden to take orders from their superiors in Rome. Their
right to appeal to papal courts was likewise limited. Catholic
seminarians were forbidden to study in Rome. "General sem-
inaries" were established and placed under the supervision of
the state. Their purpose was to educate clergy in the new spirit
of enlightenment and obedience to the state.

In 1782, alarmed by Joseph's innovations, Pope Pius VI
took the unprecedented step of traveling to Vienna to reason
with him. Joseph received him courteously, but he was unimpressed with the pope's protests and continued to interfere in
the affairs of the Church. He abolished 738 monasteries
and convents that did not perform a useful social function,
such as teaching or maintaining hospitals or orphanages. Their
property was confiscated to establish a religious fund, which
was used to establish new parishes and bishoprics, as there was
indeed a shortage in some parts of the empire. Joseph did not
stop at organizational matters of the Church. Considering the
pervasive piety of his subjects as a manifestation of superstition, he decreed simplification of Church ritual, abolished
numerous holidays, forbade many pilgrimages, ordered the
use of sacks in place of coffins for burials, and insisted that
churches, like government buildings, be built in a severe func-
tional ("Josephine") style.

PEASANT EMANCIPATION   In 1780 peasant serfdom still prevailed
in the Habsburg empire. There were some free peasants, but
most were serfs. Conditions of serfdom varied from province

to province, but in no instance were they worse than, for example, in the Russian empire. Serfs in the Habsburg empire were legally their lords' "hereditary subjects" *(Erbuntertanen)*, not property. Without their lords' permission, they could not move from the land, determine their vocation, or marry whom they wished. In return for their use of the lords' land, they had to provide *robot*[17] (labor, *corvée*) or pay rents. Unlike the Russian "souls" (serfs) or American Negro slaves, they could not be bought and sold.

Joseph long regarded serfdom as a degrading and inefficient system of rural labor. On November 1, 1781, he issued his famous Serfdom Patent *(Leibeigenschaftspatent)*, which transformed the serfs from subjects of the lords into subjects of the state, in theory at least, equal before the law. Henceforth, they could leave the land if they wished, marry whom they wished, learn a trade, or, in rare instances, go to school to learn a profession and escape the lowly peasant status altogether.

The principal limitation of the peasant emancipation was that it was not accompanied by any redistribution of the land. The nobles remained the owners of the land. The peasants could buy it—if they had capital and the nobles were willing to sell. Otherwise, they had to continue to provide the lords labor or pay rents, which was the prevailing practice. Another limitation of peasant emancipation arose from the inability of the Josephine bureaucracy to reach down to the village level and replace the nobles as unpaid policemen, judges, tax collectors, and recruitment officers. This left the nobles a powerful club to wield over the heads of the peasants. While equal before the law, they were far from equal in practice.

The Serfdom Patent was first applied in Bohemia and then was extended gradually to the other provinces, except Lower and Upper Austria, where Joseph believed (perhaps too optimistically) serfdom did not exist. The inevitable slowness with which it was implemented by frequently unsympathetic noble officials led to peasant outbreaks. The most serious case

[17] From the Czech word *robota*, meaning labor.

of such a "revolution of rising expectations" occurred in Transylvania.

The Serfdom Patent was duly promulgated at Sibiu (Hermannstadt) in Transylvania on August 16, 1783. However, the Magyar nobles in Transylvania generally ignored it. In November 1784 a disturbance over army recruitments flared up into a full-scale peasant jacquerie that had religious and national (ethnic) overtones. The rebels avenged centuries of accumulated grievances by slaughtering the Magyar nobles and burning their manors. The leader of the revolt was a Rumanian peasant, Vasile Nicola, better known by his nickname Horia. He had gone several times to Vienna bearing petitions for the redress of peasant grievances, and claimed to have been received by Joseph in audience and to have been encouraged by the emperor to lead the revolt. Joseph denied that he had received him, but he may have forgotten; he received streams of petitioners in Vienna and on his travels. In any event, the story of peasants turning trustingly to their sovereign, like children to their father, to protect them against oppressive officials who deceive him, is a classical one; it has many versions in European history. Horia's revolt also had a classical ending. Joseph would not tolerate flaunting of authority; he ordered the army to supress the revolt. Horia was publicly executed, after ghastly torture appropriate to the occasion. However, Joseph did not content himself with repression. He ordered an investigation, and it was on the basis of its finding that he decreed peasant emancipation in all of Hungary in 1785.

Joseph was aware of the limitations of peasant emancipation. He would have liked to transform the peasantry into an independent landowning yeomanry that could produce far more in taxes than the peasants did under the existing conditions. In 1785 he ordered a new survey of all land, rustical and dominical, to be made, and in 1787 a census to be taken, even in Hungary. When the new Josephine Cadaster was completed in 1789, he decreed a single land tax, which was designed to end the *robot* and distribute the tax burden evenly between peasants and landowners. All land was to be taxed at the rate of 12.22 percent of its gross annual yield. In addition, the peasants were to pay up to 17.78 percent annually to the lords, in commutation of their obligations in *robot* or rents and the tithe, which the landowners would take over. The peasants would thus be free of all obligation to the lords and pay a maximum of 30 percent of their income in taxes. Owing, however, to the outcry of the nobles, Joseph was forced to postpone the planned tax for a year. Before the year was up he died, and his successor suspended the plan. *Robot* continued in the empire until 1848.

Despite all its limitations, Joseph's peasant emancipation was a revolutionary measure. Contrary to the nobles' dire prophecies, it resulted in no mass flight of the peasants from the land. Nevertheless, it provided a safety valve for peasant discontent. When conditions in the villages became intolerable, the peasants could and did leave them for the cities, where they provided a reservoir of free, cheap, and mobile labor that stimulated the industrialization of the empire in the nineteenth century.

OPPOSITION Reformers are seldom popular in their lifetime. Joseph's abrupt, coldly rationalistic, and often tactless reforms caused his tradition-bound subjects a virtual trauma. His Toleration Patent was welcomed by the tiny Protestant minority, but it offended the Catholic majority. His reforms of the Catholic Church were watched with shocked disbelief. His centralization provoked a resurgence of regional patriotism, and his germanization the first stirrings of ethnic nationalism or, to use Béla Király's apt term, protonationalism. The emancipated peasants were glad of their new freedom, but they were disappointed with its practical limitations. The nobles found the novel idea that they were no better than peasants before the law shocking and the attempt to tax them outrageous.

The Austrian nobles, long conditioned to submit to Habsburg authority, accepted Joseph's reforms with resignation. The Bohemian nobles were more resentful. Suddenly, they remembered Bohemia's long-forgotten "state rights" *(Staatsrecht)*. Some of them even rediscovered the beauty of the Czech language. However, being aliens in Bohemia, they did not dare to resist Joseph openly. The Hungarian nobles, however, had a long tradition of resistance to the Habsburgs, and were not prepared to accept Joseph's reforms supinely. Open rebellion, such as they had attempted in the seventeenth and early eighteenth centuries, was out of the question—at least as long as the empire was at peace. However, should war break out, with foreign aid, rebellion might succeed. Therefore, the Hungarian nobles offered passive resistance and bided their time. Joseph's ambitious foreign policy soon gave them their opportunity.

War and Diplomacy

BAVARIAN EXCHANGE Joseph II did not accept the outcome of the Potato War (War of the Bavarian Succession) as definite. In 1785 he proposed a scheme that he had been entertaining for a long time, namely, to exchange the Austrian Netherlands (Belgium) for Bavaria. Belgium was far richer than Bavaria. However, being isolated from the Habsburg empire, it was difficult to govern from Vienna and impossible to defend. Charles Theodore, who did not like Bavaria and was not liked by the Bavarians, was amenable to the proposal, but once again Frederick II interfered. Catherine II, now Joseph's ally, tried to arbitrate the conflict, as a signatory of the Peace of Teschen. However, Frederick, though old and ailing, was as resolute and resourceful as ever. In 1786, just before his death, he organized the "League of (German) Princes" *(Fürstenbund)* and frustrated both Joseph's scheme and Catherine's ambition to be arbiter of German affairs.

TURKISH WAR After Frederick's death Joseph considered a rapprochement with Prussia, but Kaunic, who had spent his career fighting Prussia, dissuaded him from it. Instead, he pushed Joseph toward closer collaboration with Russia. In the meantime, Catherine had annexed the Crimea (1783), which was in violation of the Peace of Kuchuk-Kainardji. Turkey, backed by France and Britain, protested but was not prepared to go to war. Early in 1787, in defiance of European opinion, Catherine undertook a well-publicized tour of inspection in the Crimea and "New Russia,"[18] and she invited the diplomatic corps and Joseph II to accompany her. On Kaunic's advice Joseph reluctantly accepted. The tour was stage-managed with flair by Grigori Potëmkin, Catherine's former lover, proconsul in New Russia, and father of the Greek project.[19] They sailed down the Dnieper River to Kherson, the port newly established by Potëmkin at the river's mouth, where he had a triumphal arch erected with the sign "This way to Byzantium." Catherine joked to Joseph that it was only two days' sail from Kherson to Constantinople. However, Joseph was unimpressed with her daydreaming. If he permitted himself any daydreaming about the final goal of the Austrian *Drang nach Südosten,* it was probably Salonica and the Aegean.

In August 1787, goaded by Catherine's many provocations, the sultan declared war on Russia. Joseph recognized at once a *casus foederis* for Austria, and in February 1788 he declared war on Turkey. Fancying himself a competent general, he took personal command of the troops on the Danube and the Sava rivers, but he only succeeded in completely disorganizing and demoralizing them. When the Turks ventured north of the Danube into the Banat, he and the troops panicked disgracefully. In 1789 he fell ill and relinquished command to old General Laudon, an uninspired but competent professional, who restored order and morale among the troops.

The war did not go well for the allies. France was too close to outbreak of revolution to interfere. However, England was hostile and free to act. England had supported Catherine II in her first war with Turkey but was alienated by Catherine's initiative in forming the League of Armed Neutrality (1780) during the American War of Independence. Now William Pitt the Younger (1759–1806) took the lead in forming a coalition of Prussia, Holland, Poland, and Sweden against Russia and Austria. Sweden declared war on Russia, which prevented Catherine from sending the Baltic fleet to the Mediterranean

[18] New Russia consisted of the Ukrainian lands annexed by Russia from Poland in 1772 and from Turkey in 1774.
[19] It was on this occasion that Potëmkin had the sham "Potëmkin villages" built to enhance his accomplishment as governor of New Russia.

and hampered the Russian operations against the Turks. In August 1789 the Russians under the brilliant Alexander Suvorov and the Austrians under Prince Koburg dealt the Turks a crushing blow at Focsani in Moldavia, forcing them to fall south of the Danube. In September Laudon took Belgrade and advanced into Serbia and Bosnia. The Serbs, who again supported the Austrians, were organized into the Free Corps *(Freikorps).* (One of its members, Djordje Petrovic, later became famous as Kara George.) However, internal difficulties offset the Austrian advances.

SUCCESS OR FAILURE? In December when Joseph II returned mortally ill to Vienna, the situation was ominous. The Austrian Netherlands (Belgium) had revolted and expelled the small Austrian garrisons. In January 1790 it declared the independence of the United States of Belgium. Hungary was seething with discontent over Joseph's reforms and also the presence of the imperial army in Hungary for the Turkish war, with the inevitable requisitions and other hardships on the citizenry. Hungarian malcontents were openly talking of revolt and secretly negotiating with the Prussian ambassador in Vienna and in Berlin. Galicia was likewise threatening to revolt. In view of these circumstances, Joseph, deeply discouraged, on January 30, 1790, revoked all his reforms in Hungary except the Toleration Patent and the Serfdom Patent. Three weeks later, on February 20, he died.

Joseph had bitterly suggested as his own epitaph: "Here lies Joseph II, who failed in all his enterprises." Actually, he was too severe on himself. It is true that most of his reforms had failed, but the empire was never the same again. If nothing else, he had swept it clean of feudal cobwebs. By his shock treatments he had awakened his subjects from the intellectual torpor into which the Counter-Reformation had plunged them and made them alive to new European trends. His and Maria Theresa's reforms had also welded the loose Habsburg possessions into an effective state, and had greatly increased their disparate subjects' feeling for the "common monarchy" *(Gesamtmonarchie).* More than any other Habsburg, Joseph thought first of the interests of the state and the people whom it was to serve, and only then of the dynasty. His basic aims were rational and disinterested. He was the best the Habsburgs ever produced.

Leopold II

PEACE ABROAD Joseph's brother and successor, Leopold II (1790–1792), was just as enlightened as he and a far better politician. As duke of Tuscany (1765–1790), Leopold had given that duchy a model administration and had made it one of the most advanced of the Italian states. When he moved up from Florence to Vienna to head the Habsburg empire, he found the situation dangerous in the extreme. On March 31, 1790, Prussia had concluded an alliance with Turkey against Austria and on March 20 one with Poland against Russia. War on two fronts and a revolt in Hungary seemed imminent. Leopold moved deftly to defuse the explosion. First, despite Kaunic's objections, he took steps to neutralize Prussia. In the Convention of Reichenbach (Dzierzoniow in present Polish Silesia) on July 27, 1790, Leopold promised to end the Turkish war without territorial acquisitions, while King Frederick William II (1786–1797) agreed to stop supporting the Hungarians and other dissident elements in the empire. Next, he instructed his commanders to conclude an armistice with the Turks. This led, through Prussian and British mediation, to the conclusion of a separate peace with Turkey at Svishtov in Bulgaria on August 4, 1791. With the exception of a few small frontier rectifications, it marked a return to the status quo ante. Russia fought on alone until forced by an Anglo-Prussian ultimatum to agree to conclude peace too, at Jassy on January 9, 1792; under the terms of the peace Russia's southwestern boundary was extended from the Bug to the Dniester River.

COMPROMISE AT HOME At the same time Leopold effected a series of tactical retreats at home. He offered the estates of his various possessions a compromise. He would foreswear legislating by imperial fiat, restore provincial and local self-government, and abandon Joseph's program, provided that the diets would confirm by their own laws Joseph's most important reforms: religious tolerance and peasant emancipation. In Hungary and Bohemia he also offered to be crowned as king of their respective lands and restored their crown jewels, to which the Hungarians, especially, attributed almost mystical properties.

Most of the diets accepted Leopold's compromise without cavil. The Bohemian diet, in which noble malcontents had talked of reverting to the status before the Renewal Ordinance of 1627,[20] meekly confirmed the Toleration Patent, abolition of serfdom, and equal taxation of the land. It did not even insist on restoring Czech to official parity with German, but contented itself with a promise to allow Czech to be taught in some *gymnasia* and to establish a chair of Czech language and literature in the University of Prague. The Moravian diet approved the Toleration Patent more reluctantly, but it made no demands concerning the Czech language. In September 1791 Leopold was crowned king of Bohemia in Prague amidst scenes of Bohemian-Habsburg reconciliation. Administratively, the Bohemian lands reverted to the status of 1764, that is, after the completion of the Theresan administrative reforms. Return to the status of 1764 was also the basis of the compromise with the Austrian lands. In Belgium, which the Austrian troops reoccupied, Leopold restored the old constitution (the *Joyeuse Entrée*).

HUNGARY The Hungarian estates proved harder to appease. The diet of 1790–1791 was a great storm c̈enter. There was fear at the Austrian court lest the Hungarian estates imitate their French counterpart and transform themselves into a revolutionary national assembly. To prevent such a possibility, the court sought, with a sure Habsburg instinct for divide and conquer,[21] allies within Hungary. Croatia and Transylvania were separated again from Hungary and their diets restored. The Serbs were encouraged to hold a "diet" of church and lay leaders under Metropolitan Putnik which met at Timişoara (Temesvár)

[20] See p. 61.

[21] Habsburg apologists bristle at the suggestion that the Habsburgs deliberately practiced *divide et impera*. Regardless, Habsburg history is replete with examples of it. It is entirely safe to characterize it as conscious Habsburg policy.

in the Banat from September to December 1790. Amidst much vituperation against the Hungarians, the Serbs drafted a resolution demanding equality of the Orthodox Church with the Catholic, autonomy for the Serb area in southern Hungary (Vojvodina), and a minister for Serb affairs in Vienna. The court also encouraged a group of young Hungarian radicals who supported Josephinism,[22] and it even considered stirring up the peasants against the nobles, but discarded the idea as too dangerous.

Actually, the court's fears were not warranted. The Hungarian nobles were no "third estate," clamoring for liberty, equality, and fraternity; on the contrary, they were counter-revolutionaries seeking to restore the feudal order that Joseph had destroyed. The news of the Reichenbach Convention signed by Leopold and Frederick William cooled their ardor for armed uprising, for they knew that without foreign aid it had no chance of success. The diet's rhetoric proved stronger than its actions. It did nullify all of Joseph's decrees, but it enacted toleration acts of its own for the Protestants, Orthodox, and Jews and also provided for personal freedom of the peasants. However, it resolutely refused to agree to taxation of the nobles' land. With much satisfaction, it ordered Joseph's cadaster and the results of the census of 1787 burned. It rejected German as the official language in Hungary and as the language of instruction in the schools. It proposed to replace German with Magyar (the "language of the fatherland"). This proposal encountered stiff opposition from the Croat delegates in the diet— a harbinger of Hungary's bitter linguistic quarrels in the nineteenth century. The Croats were as vehement as the Magyars in denouncing Josephinism, but they did not see why Magyar should be the language of the fatherland any more than Croat and insisted on restoring neutral Latin. In the end, this was agreed upon. However, Magyar was to be taught in the *gymnasia,* and it was adopted as the official language in many of the counties. The Serb demand that Orthodox bishops be admitted to the diet, the same as Catholic, was grudgingly granted

[22] See p. 145.

(though without the right to vote), but the other Serb demands were rejected. Although more reluctantly and with many more reservations than other diets, the Hungarian diet thus accepted Leopold's compromise. He, in turn, confirmed Hungary's special position in the empire in his coronation oath.

In Transylvania the Rumanians, prompted by the Serb example, also asked for permission to hold a "diet," but they were rudely rebuffed by the governor, György Banffy, who was a Magyar noble. The Rumanian Uniat and Orthodox clergy, therefore, united in presenting a memorandum to Leopold II called *Supplex Libellus Valachorum* (Booklet of the Pleas of the Vlachs), in which they proudly claimed to be descendants of the original Daco-Roman population of Transylvania and demanded equal rights with the Magyars, Szekels, and Saxons, whom they treated, by implication, as newcomers to the province. Leopold passed the memorandum with a sympathetic endorsement to the Transylvanian diet, where it produced stupefaction among the Magyars. The pretentions of the despised Rumanian peasants seemed to them sheer impudence. The only Rumanian in the diet, the Uniat bishop Ioan Bop, was angrily set upon to explain the memorandum. Frightened by the Magyar wrath, he cravenly disavowed it. It was naturally rejected with insults appropriate to the Rumanian "insolence."

In pacifying the empire without giving away anything essential, Leopold proved real statesmanship. He might have led the empire along the path of further reform, but he died suddenly on March 1, 1792, when he was only forty-five years old. With his death the period of reform begun under Maria Theresa came to an end, and an era of reaction set in. It was to last until 1848.

The Habsburg Empire and the French Revolution

CHALLENGE OF THE FRENCH REVOLUTION   With its democratic and nationalistic ideas, the French Revolution presented a real threat to the multinational, absolutist Habsburg empire. The Habsburg court, however, perceived this danger only gradually.

Joseph II disapproved of Louis XVI's convocation of the

French Estates General, for he did not approve of representative institutions. However, he was not unduly perturbed by it. After the fall of the Bastille he believed that France would be preoccupied with internal affairs for many years to come and, consequently, unable to play an important part in European affairs. When the Count of Artois, Louis' younger brother (later Charles X), who had fled abroad, appealed to Joseph to intervene in France to restore the *ancien régime,* the emperor refused and sternly counseled him to return to France and obey the king and the National Assembly.

Leopold II and the venerable Kaunic were likewise reluctant to interfere in, or break with, France. However, revolutions have a tendency to transfer their internal conflicts abroad. Leopold could not ignore the repercussions of the revolution in Belgium and the west German states. He was also moved by the appeals of his sister Marie Antoinette to save the tottering French monarchy. He met with Frederick William II at Pillnitz in Saxony to discuss the problems arising out of the French Revolution, and on August 27, 1791, they issued a joint declaration calling on European monarchs to restore Louis XVI to full authority in France. They made it clear, however, that they would intervene in France only if all European powers, including England, would consent to it, which was doubtful. The Declaration of Pillnitz enraged the French revolutionaries. They eagerly seized on it to discredit Louis XVI. Thus, relations between France and the European monarchies were further strained.

In 1792 the aged pro-French Kaunic was retired and replaced with Count Philipp Cobenzl, who concluded an alliance with Prussia against France (February 7, 1792). Three weeks later, on March 1, Leopold died, and on April 20 the French Legislative Assembly declared war on "the king of Hungary and Bohemia"[23] to defend "the liberty and independence of the French nation." The cycle of the French Revolutionary and Napoleonic wars had begun.

[23] This formula was used to indicate that France was making war on the Habsburgs, not on the German empire or its people.

FRANCIS I The king of Hungary and Bohemia was Leopold's son Francis II (I)[24] (1792–1835). The impression made on him by the revolutionary wars that filled out the first half of his long reign wiped out any trace of the enlightened education that he had received from his father and uncle. A timid, untalented, and narrow-minded man, whose denseness of mind was relieved only by a primitive cunning and sly bonhomie, Francis was as un-Josephinian, obscurantist, and reactionary a monarch as could be imagined. His principle virtue was his application to work. He was not, however, a good administrator but a bureaucratic pedant, who often wasted his time on trivia. Until 1805 he was assisted by a "cabinet minister" *(Kabinettminister)*, Count Franz Colloredo, his former tutor, who controlled the work of the other ministers. Thereafter, Francis acted as his own prime minister, dealing with each minister separately, which resulted in poor coordination of policy between departments.

Fortunately for the empire, the stress of war brought to the fore able men to assist the emperor: notably, Count Philipp Stadion, foreign minister and fiscal reformer; Archduke Charles (Francis' brother), reformer of the army and prolific writer on military strategy; and, last but not least, Metternich, an astute diplomat. Under the great servants of the empire, the ordinary Habsburg bureaucrats continued in their plodding but steady way, often in an enlightened Josephinian spirit By 1811 they completed the work begun under Maria Theresa on the civil code. Applied only in the Austrian half of the empire, the new General Civil Code *(Allgemeine Bürgerliche Gesetzbuch)* was quite as advanced as Napoleon's Code Civil.

POPULAR RESPONSE AND REACTION Ultimately. the political and social ideas of the French Revolution had a strong influence on the peoples of the Habsburg empire, but their immediate impact was slight. In 1794 the police discovered two "Jacobin plots," one at Vienna and one at Budapest. The former was no plot at all, but only a small group of intellectuals who sympa-

---

[24] Francis changed the ordinal in 1804 when he became emperor of Austria. As such, he was Francis I. See p. 149.

thized with the ideas of the French Revolution and opposed the war. The latter was indeed a plot, but it was scarcely dangerous. Its instigator was an enlightened Franciscan, Father Ignaz Martinovics, who had traveled abroad and had been to France. In 1790 he had been engaged by Leopold's police to propagandize the cause of reform and progress as a means of checking the feared nobles' revolt.[25] Frustrated by the reaction that ensued under Francis, he organized a group of like-minded young radical intellectuals in the secret Society of Liberty and Equality, the program of which called for proclaiming a Hungarian republic, legal equality, and civil freedoms. Within the social and psychological conditions then prevailing in Hungary, the program had no chance of success—even if it had been supported by the French revolutionaries, which was not the case. However, the court, frightened by the Reign of Terror in France, overreacted. It treated the "plots" with utmost seriousness. The "Jacobins" were tried and convicted of treason. Seven of them, including Martinovics, were hanged and the rest sentenced to long prison terms.

Apart from a handful of radical intellectuals, the French Revolution held little appeal to any significant segment of the population. The "middle class" of tradesmen were, unlike the French bourgeoisie, neither numerous nor forward-looking. Steeped in a political, religious, and social conservatism, they discerned no advantage in the French Revolution. As a matter of fact, they were appalled by its antimonarchist and anticlerical aspects. For the nobility, the French Revolution obviously held little attraction. Somewhat *frondeur* under Joseph II, especially in Hungary, they now nestled close to the throne in which they saw the best safeguard of their privileges. Apart from redistribution of land, the appeal of the "fruits of the French Revolution" (abolition of serfdom, religious freedom, and legal equality) to the peasantry was likewise slight, for they had already received them from Emperor Joseph II and his dutiful bureaucrats. There was as yet no significant city proletariat in the empire that might respond to the French Revolution.

[25] See p. 141.

Far more important than the response of the peoples of the Habsburg empire to the ideas of the French Revolution was their reaction to its military threat. The dangers of the French Revolutionary and Napoleonic wars produced a strong upsurge of loyalty to the dynasty and anti-French nationalism.[26] Because of the basic loyalty of its subjects, the empire showed an amazing resilience in the face of repeated military defeats.

FIRST COALITION   The Habsburg empire played a major role in the French Revolutionary and Napoleonic wars. It was the continental kingpin of the anti-French coalitions. Only Britain matched it in resolution and implacable hostility to France. However, Britain was protected from the French armies by its insular position and the efficient British navy, whereas Austria was fully exposed to their attacks. Four times Austria went down in defeat, only to rise again and join the next anti-French coalition.[27]

The Austro-Prussian alliance of 1792 was the nucleus of the First Coalition (1792–1797). In 1792 the Austrian and Prussian armies under the command of the aged duke of Brunswick invaded France. On July 25, 1792, the duke issued a notorious manifesto bombastically threatening to destroy Paris if Louis XVI were harmed. Instead of saving the French monarch it had the opposite effect; it precipitated Louis' downfall and the rise of the National Convention (1792–1795), which took energetic steps to defend France. On November 19, 1792, at a moment of exaltation over the French victory at Valmy, the Convention retorted to the allied threat to restore the French monarchy by threatening to export the French Revolution abroad; it offered French "help and fraternity to all peoples who wanted to recover their freedom." On February 1, 1793, it declared war on Britain, Holland, and Spain. The French revolutionary armies

[26] See pp. 153–154.

[27] The intensity of Austrian resistance to revolutionary France may be best seen if compared to Austrian resistance to the Allies in World War I. Napoleon defeated Austria four times and occupied Vienna twice. Yet Austria survived. The Allies never squarely defeated Austria or occupied Vienna and Budapest in World War I. Yet Austria disintegrated in 1918.

began to erect a band of satellite republics from the Netherlands to Italy.

PARTITIONS OF POLAND   Prussia chose this moment to deceive its Austrian ally and basely betray its Polish ally. On January 23, 1793, behind Austria's back, Prussia agreed with Russia on the Second Partition of Poland. Catherine II had loudly denounced the French Revolution but rather than come to Louis XVI's aid, she preferred to use the distraction of Europe to deal with the "Jacobins on the Vistula," who (with Prussian encouragement and against her wishes) had adopted a constitution (May 3, 1791).

The court in Vienna resented being left out of the Second Partition. In 1793 the pro-Prussian Cobenzl was replaced with Baron Johann Thugut in the foreign office. In 1795 he negotiated with Russia compensations in Poland, whereupon Prussia left the First Coalition (Peace of Basel, March 5, 1795) to join Russia and Austria in the Third (final) Partition of Poland (October 24, 1795). Austria received Cracow and a substantial area in west-central Poland, which was given the name of West Galicia.

PEACE OF CAMPO FORMIO   In 1795 Spain likewise left the First Coalition, but Austria went on doggedly fighting France until crushed by the young General Napoleon Bonaparte, whom the directory (1795–1799) had placed in command of the French armies in Italy. During his First Italian Campaign (1796–1797) Bonaparte conquered Piedmont, Milan, and Venice and advanced into Carniola and Styria. Austria was forced to withdraw from the First Coalition. Under the Peace of Campo Formio (October 17, 1797) Austria abandoned Belgium and Milan to France, and received in compensation Venice, including its possessions across the Adriatic Sea, Dalmatia and (littoral) Istria.

The affairs of Germany were to be settled at a general peace congress that met at Rastadt. Prussia at Basel and Austria at Campo Formio had secretly agreed to abandon all of the left bank of the Rhine to France. The dispossessed German princes were to be compensated elsewhere. However, because of

Austrian and Prussian jealousy, which put the French in the role of arbiters of German affairs, the Congress of Rastadt came to nothing.

SECOND COALITION In 1798 Bonaparte tried to strike at England, which refused to make peace, through Egypt. England took the lead in forming the Second Coalition (1799–1801). Austria and Russia, the latter under the erratic Tsar Paul I (1796–1801), joined it. The plan of the allies called for the British and the Russians to land in, and expel the French from, the Netherlands; for the Austrians to expel the French from southern Germany and Switzerland; and for the Austrians and the Russians to drive them out of Italy. The Anglo-Russian force that landed in the Netherlands met with disaster. However, the Austrians under Archduke Charles succeeded in forcing the French to retire from southern Germany behind the Rhine. In Italy, largely owing to the genius of Russian General Alexander Suvorov, the Russians and the Austrians completely crushed the French. Suvorov then wanted to invade France, but the Austrians feared that this would be courting disaster. Instead, Suvorov was sent to Switzerland, where he escaped a French trap only by his famous retreat across the St. Gotthard to Germany.

Paul I was angered by what he thought was English and Austrian readiness to fight to the last Russian soldier and also by English policy in the Mediterranean. In October 1799 he abruptly withdrew from the Second Coalition. At the same time Bonaparte returned from Egypt, overthrew the Directory, and established the Consulate (1799—1804). In his Second Italian Campaign (1800–1801) he repeated the feats of the First Campaign and constrained Francis II to sue for peace.

PEACE OF LUNÉVILLE Under the Peace of Lunéville (February 9, 1801) Austria lost Tuscany but was to be compensated for it in Germany. Solution of the German problem, which had been left unsettled by the abortive Congress of Rastadt, was entrusted to a "deputation" (committee) of the German diet consisting of representatives of the principal German princes. After a good deal of bargaining, which was arbitrated by Napoleon's foreign minister Charles Talleyrand, the committee presented its recommendations *(Reichsdeputationshauptschluss)* to the diet and they were approved on March 23, 1803. They provided for secularization of the remaining ecclesiastical states and abolition of the mass of petty German states. Austria's compensations were relatively small. It received two small bishoprics, Brixen (Bressanone) and Trent (Trento), in the Tyrol, for the loss of two small possessions in southern Germany, and the larger archbishopric of Salzburg for the loss of Tuscany.[28]

By French design, the principal beneficiaries of the simplification of Germany's map were the German "middle" states, such as Bavaria and Württemberg. They were made large enough to be able to resist complete domination by Austria or Prussia but not large enough to be able to defy France.

EMPEROR OF AUSTRIA   When these changes were made in Germany, the Holy Roman Empire was already under the shadow of dissolution. When and if it disappeared from the stage of history, Francis II would be left without a proper dignity among European monarchs, other than his titles archduke of Austria, king of Hungary, king of Bohemia, and so forth. The fact that on May 18, 1804, Napoleon made himself "emperor of the French,"[29] gave the matter particular. urgency. Therefore, on August 11, 1804, Francis II issued a patent establishing the title and dignity of hereditary "emperor of Austria" for himself and his successors.

The new title was a dynastic rather than territorial one. The patent established an *emperor,* not an *empire,* of Austria. It stressed that the new rank did not affect the rights and constitutions of any of the Habsburg possessions, in particular those of Hungary, and would not loosen the ties of the Habsburg *Erblande* and the Kingdom of Bohemia to the Holy Roman Empire. Nevertheless, legal niceties notwithstanding, the patent did just that: it gave the Habsburg possessions a new identity

[28] Technically, Salzburg became a secundogeniture under Archduke Ferdinand, who was previously in Tuscany.

[29] Napoleon was crowned emperor of the French on December 2, 1804.

and loosened their ties to Germany. They had constituted a defacto empire for almost 300 years, but they never had a common name. Now they became generally, albeit unofficially, known as the empire of Austria. By acquiring a common identity, their unity was inevitably strengthened and Austria's and Bohemia's ties to the Holy Roman Empire were weakened.

THIRD COALITION   In 1802, by the Treaty of Amiens, even Britain made peace with Napoleon. Briefly all of Europe was at peace. However, as early as 1803 war broke out again between France and Britain. In 1804 Napoleon assembled a fleet at Boulogne to invade England. Britain, under William Pitt's energetic leadership, countered the threat by organizing the Third Coalition (1805–1807). By offering subsidies, Pitt secured Russia's and Sweden's adherence to it in April and Austria's in August 1805. Spain, Bavaria, and other South German states joined France.

Expecting the main theater of war to be in Italy again, Archduke Charles led the main Austrian army there, while a smaller army under Archduke Ferdinand and General Mack went to southern Germany. Contrary to Vienna's expectations, Napoleon decided to make Germany the main theater. In September 1805 he broke up camp at Boulogne and by forced marches advanced into Germany with extraordinary speed. At Ulm he surprised and surrounded the army under General Mack and forced it to surrender (October 17). He then rushed down the Danube valley toward Vienna. Although Archduke Charles was recalled from Italy, he returned too late to save the capital; it fell to Napoleon on November 13. Napoleon then pursued Emperor Francis, who had retreated northward into Moravia, there to await the arrival of Russian help under Tsar Alexander I (1801–1825) and General Michael Kutuzov. On December 2, the first anniversary of his imperial coronation, Napoleon won his most resounding victory by decisively defeating the combined Austrian and Russian armies at Austerlitz (Slavkov) in Moravia (the "Battle of the Three Emperors"). Alexander I hastily retreated from the country, and Francis I requested an armistice and sued for peace.

Francis II and Napoleon after the battle of Austerlitz, 1805. Painting by Antoine Jean Gros. (*Giraudon*)

PEACE OF PRESSBURG   On December 26, 1805, Francis I accepted the humiliating Peace of Pressburg (Bratislava). Under its terms Austria was forced to relinquish Venice, Dalmatia, and Venetian Istria to Napoleon's satellite kingdom of Italy; the Tyrol (with Brixen and Trent) and Voralberg to Bavaria; and the remaining Habsburg possessions in Germany to Napoleon's other German allies. Austria was permitted one concession, namely to annex Salzburg outright.[30]

A direct outcome of Napoleon's victory was the dissolution of the Holy Roman Empire. On August 6, 1806, after Napoleon organized the Confederation of the Rhine, Francis I laid down the German crown, and the Holy Roman Empire formally came to an end. The Habsburg empire, which had long been obscured by its empty facade, now stood alone in view.

In 1806 King Frederick William III (1797-1840) of Prussia belatedly joined the Third Coalition, and was promptly punished for his imprudence. Napoleon polished off the Prussian army in the twin battles of Jena and Auerstädt (October 14) and occupied Berlin (October 27). The king fled to East Prussia. Tsar Alexander I, although at war also with Turkey from 1806, held out until 1807. However, after the bloody battles of Eylau and Friedland in East Prussia, he, too, sued for peace. At the famous meeting of Napoleon and Alexander at Tilsit, the two adversaries not only concluded peace but also an alliance. Under the treaties of Tilsit (July 7-9, 1807) Prussia alone was made to pay for defeat. Russia lost no territory, but Prussia had to relinquish its Polish provinces (except West Prussia) to make possible Napoleon's Polish satellite—the Duchy of Warsaw under the Saxon king Frederick Augustus I.

A side effect of the situation that was overlooked at the time, but was of considerable importance for Austria later, was that Kara George, the leader of the First Serb National Uprising (1804-1812) against the Turks, turned from Austria to Russia for support. It was with the help of Russian troops that he liberated Serbia, albeit only temporarily. The Serbs never forgot the fact.

---

[30] The much-moved Archduke Ferdinand, who had been recently installed in Salzburg, was transferred to Wurzburg.

REVIVAL   The humiliations of the Peace of Pressburg produced strong reactions at the court of Vienna and in the empire as a whole. Count Philipp Stadion (1763–1824), who replaced Cobenzl as foreign minister, became the principal spokesman at the court for mustering the empire's forces for a reckoning with Napoleon. Archduke Charles, who was at the head of the War Office, undertook to reorganize, modernize, and increase the imperial army. In 1807, to answer the French system of "nation in arms," Francis I decreed general conscription for a newly founded home-defense force (*Landwehr*) in Austria and Bohemia. Hungary grudgingly consented to an increase of the Hungarian contingent in the imperial army.

Financing the rearmament presented a serious problem. British subsidies were discontinued after the Peace of Pressburg. The loss of Belgium and the Italian lands diminished the government's income. Hungary and Galicia could not be made to pay a proportionate share of the cost of rearmament without a risk of revolt. Austria itself was poor. As usual, therefore, the burden fell heavily on the Bohemian lands. To solve the problem, the government raised taxes, debased the coinage, and printed paper money, all of which produced a runaway inflation.[31] The inflation had one beneficial side effect: it favored the peasants and kept their unrest down throughout the wars. Since their taxes and dues were fixed, it was easier for them to pay them in the inflated currency. Many peasants were able to buy themselves out of the obligation of *robot* and also buy some of the rustical land and so become independent farmers. Artisans and manufacturers likewise benefited from the inflation, often accumulating enough capital to finance industrialization. However, the effect of this was felt only after the wars.

NATIONALISM   The humiliations that Napoleon heaped on Germany and the Habsburg empire provoked modern (that is,

---

[31] By 1811 paper money fell to 11.25 percent of its face value. The government then issued a new paper currency that had one-fifth the value of the old. In effect, it repudiated four-fifths of its debt. The operation was frankly called state bankruptcy.

ethnic) German nationalism, which the Austrian Germans fully shared. Less noticed and less important at the time was the quickening of the nationalism of the non-German peoples of the empire. The Magyars, Poles, Czechs, Slovaks, Rumanians, and Southern Slavs were touched too by nationalism, which, however, did not mature until the Revolutions of 1848.

Although German-Austrian nationalism was quite *Habsburgtreu,* Francis I characteristically distrusted it, for he distrusted all popular spontaneous movements. When a petitioner was recommended to him as a patriot, he is reported to have said: "I hear he is a patriot for Austria. But the question is whether he is a patriot for me."[32]

Francis disapproved also of the preparations for an uprising of the stoutly pro-Habsburg Tyrolean peasants against the pro-French Bavarians. In his narrow view it was not for subjects to take matters into their own hands and rebel against the legal authorities, be they foreign and anti-Habsburg, but only to obey in silence and keep working (*Maul halten und weiter dienen*). Instinctively, he may have been right. Napoleon's arrogance indeed provoked popular European nationalism that was directed against France. However, nationalism was also deleterious to the principle of monarchy. Napoleon's personal charisma, moreover, had an incalculable effect on the European popular imagination. Beethoven (1770–1827), a native of Bonn but a resident of Vienna from 1792 on, gave it artistic expression in his Third, or Eroica, Symphony (1802–1804). Napoleon's rise from obscurity to imperial dignity and his unceremonious toppling and juggling of ancient European thrones, as if they were mere army command posts, dealt an irremediable blow to the principle of divine-right monarchy.

WAR OF 1809 In 1808 the Duke of Wellington landed in Portugal and launched the Peninsular War. Together with the Spanish guerrilla warfare, it tied down an increasing number of French forces. By 1809 Stadion was convinced that the time was ripe for

[32] Oscar Jaszi, *The Dissolution of the Habsburg Monarchy* (Chicago, 1961), p. 86.

Austria to challenge Napoleon. Although Archduke Charles warned that the reorganization of the army was not complete, Stadion optimistically assumed that Austria's example would sway the German princes and Tsar Alexander I. In February the Tyrolean uprising broke out, and on April 9 Francis I declared war on France. In a fiery proclamation to his troops Archduke Charles appealed to the whole German people to embark on a war of liberation. He then marched into Germany. Smaller armies under Archdukes John and Ferdinand were sent to Italy and the Grand Duchy of Warsaw, respectively. But neither Prussia nor the other German princes stirred. Tsar Alexander I, as Napoleon's ally, actually declared war on Austria, although he did so reluctantly. The Russian army studiously evaded fighting the Austrians, and tried hard to hamper its Polish "allies." They nearly came to blows at Cracow. Austria was left to face Napoleon's wrath alone.

Napoleon turned over command in Spain to a subordinate and hurried to the scene of his earlier triumph in Central Europe, muttering angrily about Austrian perfidy. He managed, with amazing speed, to separate the Austrian armies north and south of the Danube and seize Vienna, virtually without firing a shot (May 13). Two days later he issued a proclamation to Hungary, to which Francis I had fled, to rise, but there was no response. The Hungarians loyally stood by the Habsburgs. The noble *insurrectio* (levy) was called out—for the last time in history. Fortunately for it, this colorful but largely useless host was never put to the test of battle against the French veterans.

On May 21 when Napoleon ventured east of Vienna, he was intercepted and sharply repelled by Archduke Charles at Aspern. However, on July 5 and 6, at Wagram on the Marchfeld, Napoleon defeated him by massing his "grand battery" of 100 guns, the largest concentration of guns that had been used until then. Six days later Archduke Charles asked for an armistice. The Austrian attempt to lead a war of liberation came to an ignoble end. The Tyrolese were abandoned to their fate. They went on fighting heroically under Andreas Hofer (1767–1810), a sturdy innkeeper, until completely overwhelmed by the Bavarians and the French. Hofer was captured in November and later shot at Mantua; this assured him a permanent place in Austrian history as a national hero.

PEACE OF SCHÖNBRUNN   The peace that was dictated to Francis I at Schönbrunn on October 14, 1809, was vindictive and harsh in the extreme. Austria had to cede to France Carniola, part of Carinthia, Trieste, Istria, Croatia south of the Sava River, and the Croat Littoral, all of which provinces, with Dalmatia, were formed into the "Illyrian Provinces" and attached directly to France; Austria had to surrender to the Grand Duchy of Warsaw its acquisitions under the Third Partition of Poland, to Russia the district of Tarnopol, and to Bavaria Salzburg and some border districts. Moreover, Austria had to pay a large indemnity to France, reduce its army to 150,000 men, break off relations with Britain, and join the Continental System. The last requirement was perhaps superfluous, as Austria was now completely cut off from access to the sea.

METTERNICH   The Peace of Schönbrunn marked the complete failure of Stadion's policy. He resigned just before it was signed. As his successor, Francis I appointed Prince Clemens Metternich (1773–1859), a scion of a distinguished but impoverished West German (not Austrian) family[33] whose members had to seek employment in state or imperial service to support themselves. He was educated at Strassburg at the height of enlightened rationalism, and remained a rationalist, albeit an unenlightened one, to his end. The rising tide of romanticism never influenced him.

Indolent and pleasure-loving but charming and clever, Metternich was a superb diplomat but scarcely a statesman—if by statesmanship is meant the ability to discern the dominant social and political forces of the times and harness or accommodate them to the needs of the state. He fancied himself a philosopher, but lacked profundity. In fact, his writings reveal a singular triviality of mind. As Francis' ambassador to Napoleon's

[33] Metternich was born in Koblenz on the Rhine.

court (1806–1809), he had an opportunity to observe at first hand the impact of the ideas of the French Revolution in France, but this left not the slightest stain on the shining blankness of his mind. He thought of international relations, as was usual in the eighteenth century, as a clever game, to be "played" by cabinets, and he never saw the bearing social and economic forces had on them. He never understood nationalism, although he was to live up to the eve of the battles of Solferino and Magenta (1859), which destroyed the dikes that he had built against Italian nationalism. His fame was based principally on his role during the post-Napoleonic period (the "Age of Metternich") when he was the "coachman of [conservative] Europe," busily building barriers against the rising tide of liberalism and nationalism (the "Metternich system") until these burst through in 1848, sweeping him, among others, to a well-deserved disgrace. Seldom was a major statesman so belied by history during his lifetime. Yet in his monumental vanity he never saw it; he remained convinced to the end that he had been right and would have succeeded if only others had held firm. In the long line of gravediggers of the Habsburg empire he held a front place.

WATCHFUL OPPORTUNISM Francis I gave Metternich a free hand in the conduct of foreign affairs while retaining control of domestic affairs in his own hands. Metternich preferred diplomacy to military solutions of foreign problems. After Stadion's fiasco he was determined that Austria should not take any unnecessary risks. During the remainder of the Napoleonic era his policy was one of cautious and watchful opportunism. He allied Austria to France, but he was ready to betray France the moment Napoleon stumbled. In 1810 he arranged the marriage of Francis' daughter Marie Louise to Napoleon, reviving thus for the instant Maximilian I's policy of letting others fight while Austria married.[34] He did not, however, wish for Austria to be dependent on France. In 1810 when Napoleon suggested that Austria annex Serbia, he declined, even though the army leaders pressed for annexation as compensation for Austria's losses

[34] See pp. 6–7.

in Italy and the transfer of Illyria to France. The hard-pressed Serbs would have probably welcomed it at the time. However, expansion in the Balkans would have strained Austria's relations with Russia and increased its dependence on France.

Metternich's opposition to Balkan expansion was not merely a tactic of the moment, but his permanent policy. A West German, his interest lay in Western Europe, especially Germany and Italy. He knew little and cared less about the historical Habsburg eastern policy. The Orient, he said, began at Rennweg (the eastern route out of Vienna). He believed that Austria's interests in the Balkans were best served by maintaining the territorial integrity of the Ottoman Empire as a bulwark against both Russian and French influence in the area. To the end of his office, therefore, he remained coldly hostile to all Balkan nationalist movements.

FOURTH COALITION   In 1812 when Napoleon's invasion of Russia led to formation of the Fourth Coalition, Metternich adopted a cautious policy. Austria agreed to provide a corps of 20,000 men, which was to form the right wing of Napoleon's Grand Army in Russia. Instead, however, the corps under Prince Karl Schwarzenberg moved to the rear of the Grand Army, into the Duchy of Warsaw, where it did what it could to impede Polish assistance to Napoleon. Austria thus reciprocated Russia's attitude in 1809.

In 1813, when after Napoleon's debacle in Russia Alexander I launched the war of liberation, Metternich maintained a cautious wait-and-see stance. Schwarzenberg did not imitate General York, his Prussian counterpart on the left wing of the Grand Army who went over to the Russians. Instead, he got out of the way of the west-moving Russian army and marked time. Austria waited to see which way the balance would tip. It was not until June 1813, when Napoleon asked for an armistice, that Metternich took a stand. In the secret Treaty of Reichenbach (June 27, 1813) Austria concluded an alliance with Russia and Prussia and undertook to declare war on France if Napoleon rejected the allied terms. On August 12, after Metternich's failure to mediate peace between Napoleon and the allies at the

Conference of Prague (July 28–August 11), Francis I declared war on his son-in-law, and Austria openly joined the Fourth Coalition. The Austrian army under Schwarzenberg and his chief-of-staff, General Josef Radetzky, took part in the decisive "Battle of the Nations" at Leipzig (October 16–19, 1813) and the ensuing hard-fought battles leading to the triumphal entry of the allies into Paris (March 31, 1814) and Napoleon's downfall and exile. For the Austrian army this campaign was the last victory in history over a major opponent.[35] The allies made peace with Louis XVIII (1814–1824), whom they had brought along in their "baggage van," in Paris on May 30, 1814.

CONGRESS OF VIENNA   In recognition of Austria's contribution to their victory, the allies chose Vienna as the site of the peace congress (September 1814–June 1815). Because of Metternich's diplomatic skill, Austria scored a brilliant success at the Congress; it recovered or received compensation for all the lands it had held in 1792, and retained most of the lands that it had gained during the wars.

Metternich was too realistic to attempt to recover Belgium. It was not contiguous to the Habsburg empire and consequently difficult to govern and defend. Instead, he sought compensation in Italy. Austria recovered not only Milan but all of Lombardy and Venetia in Italy and Venetian Istria and Dalmatia across the Adriatic. It also regained Tuscany (as a secundogeniture) and received Modena (as a tertiogeniture). For reasons similar to those that led him to forsake Belgium, Metternich abandoned the scattered Habsburg *Vorlande* in Germany, but he insisted on the restoration of Salzburg and the Tyrol by Bavaria. As for Germany as a whole, he was too rationalistic to resurrect the Holy Roman Empire. Instead, he promoted the German Confederation under the chairmanship of Francis I. In Poland he would have liked to recover Austria's share of the Third Partition (West Galicia), but there he encountered the opposition of Alexander I, who had committed himself to the

---

[35] In 1848–1849 Austria defeated Piedmont and in 1864 shared a victory with Prussia over Denmark — scarcely worthy adversaries. Austria lost all other wars.

Poles to maintain the Grand Duchy of Warsaw (renamed the Kingdom of Poland). The Polish and the related Saxon question nearly precipitated war between the allies. In the end, Metternich acquiesced in the creation of the Kingdom of Poland and the establishment of Cracow as a free city. Russia, however, restored Tarnopol to Austria. Finally, in the Second Peace of Paris (November 30, 1815) after Napoleon's Hundred Days adventure, Austria received a war indemnity from France.

Altogether, the Habsburg empire emerged from the wars strengthened and enlarged, and with its prestige restored. However, the triumph was more apparent than real. The peace settlement, which was based on the principle of legitimacy and balance of power and ignored the new concepts of nationalism and democracy, proved fragile. Austria's involvement in German and Italian affairs committed it to oppose German and Italian unification, and in this it was doomed to failure, as events were to prove. Worse still, the Metternich System, involving repression of nationalism and democracy at home, set off a chain reaction of events which led to the empire's downfall. The Congress of Vienna thus marked not only Austria's last triumph but also the beginning of its decline.

Bibliographical Note

Since the "Berkshire Studies in History" series is designed primarily for undergraduate students and few of them are well versed in foreign languages, only studies in English are indicated.

There is a great shortage of general surveys of the Habsburg empire's history, especially during the period of its formation and evolution before the end of the eighteenth century, whether in English or any other language, including the languages of its own peoples. Although each of the eleven nationalities of the Habsburg empire produced a prolific historical literature, invariably each took a national or regional rather than a multinational or empire-wide approach to its history; that is, each studied only those aspects that related to the particular nationality or the historical region that each claimed as its own.

Among the empire's peoples, the German Austrians identified most closely with the Habsburg dynasty and gave the greatest attention to Habsburg "imperial history" (*Kaisergeschichte*), that is, the history of the Habsburg German policy. Studies by German-Austrian historians are essentially histories of German Austria and Habsburg imperial history. Habsburg imperial history, however, was by no means identical with the history of the whole empire and all its peoples. Few of the empire's many distinguished historians attempted to synthesize all of the empire's history, no doubt because of its extreme complexity and its multinational character, and the consequent need of unusual linguistic training to tackle it, but also perhaps because the nationalities, imbued in the nineteenth century with a growing spirit of ethnic nationalism and intolerance, took little interest in one another, except perhaps a malevolent one. In fact, it has been primarily outsiders to the empire who have tended to look at it as a unit and have attempted to synthesize its history.

Unfortunately, most such attempts are either dated or, if more recent, deal only with the empire's history during its period of decay and dissolution in the nineteenth and twentieth centuries. Among the former, one may cite Louis P. Leger, *History of Austro-Hungary* (New York, 1913), a translation from the French (the original dates from 1895); and Henry W. Steed *et al.*, *A Short History of Austria-Hungary and Poland* (London, 1914), which is a collection of articles reproduced from the *Encyclopedia Britannica*. Among the latter, C. A. Macartney, *The Habsburg Empire, 1790-1918* (New York, 1969), covers more than its title indicates. Its long introductory chapter, "The Monarchy in 1780" (pp. 1–118), although topically rather than chronologically arranged, gives an admirable survey of all aspects of the empire's history to 1780. Very useful also is *The Habsburg and Hohenzollern Dynasties in the Seventeenth and Eighteenth Centuries* (New York, 1970), which Macartney edited for the "Documentary History of Western Civilization" series; it gives many documents, with explanatory comments, on early Habsburg history that are hard to come by elsewhere.

Useful to consult for the empire's development before the end of the eighteenth century are appropriate chapters in the national histories of its various peoples. For the Hungarians, see C. A. Macartney's brilliant *A Short History of Hungary* (Edinburgh, 1962); Denis Sinor, *A Short History of Hungary* (London, 1959); Emil Lengyel's popular *1000 Years of Hungary* (New York, 1958); Domokos G. Kosáry, *A History of Hungary* (Cleveland, 1941); and Pál Teleki, *The Evolution of Hungary and Its Place in European History* (New York, 1923). With the exception of Macartney, who gives the non-Magyars of Hungary a few passing nods, the authors treat Hungary as if it had been a national Magyar state. For the Czechs and Slovaks, see S. Harrison Thomson, *Czechoslovakia in European History* (2nd ed., Princeton, N.J., 1953) and Robert W. Seton-Watson, *A History of the Czechs and Slovaks* (London, 1943). Seton-Watson has also written *A History of the Roumanians* (London, 1934) which includes the history of the Rumanians of Transylvania. It may be supplemented with Keith Hitchins' study *The Rumanian National Movement in Transylvania, 1780–1849* (Cambridge, Mass., 1969), which covers more than its title indicates; it goes back to the formation of the Uniat Church of Transylvania at the end of the seventeenth century. For the Yugoslavs, see Stephen Clissold (ed.), *A Short History of Yugoslavia from Early Times to 1966* (New York, 1966), which covers the South Slav provinces of the Habsburg empire; and the dated but still useful *History of Serbia* (London, 1917) by Harold W. Temperley. For the Poles, who did not enter the empire until 1772, see appropriate chapters in W. F. Reddaway *et al.* (eds.), *The Cambridge History of Poland* (2 vols.; London, 1950) vol. II, 1941.

For the history of the Habsburg dynasty, see the short but brilliant *The House of Habsburg: Six Hundred Years of a European Dynasty* (Garden City, N.Y., 1965) by Adam Wandruszka and the larger but more popular *The Habsburgs* (Garden City, N.Y., 1966) by Dorothy G. McGuingan. Both are preferable to the earlier. *The Imperial Crown: The Story of the Rise and Fall of the Holy Roman and the Austrian Empires* (New York, 1939) by Paul Frischauer, which is much too journalistic. For the political and dynastic relations between the Austrian and Spanish Habsburgs, see Bohdan Chudoba's scholarly *Spain and the Empire, 1519–1643* (Chicago, 1952).

There is no work in English dealing specifically with the foundation of the Austrian Habsburg empire and the sixteenth-century Austrian Habsburgs. However, aspects of the story may be gleaned from studies of Germany, the Protestant Reformation, and Ottoman expansion in the sixteenth century. The rise of the Austrian Habsburg empire is treated as a part of the history of Greater Germany by Hajo Holborn in *A History of Modern Germany* (3 vols; New York, 1967–1969), Vol. I, *The Reformation,* and also by Friedreich Heer in *The Holy Roman Empire* (New York, 1968). Much useful information may be gleaned from *The Slavs in European History and Civilization* (New Brunswick, N.J., 1962) by Francis Dvornik, who treats the Habsburg empire virtually as a Slav empire, much as German historians treat it as a German empire. On the interaction of the German Reformation and Ottoman expansion, see Stephen A. Fischer-Galati, *Ottoman Imperialism and German Protestantism, 1521–1555* (Cambridge, Mass., 1959). For the Habsburg-Ottoman struggle over Hungary in the sixteenth century, see Roger B. Merriman, *Suleiman the Magnificent, 1520–1566* (Cambridge, Mass., 1944), which, though not based on the latest research in Ottoman history, is very readable and still probably the best introduction to the policy of the great Ottoman sultan. On the involvement of Turkey in European alliances and its impact on the Habsburg empire, see Dorothy M. Vaughan, *Europe and the Turk: A Pattern of Alliances, 1350–1700* (Liverpool, 1954) and Paul Coles, *The Ottoman Impact on Europe* (New York, 1968).

The Habsburg empire in the seventeenth century fares better in English-language historiography. Habsburg involvement in the Thirty Years' War is briefly but clearly treated in *The Thirty Years War* (London, 1938) by Cecily V. Wedgwood and in the biography of their great soldier, *Wallenstein: Soldier Under Saturn* (London, 1938) by Francis Watson. The transformation of the Habsburg central administration after Westphalia, from primarily "imperial" to primarily "Austrian," has been clarified by Henry F. Schwarz in *The Imperial Privy Council in the 17th Century* (Cambridge, Mass., 1943). The disastrous outcome for the Bohemian Protestants of the Battle on the White Mountain is told by Ernst Sommer in *Into Exile: The History of the Counter-Reformation in Bohemia, 1620–1650* (London, 1943) and by Matthew Spinka in his biography, *John Amos Comenius: That Incomparable Moravian* (Chicago, 1943).

The martial reign of Leopold I has been treated in several studies of the 1960s: John Stoye, *The Siege of Vienna* (New York, 1964); Thomas M. Barker, *Double Eagle and Crescent: Vienna's Second Siege and Its Historical Setting* (Albany, N.Y., 1967); and William B. Munson, *The Last Crusade* (Dubuque, Iowa, 1969). Stoye deals only with the memorable siege of Vienna in 1683; Barker describes also the whole Austrian military organization under Leopold I, and Munson the diplomacy of the Holy League from 1683 to 1699. The Habsburgs' greatest soldier has at last found an adequate English biography in *Prince Eugen of Savoy* (London, 1964) by Nicholas Henderson. The earlier biography, *Prince Eugene, 1663–1736: A Man and a Hundred Years of History* (New York, 1934) by Paul Frischauer was much too popular. The important role of the Military Frontier in the defense of the Habsburg empire against Turkey has been treated by Gunther E. Rothenberg in two volumes, *The Austrian Military Border in Croatia, 1522–1747* (Urbana, Ill., 1960) and *The Military Border in Croatia, 1740–1881* (Chicago, 1966). Austria's and Russia's policy toward Turkey under Charles VI has received rather unsatisfactory treatment in Lavender Cassels, *The Struggle for the Ottoman Empire, 1717–1740* (London, 1966).

The economic revival and reform of the Habsburg empire in the eighteenth century has led to several excellent studies. Herman Freudenberger's article "Industrialization in Bohemia and Moravia in the Eighteenth Century," *Journal of Central European Affairs,* XIX (January, 1960), deserves notice because of its pioneering character. The

Theresan and Josephine peasant reforms have been treated, in Austria by Edith M. Link, *The Emancipation of the Austrian Peasant, 1740–1798* (New York, 1949), and in Bohemia by William E. Wright, *Serf, Seigneur, and Sovereign: Agrarian Reform in Eighteenth-Century Bohemia* (Minneapolis, 1966). Robert J. Kerner, *Bohemia in the Eighteenth Century: A Study in Political, Economic, and Social History with Special Reference to the Reign of Leopold II, 1790–1792,* (2nd ed.; Orono, Me., 1969), though focusing on the Leopoldine compromise with the Bohemian nobility, gives the whole background of Theresan and Josephine reforms in Bohemia. Similar in approach is Béla Király, *Hungary in the Late Eighteenth Century: The Decline of Enlightened Despotism* (New York, 1969); the story of the Leopoldine compromise with the Hungarian nobility is introduced by a mass of information on Hungarian institutions and development in the eighteenth century, and largely supersedes Henrik Marczali, *Hungary in the Eighteenth Century* (Cambridge, Eng., 1910). Joseph's religious policy is treated by Charles H. O'Brien in "Ideas of Religious Toleration of Joseph II: A Study of the Enlightenment among Catholics in Austria," *Transactions of the American Philosophical Society,* New Series, Vol. 59, Part 7 (Philadelphia, 1969). Joseph's enlightenment is the subject of Paul P. Bernard, "The Origins of Josephinism: Two Studies," *The Colorado College Studies,* VII (Colorado Springs, 1964). The whole range of German-Austrian intellectual development, from the late seventeenth century to the early nineteenth, has been analyzed by Robert A. Kann in *A Study of Austrian Intellectual History: From Late Baroque to Romanticism* (New York, 1960); his treatment of the Austrian enlightenment is particularly valuable.

The strong personalities of Maria Theresa and Joseph II have attracted numerous biographers. Unfortunately, of the four biographies of Maria Theresa available in English—James F. Bright (London, 1897), Mary M. Maxwell (London, 1911), J. Alexander Mahan (New York, 1932), and Margaret Goldsmith (London, 1936)—none is quite satisfactory. George P. Gooch, *Maria Theresa and Other Studies* (New York, 1952) contains also a sketch of Joseph II. Of the three biographies of Joseph II in English, James F. Bright, *Joseph II* (London, 1897) stresses, like its companion volume on Marie Theresa, diplomatic history; Saul K. Padover, *The Revolutionary Emperor* (New York, 1934) is admiring and uncritical; and Paul R. Bernard, *Joseph II* (New York, 1968), though short, is critical and well balanced. Paul R. Bernard, *Joseph II and Bavaria* (The Hague, 1965), is a thorough study of Joseph's attempt to annex Bavaria or exchange it for Belgium, which supersedes Harold

W. Temperley, *Frederick the Great and Kaiser Joseph: An Episode of War and Diplomacy in the Eighteenth Century* (London, 1915). *The First Partition of Poland* (New York, 1962) by Herbert H. Kaplan is a fresh look at that old problem, while *The Second Partition of Poland* (Cambridge, Mass., 1915) by Robert H. Lord remains unsuperseded. There is nothing in English on Joseph's eastern policy and the Turkish war of 1789–1791. Chapters on the reigns of Joseph (pp. 119–133) and Leopold (pp. 134–146) in Macartney, *The Habsburg Empire*, mentioned above, should also be consulted.

The period of the French Revolution and Napoleon has inspired several good studies of the Habsburg reaction to that cataclysm. Ernst Wagermann, *From Joseph II to the Jacobin Trials* (London, 1959) is an original study of the response of the German-Austrian and Hungarian intellectuals to the French Revolution. Walter C. Langsam, *The Napoleonic Wars and German Nationalism in Austria* (New York, 1930) deals with the very different German-Austrian nationalistic reaction to Napoleon. Langsam has also written a study of Francis I to his accession, *Francis the Good: The Education of an Emperor, 1768–1792* (New York, 1949). The Habsburg diplomatic reaction to Napoleon is dealt with in Enno E. Kraehe, *The Contest with Napoleon, 1799–1814* (Princeton, N.J., 1963), which is the first volume of a projected larger study on Metternich's German policy; Josephine B. Stearns, *The Role of Metternich in Undermining Napoleon* (Urbana, Ill., 1948); and C. S. B. Buckland, *Metternich and the British Government from 1809 to 1813* (London, 1932). Biographies of Metternich, none very satisfactory, continue to proliferate: Arthur Herman (New York, 1932), Algernon Cecil (London, 1933), Helen du Coudray (London, 1935), and Constantin de Grunwald (London, 1953). For the Congress of Vienna, see the standard Charles K. Webster, *The Congress of Vienna, 1814–1815* (London, 1934); the popular and readable Harold Nicolson, *The Congress of Vienna; A Study of Allied Unity, 1812–1822* (New York, 1946); and the specialized Hannah A. Straus, *The Attitude of the Congress of Vienna toward Nationalism in Germany, Italy, and Poland* (New York, 1949). Finally, Macartney's chapter on Francis I in *The Habsburg Empire* (pp. 147–198) is recommended.

Index

Aachen, 3n., 108
Aargau, 3n.
Acadia, 89
Adrianople, 72
Agriculture, 59, 114, 115, 121, 122
Ahmed Köprülü, 67, 70, 72
Ahmet Pasha, 99
Alba Iulia, 66, 78
Albania, 85; Turkish conquest
    of, 22–23
Alberoni, Giulio, 97
Albrecht II, king of Germany,
    5–6, 22
Alexander I, tsar of Russia, 150,
    152, 155, 159–160
Alexis I Mikhailovich, tsar of
    Russia, 69n.
Altmark, Truce of, 54
American colonies, Franco-
    British conflict in, 108, 111
American War of Independence,
    137
Anabaptists, 38, 42
Andrew II, king of Hungary,
    19, 75
Angevin dynasty, 20–21
Anna Ivanovna, empress of
    Russia, 99, 100
Anne, queen of Bohemia and
    Hungary, 29
Apafy, Mihály (Michael), 69,
    70, 77, 78
Architecture: baroque, 44–45,
    68–69, 92; Gothic, 4, 15, 44
Árpád, 17

Árpád dynasty, 17–19
Arsenije III Crnojević, 80–82
Arsenije IV Jovanović, 99–100
Artois, Count of, 143
Asiento, 89
Aspern, battle of, 155
Attica, Morosini's advance into,
    83
Auerstädt, battle of, 152
Augsburg: Confession of, 40–41,
    44; League of, War of the, 79,
    82, 83, 86, 87; Peace of, 9, 54
Augustus III, king of Poland and
    elector of Saxony, 98, 108,
    110–112, 123
Austerlitz, battle of, 150
Austria: Anterior, 31; Alpine
    duchies, 3, 4, 7; Austrian
    duchies, 2–5, 7; the Babenberg
    dynasty, 3; Catholic Counter-
    Reformation, 39, 44, 46–47,
    50, 51, 52, 64–65, 68, 92, 102,
    131; chancellery of, abolished,
    115; diets of, 5; "Eastern
    March" (Ostmark), 2–3;
    economic development, 4,
    58–60, 114–115, 153; estates
    of, 4–5, 51; first dynasty, 3;
    German colonization, 4; and
    German nationalism, 153–156;
    and Habsburg dynasty, 1–3;
    hereditary lands (Erblande),
    2, 4, 7, 30–31, 149; and the
    Holy Roman Empire
    (Germany), 2–8; "House of

Austria (*cont.*)
Austria," 4–5, 67, 92, 109–110; Lower (*see* Lower Austria); medieval efflorescence, 4; Pragmatic Sanction, 92–93; Protestant Reformation, 38–40; social development, 4–5, 58–60, 114, 133; union with Bohemia and Hungary, 2, 4, 22, 28–31; Upper (*see* Upper Austria)
Austrian Succession, War of the, 103–105, 107–109
Austro-Hungarian Compromise, 78
Avars, 2–3
Azov, 83, 90, 100

Babenberg dynasty, 3
Balance of power, 67–68, 86, 87, 99, 160
Balkans, 35; Austro-Russian rivalry in, 90; Habsburg interests in, 79–85, 96–97; Habsburg policy in, origins of, 79–80; Turkey and, 11, 21–23, 79, 96
Banat, The, 85, 95, 97, 100, 137, 140–141
Banffy, György, 142
Barbary pirates, 10
Basel: Compacts of, 16, 17, 24, 29, 42; Council of, 16; Peace of, 147
Basta, Giorgio, 45–46
Bastille, fall of, 143
Báthori, István (Stephen), king of Poland, 45
Báthori, Krystóf (Christopher), 45
Báthori, Zsigmond (Sigismund), 45–46
"Battle of the Nations," 159
"Battle of the Three Emperors," 150
Bavaria: France and, 149, 150; Peace of Pressburg and, 152; and Silesian wars, 105, 107; and War of the Spanish Succession, 87, 88; proposed exchange of, 136
Bavarian Succession, War of the, 126–127, 136
Beethoven, Ludwig van, 154
Bél, Matej (Matthew), 120
Belgium, 104, 107–108; Austria and, 109, 112, 140, 147, 159; French Revolution and, 143, 147; overseas trade, 93; Peace of Utrecht and, 88; revolt in, 138; War of the Spanish Succession in, 88
Belgrade: Habsburg occupation of, 79, 97, 138; Peace of, 100; Turkish occupation of, 22, 23, 26, 72, 74
Berlin: Congress of, 100; Napoleon's occupation of, 152; Peace of, 107, 108, 111–112; Russian raid, 111
Berlios, Louis Hector, 91*n*.
Bessenyei, György, 119
Bethlen, Gábor (Gabriel), 46, 52, 53, 65–67
Bible: King James Version, 43; New Testament, 40, 41, 66; translations, 38, 40, 41, 43, 66
Bible of Kralice (Czech), 41, 43
Bihari, John, 91*n*.
Biró, Mátyás (Matthias), 40, 41
Blahoslav, Jan, 42–43
Blenheim, battle of, 88–90
Bocskay, István (Stephen), 45–46, 53, 65, 67
Bohemia, 11–17; agriculture, 115; American gold and silver, influx of, 59; Austria and, 2, 3, 28, 115–117; and battle of Mohács, 27; Bavarian-French invasion of, 115; and Brandenburg, 14–15, 17; carpetbagger nobility, 64, 77, 94; Catholic Church, 43; centralization and bureaucratization of administration, 115–116; Charlemagne's invasion of, 12; Chancellery, 30, 62, 115; constitution, alteration of, 61;

coronations, 61–62; Counter-Reformation in, 43, 62–64, 92; cultural revival, 92, 117; Darkness, period of, 62; dependence on Germany, 12, 13; depopulation, 62; diets, 14, 16, 24, 28, 43–44, 51, 62, 117, 140; and division of Habsburg possessions, 47; economic revival, 92, 94; election in (1526), 2, 28–29; and England, 51, 52; estates, 14, 28, 30–31, 51, 115; father of the country, 14–15; feudal, golden age of, 14–15; French cultural influence in, 15; German colonization, 13; German influence in, 12, 13; German invasion of, 13; germanization of, 13, 64, 116–117; and Great Moravia, 12; Habsburg centralism in, 61; Habsburg claim to, 2, 7, 27; as hereditary Habsburg possession, 61–62; and Holy Roman Empire, 2; home-defense force, 153; Hungary, union with, 22, 24, 28–29; Hussite movement, 15, 21, 42, 92; Hussite wars, 16–17, 23–24, 43, 50, 52; independence, end of, 51–53; industries, 94; inflation, 59; Jagellon kings, 7, 24–26; Jesuits in, 43, 62, 89, 92; knights, 60, 64; languages, 116–117, 130; Leopold II and, 140; literary efflorescence, period of, 42–43; and Lusatias, 14–15, 17, 24, 62; Luxemburg dynasty, 5, 14, 17; Maria Theresa and, 115–117; mining, 13, 59; and Moravia, 12, 14, 24; national kings, 23–24; neo-Utraquists, 42, 44; and Patent of Toleration, 131; peasant outbreaks, 25, 114; and Poland, 12; population (1787), 121; Přemyslid dynasty, 3, 11, 12, 14; price revolution,

59; princes, 13; Protestant army, 50; Protestant estates, 50, 52; Protestant Reformation in, 42–44; Protestant revolt, 49–53, 62; Protestants in, 42, 43, 47, 50, 52, 53, 92; recatho-licization of, 62–63; religious refugees, 63; royal absolutism in, 61; Schwarzenberg estates, 64; and Serfdom Patent, 133; and Silesia, 12, 14, 17, 24; Silesian wars in, 105, 107; silver, discovery of, 13; social organization, 13; social transformation, 60; subjection of, 61–62; and Thirty Years' War, 49–53, 62; Transylvania and, 52; Turkish menace and, 11, 32; Utraquist Church, 42–44. See also Czechs; Habsburg empire; Habsburgs; Prague *and* names of rulers

Bohemian Chancellery, 30, 62, 115
Bohemian Confession, 44, 47
Boleslav I, duke of Bohemia, 12, 13
Bonneval, Claude de (Ahmet Pasha), 99
Booklet of the Pleas of the Vlachs, 142
Bop, Ioan, 142
Bořivoj, Prince, 12
Bosnia: Habsburg advance in, 79, 99, 138; Hungary and, 21; Turkish conquest of, 22–23
Bouquoy, Karl, 52
Bourbons, 108
Brahe, Tycho, 44, 60
Brandenburg, Bohemia and, 14–15, 17, 103–104
Branković, Djordje (George), 80
Bratislava, 29, 36–37, 71, 73, 75, 105, 119. *See also* Pressburg
Britain (*see* England)
Brunswick, duke of, 146
Buda, 21, 35–37, 119; Ferdinand's seizure of, 30; Royal Palace in, 123; and Pest, 123; Turkish occupation of, 20, 32, 33, 74

Bukovina, 125–126
Bulgaria: Habsburg advance into, 79; Russian occupation of, 124; Turkish destruction of, 11, 21, 35; Uniat Church, 79*n*., 82
Bulgars, 95
Burgundy, 6
Byzantine empire, 11, 127
Byzantine missionaries, 12

Calvinism, 9, 38, 40–42, 76
Calvinists, 41, 51, 57, 89; Magyar, 41, 46, 66, 120
Canisius, St. Peter, 39
Caraffa, Antonio, 74, 75, 77
Carinthia, 3, 4, 31, 40, 156
Carniola, 3, 4, 31, 40, 147
Carolina Resolutio, 92
Carolingian empire, division of, 3, 12
Catherine I, empress of Russia, 98*n*.
Catherine II, empress of Russia, 111, 117, 123, 124, 127, 136–138, 147
Catholic Church, 8, 17, 38, 39, 65, 68, 76, 77; battle of Mohács and, 27, 40; Bohemian, 43; Great Schism in, 15; Hungarian, 121; Joseph II and, 132, 135; Utraquist Church and, 42
Catholic Counter-Reformation (*see* Counter-Reformation)
Catholic League, 47, 52
Catholicism, 42, 51, 53, 57, 61, 63, 66, 76, 121
Catholics, 38, 60–61; Austrian, 65; Bulgarian, 79; Czech, 63–64; German, 57; Polish, 125; Spanish, 8; in Transylvania, 41–42
Charlemagne, 2, 12
Charles, archduke of Austria, 144, 148, 150, 153, 155
Charles V, duke of Lorraine, 73, 74, 79
Charles IV, emperor, 5, 14–15

Charles V, emperor, 6–10, 26, 30, 87
Charles VI, emperor, 87, 88, 101, 103; alliance with Venice, 96; and the Balkans, 96, 97; *Carolina Resolutio,* 92; mercantilist interest, 93; Peace of The Hague and, 98; Peace of Vienna and, 99; Pragmatic Sanction, 92–93, 99, 101, 103–105; reign, character of, 91–92, 94
Charles VII, emperor, 105, 107
Charles I, king of England, 67
Charles II, king of England, 86
Charles X, king of France, 143
Charles I, king of Hungary, 20–21
Charles II, king of Spain, 87
Charles XII, king of Sweden, 90, 98*n*.
Charles X Gustavus, king of Sweden, 69*n*.
Charles Theodore, 126, 136
Chelčický, Peter, 24
Chesme Bay, battle of, 124
Christian IV, king of Denmark, 54
Christina, queen of Sweden, 54
Churchill, John, 88
Cithara Sanctorum, 41
Clement XIII, pope, 118
Clement XIV, pope, 117
Cobenzl, Philipp, Count, 143, 147, 153
Colloredo, Franz, Count, 144
Comenius, John Amos, 63
Confederation of the Rhine, 152
Confessio Bohemica, 44
Confessio Pentapolitana, 40–41
Constance, Council of, 15
Constantinople, 11, 22, 90, 137
Continental System, 156
Copernicus, Nicolaus, 60
Corpus Catholicorum, 57
Corpus Evangelicorum, 57
Cossacks, 52*n*., 58*n*.
Counter-Reformation, 8, 38–39, 42–49, 60–61, 68; Ferdinand II

and, 65; Joseph II and, 131;
Maria Theresa and, 102. *See
also under* names of countries
Cracow, 147, 155, 160
Crécy, battle of, 14
Crimea, 136–137
Croatia, 18, 19, 27, 33, 37, 95;
Counter-Reformation in, 46;
diet, 29, 34, 37, 46, 140;
Magyar nobles in, 96;
Military Frontier, 34; peasant
revolt, 46; Protestant
Reformation in, 40; Royal
Hungary and, 37
Croats, 40, 95–96, 121, 141
Cromwell, Oliver, 67, 86
Cuius regio, eius religio, 9
Cumberland, duke of, 107–108
Cyril, St. (Constantine), 12
Czech Brethren, Unity of, 24,
42–43, 62, 63
Czech language, 61, 62, 117, 130,
135, 140
Czech nationalism, 117, 154
Czechs, 11–13, 15–17, 63–64, 92,
117; and Catholicism, 63–64;
Lutheranism and, 42;
Protestant, 43; religious
literature, 41, 42–43, 63.
See also Bohemia

Dalmatia: Peace of Campo
Formio and, 147; Turkish, 85;
Venice and, 18, 21, 85
Dalmatin, Antun, 40
Damad Ali, 96–97
Damnation of Faust, 91n.
Danube River, 18, 20–22, 27,
54, 81n., 83, 85, 97, 99–100,
123, 124, 137, 138
Declaration of Pillnitz, 143
Denmark, 54, 90
Diploma Leopoldina, 78
Diplomatic Revolution, 108–110
Djaković, Isaia, 80–81
Don Carlos, 99
Dubois, Guillaume, 97–98
Dutch War, 71, 86

East India Company, 115
Eastern March, 2–3
Eck, Johann, 42
Edict of Nantes, 86
Edict of Restitution, 54
Egypt, Napoleon's campaign
in, 148
Elizabeth Farnese, 97, 99
Elizabeth Petrovna, empress
of Russia, 110, 111
England: and Austria, 86, 88,
105, 109, 137, 150; Bohemia
and, 51, 52; Church of, 42;
France and, 67, 86, 105, 110,
146–148, 150; Glorious
Revolution, 86; Grand
Alliance, 87–89; and Holy
League, 83; and League of
Augsburg, 86; and Ottoman
empire, 83–84, 97; overseas
colonization, 94; Pragmatic
Alliance, 105; Pragmatic
Sanction, 93; and Prussia,
109–111; and Russia, 109, 110,
137, 150; and Scotch rebellion,
108; and Seven Years' War,
110, 111; and Spain, 67;
Sweden and, 150; Whigs, 88.
See also names of rulers
Enlightenment, 102, 117, 118, 128
Erblande (Habsburg hereditary
lands), 2, 4, 7, 28, 30, 31, 61,
149
Essay on Man, An, 119n.
Esztergom, 65, 66
Explanatio Leopoldina, 75–76, 92
Eylau, battle of, 152

Felbiger, Johann, 117
Ferdinand, archduke, 149n.,
150, 152n.
Ferdinand I, emperor, 7, 9,
26–34, 36–39, 43
Ferdinand II, emperor, 47,
49–54, 56, 64; and battle on
the White Mountain, 61, 75;
and Counter-Reformation,
65; Edict of Restitution, 54;
Renewal Ordinance, 61, 140

Ferdinand III, emperor, 56, 67, 68
Ferdinand of Aragon, 6–7
Fischer von Gerlach, Johann, 69
Florence, Council of, 76, 78
Florian, St., 92
Focsani, battle of, 138
Fontenoy, battle of, 107–108
France: Austria and, 67, 98, 102, 104, 109–110, 126, 137, 143, 146–148, 150, 153–155, 159, 160; Bavaria and, 149, 150; Bourbons, 108; Dutch War, 71, 86; eastern barrier, 10; and England, 67, 86, 105, 110, 146–148, 150; and Germany, 70, 86, 148, 150; and Holland, 71, 86, 146; Huguenot refugees, 86; and Hungary, 70–71, 73, 90, 155; Most Christian Kings, 10; overseas colonization, 94; Peace of the Pyrenees and, 67; and Poland, 10, 158; and Polish succession, 98; and Pragmatic Alliance, 107–108; Protestants in, 67, 86; Prussia and, 143, 146, 152; Reign of Terror, 145; Revolution, 142–146; Russia and, 147, 148, 150, 152, 158; and Seven Years' War, 111; and Silesian wars, 105, 107; Spain and, 26, 67, 87, 98, 146, 147, 150; and Sweden, 10, 54; and Thirty Years' War, 53, 54, 56; and Turkey, 10, 26, 70, 83, 85, 90; and War of the Spanish Succession, 87, 88. *See also* Napoleonic wars *and* names of rulers
Francis, duke of Lorraine (*see* Francis I, emperor)
Francis I, emperor of Austria (*see* Francis II, emperor)
Francis I, emperor, 98–99, 101–103, 107, 108, 113–114
Francis II, emperor, 144–145, 149, 152–159
Francis I, king of France, 26

Frankopan, Ferenc, 71
Frederick IV, Elector Palatine, 47
Frederick I (Barbarossa), Emperor, 13
Frederick III, emperor, 6
Frederick V, king of Bohemia, 51–53
Frederick I, king of Prussia, 103–104
Frederick II, king of Prussia, 104, 105, 107–112, 123–125, 136
Frederick Augustus I, king of Saxony, 152
Frederick William (the Great Elector), 69n., 86, 103
Frederick William I, king of Prussia, 104
Frederick William II, king of Prussia, 139, 141,.143
Frederick William III, king of Prussia, 152
French and Indian War, 108
French Revolution, Habsburg empire and, 142–146
Friedland, battle of, 152

Galicia, 112, 125–126, 130–132, 138, 153; West, 147, 159
Galicia and Lodomeria, Kingdom of, 125
George I, king of Bohemia, 23–24
George II, king of England, 109, 111
George III, king of England, 111
German-Austrian nationalism, 153–154
German Confederation, 159
German language, 61, 62, 116–118, 120, 130, 141
Germany: American gold and silver, influx of, 59; anarchy, 14; Bohemia invaded by, 13; and Bohemian Protestant army, 50; Bohemian religious refugees in, 63; colonization, 4, 13; Congress of Vienna, 159; cultural decline, 60;

cultural revival, 117; diet, 148–149; diet of Regensburg, 70; France and, 70, 86, 148–149, 150; French Revolution and, 143; Grand Alliance, 87; Great Interregnum, 3; Habsburg possessions in, 31; Habsburg prominence in affairs of, 5–6; and Hungary, 70, 73; inflation, 59; Peasant War, 39; Protestant armies, 63; Protestant Reformation in, 8–9; Protestant Union, 47, 50, 51, 53; Protestants in, 8, 10, 42, 47, 51–52, 57, 86; Schmalkaldic League, 8–9, 43; Schmalkaldic War, 9, 32; Thirty Years' War and, 53–57; Turkey and, 32, 70; War of the Spanish Succession in, 88, 105. *See also* Holy Roman Empire; Habsburg *and* names of rulers

Gindely, Anton, 34

Goethe, Johann Wolgang von, 117

Golden Bull of Charles IV, 14

Golden Bull of Andrew II, 19, 75

Grand Duchy of Warsaw, 155, 156, 158–160

Great Moravia, 3, 12, 17

Great Northern War, 90, 98*n*., 104

Greek Catholic (Uniat) Church, 76, 78

Greek Orthodox Church, 41, 76, 81, 141–142

Greek project, 127, 137

Gustavus II Adolphus, king of Sweden, 54

Habsburg, House of, division in, 9–10

Habsburg empire: area (1740), 104; army, 30, 34, 68, 96, 113–114, 153, 159; Austria, Bohemia and Hungary core of, 2; Austro-Bohemian integration, 30–31, 61–62, 105–106, 115–117, 129–130, 135–136, 140; Austro-Hungarian dualism, 91, 112, 115, 118–119, 129–130, 136, 140–142; and the Balkans, 79–80, 82–85, 96–97, 99–100, 102, 136–138, 152, 158; the Belgian provinces, 88, 109, 112, 138, 140, 147, 159; bureaucratization, 116, 129; Catholic Counter-Reformation, 38–57, 60–61, 62–67, 68, 71, 75–76, 78, 91, 92, 102, 131, 138; central administration, 30, 61–62, 68, 109, 115–116, 129–130, 139–140, 144; centralization, 30, 115–116, 129–130; and the Congress of Vienna, 159–160; consolidation and expansion, 58–100; economic development, 58–60, 93–94, 114–115, 153; emperor of Austria, 149–150; and England, 51–52, 83, 86–89, 105–108, 109–111, 137, 146–147, 148, 150, 153; formation of, 1, 2, 28–57; and France, 10, 53–57, 67, 70, 85–89, 90, 98–99, 102, 104–108, 109–112, 124, 126, 137, 143, 146–149, 150–152, 155–156, 157–159, 160; and the French Revolution, 142–146; germanization, 64, 71, 116–117, 130, 135, 141; and the Grand Duchy of Warsaw, 152, 155, 158, 160; and the Holy Roman Empire (Germany), 2, 30, 47, 51, 53–57, 61, 70, 103, 107, 126, 136, 149–150, 152, 159; the Italian provinces, 88, 97–98, 108, 109, 112, 147, 148, 150, 152, 153, 156, 159; languages, 38–39, 61, 116–117, 130, 140, 141–142; Military Frontier, 34, 81–82; nature of, 1–2; and the Ottoman empire, 10–11, 31–35, 45–46, 69–70, 71–75, 82–85, 90, 91*n*., 96–97, 99–100, 124, 125, 136–138, 158; and Poland, 52*n*., 58*n*., 73–74, 98–

Habsburg empire (*cont.*)
99, 123–125, 137, 147, 160; the
Polish provinces, 112, 125,
138, 147, 153, 159–160;
population, 104, 121; Pragmatic Sanction, 92–93;
Protestant Reformation, 38–44;
and Prussia, 103–108, 109–112,
123–125, 126, 136, 137–138,
146, 147–148, 152, 155, 158;
reform and reaction, 101–160;
and Russia, 10, 74, 79–80, 83,
85, 90, 98, 99–100, 104–105,
109–111, 123–127, 136–138,
148, 150, 152, 155, 158; and the
Serbs, 34, 35, 80–82, 95, 97,
99–100, 120, 121, 138, 140, 142,
152, 158; social development,
58–60, 114, 132–135, 153; and
Spain, 7, 9–10, 53–56, 67, 87–89,
97–99, 104, 108, 146, 147, 154–
155. *See also under* specific
main entries
Habsburg-Jagellon agreement,
26, 28, 29
Habsburg-Lorraine dynasty,
101*n.*
Habsburgs: Austria and, 1–8;
Austrian lines, establishment
of, 31; division of, 9–10;
family cohesion and solidarity
4; family traditions, 4; Franco-
Turkish alliance and, 10;
hereditary lands (*Erblande*),
2, 4, 7, 28, 30, 31, 61–62;
intermarriage, 9; male, decline
in number of, 31; possessions,
2, 4, 7, 10, 29, 31, 34; treaties
with foreign powers, 4; Tyrolese line, extinction of, 31;
Viennese line, extinction of,
31. *See also under* specific
main entries
Haugwitz, Friedrich Wilhelm,
102–103, 112
Hawk's castle, 3*n.*
Hedvig (Jadwiga), queen of
Poland, 21
Henry VII, emperor, 14

Henry VIII, king of England, 26
Henry, prince of Prussia, 124
Hochstädt, battle of, 88–90
Hofer, Andreas, 155–156
Hohenzollern dynasty, 17,
103–105
Holland: and Austria, 86, 87,
105; Bohemian religious
refugees in, 63; France and,
71, 86, 146; Grand Alliance,
87; and Holy League, 83;
and League of Augsburg, 86;
and Ottoman empire, 83
Holy League, 74, 79, 83, 90
Holy Roman Empire: Bohemia
and, 2; decentralization of,
4; disintegration of, 6, 56–57;
dissolution of, 2, 13, 149, 152;
feudalization of, 4; founder of,
3; Habsburg empire and, 2;
Hungary and, 2; importance
of, decline in, 57, 61. *See
also* Germany and names of
emperors
Hungary, 17–27; agriculture,
121, 122; American gold and
silver, influx of, 59; Angevin
dynasty, 20–21; annexations,
18; army, 118, 153; Árpád
dynasty, 17–19; Austria and,
2, 77, 78, 85, 90, 105, 115, 118–
123, 129; battle of Mohács
and, 26–29, 37, 74, 125; Black
Army, 23, 27; Bohemia, union
with, 22, 24, 28–29; Catholic
Church, 18, 121; Chancellery,
30; colonization, 18–19, 94–96;
constitution, 75, 89, 105*n.*, 112,
118; coronations, 20; Counter-
Reformation in, 45, 65–66,
71, 75–77, 92, 120; diets, 19, 22,
25, 36, 37, 72, 75, 93, 140; and
division of Habsburg possessions, 47; Dózsa Rebellion,
25, 29, 72; economic development, 121–123; election of
the Habsburgs in (1526), 2,
29–30; estates, 19, 30, 75, 91,
140; ethnic groups, 120–121;

ethnographic picture, changes in, 95; France and, 70–71, 73, 90, 155; Franco-Turkish alliance and, 10; Germany and, 70, 73; Golden Bull, 19, 75; Habsburg (see Royal Hungary); Habsburg claim to, 2, 7, 27; Habsburg-Ottoman stalemate in, 33–34; Habsburg triumph in, 74–77; and Holy Roman Empire, 2; House of Magnates, 37; House of Nobles, 37–38; industrial development, 122–123; inflation, 59; Jagellon kings, 24–26; *kuruc* insurrection, 71–72; languages, 120, 130, 141; Leopold II and, 140–142; Magyar cultural revival, 119; Magyars, 17–19, 35, 40, 41, 95, 96, 120, 121, 141–142; Maria Theresa and, 116, 118–123; modern, magnate families of, 77; Mongol (Tartar) invasion of, 18; multinational character of, 19; national kings, 23–24; nationalities in, distribution of, 95–96n.; nobility, decline of, 37; origins, 17; partition of, 32–33, 37, 38, 95, 96; Parts, 33, 35–36; peasant emancipation, 134; peasant status, 122; peasant uprisings, 25, 29, 89; and Poland, 21, 22, 73, 74, 79; population after Turkish withdrawal, 94n.; population growth, 121; Protestant Reformation in, 40–41; Protestants in, 47, 53, 65, 71, 72, 75, 77, 92, 120; Rákóczi insurrection, 89–91; rearmament, 153; sandal noblemen, 122; silver mines, 20, 59; social transformation, 60, 119–121; struggle for, 31–32; Thököly insurrection, 71–72, 74; and Transylvania, 77–78; *Tripartitum*, 25–26, 37n., 75; Turkish (see Turkish Hungary); Turkish invasions

of, 11, 22–23, 26–27, 31–35, 40; Turkish wars, 45, 69–70, 72–74, 94–97; Wesselényi conspiracy, 70–72, 75. See also Habsburg empire; Habsburgs *and* names of rulers
Hunyadi, János (John), 22, 23
Hus, John, 15, 42
Hussite hymns, 41
Hussite movement, 15, 21, 42, 92
Hussite wars, 16–17, 23–24, 43, 50, 52

Inner Austria, 31, 34, 39; Counter-Reformation in, 46–47, 65; Ferdinand II as ruler, 51; peasant revolt, 46; Protestants in, 39, 65
Innocent XI, pope, 74
Isabella of Castile, 6–7
Isabella of Portugal, 7
Istanbul, 11, 26, 31, 32, 46. See also Constantinople
Istria, 3, 4, 147, 156; Internal, 31; Venetian, 159
Italy: Austria and, 109, 112; Congress of Vienna, 159; Franco-Turkish alliance and, 10; Habsburg influence in, 97–98; Habsburg link to, 4; Habsburg possessions in, 7; Napoleon's campaigns in, 147, 148; Renaissance in, 38; Silesian wars in, 105; and War of the Polish Succession, 98, 105; War of the Spanish Succession in, 88
Ivan IV Vasilievich (the Terrible), tsar of Russia, 26
Ivan V, tsar of Russia, 79

Jacobin plots, 144–145
Jagellon dynasty, 7, 24–26
James I, king of England, 51
James II, king of England, 86
Jena, battle of, 152
Jesuits, 38, 39, 43, 45, 47, 49–51, 62, 65, 66, 75, 78, 82, 89, 92, 117, 119

Jews, 96n., 131–132, 141
Jiskra, Jan (John), 22
Joan the Mad, 6–7
John VII, Byzantine emperor, 76n.
John, king of England, 19
John III Sobieski, king of
  Poland, 73, 74
John of Luxemburg, king of
  Bohemia, 14
John of Nepomuk, St., 92
Joseph I, emperor, 88, 90–92
Joseph II, emperor, 63, 75, 78,
  95n., 103, 105, 118, 126–141,
  145; Bavarian exchange, 136;
  and Catholic Church, 132,
  135; centralization and german-
  ization policy, 129–130; charac-
  ter, 127–129; and Counter-
  Reformation, 131; foreign
  policy, 136–139; legal reforms,
  130–131; and Louis XVI, 142–
  143; opposition to reforms
  of, 135–136, 139; and partition
  of Poland, 124; Patent of
  Toleration, 131, 135, 138, 140;
  peasant emancipation, 132–135;
  Serfdom Patent, 133–134, 138
Joseph Ferdinand of Bavaria, 87

Kara George (George Petrović),
  138, 152
Kara Mustafa, 72–74
Károli, Kálman, 41
Kaunic, Wenzel Anton, 102,
  109, 124, 126, 136, 137, 139, 143
Kepler, Johannes, 44, 60
Khlesl, Melchior, 50
King George's War, 105
King William's War (see League
  of Ausburg, War of the)
Kollonics, Leopold, 71, 75
Königsegg, Lothar, 99
Komenský (Comenius), Jan
  Amos, 63
Kunersdorff, battle of, 111
Kutuzov, Michael, 150

Ladislav Posthumus, king of
  Hungary and Bohemia, 5, 22, 23

Latin, 38–39, 61, 116, 118, 120,
  130, 141
Laudon, Gideon Ernst, 114, 137,
  138
League of Armed Neutrality, 137
League of Ausburg, 86; War of
  the, 79, 82, 83, 86, 87
League of the Rhine, 70
Lechfeld, battle on the, 17
Leibnitz, Gottfried Wilhelm von,
  60
Leopold I, emperor, 68–77, 83,
  85, 87, 90; and Balkan in-
  vasion, 79; and Hungarian
  constitution, 75, 89; and
  League of Augsburg, 86; Serb
  Privilege, 80–82; and Transyl-
  vania, 77, 78; and War of the
  Spanish Succession, 87, 103–
  104
Leopold II, emperor, 139–145
Leopold of Babenberg, 3
Leopold the Margrave, St., 92
Letter of Majesty, 47, 49, 52
Liechtenstein, Karl, 52
Lorraine, 95, 99; Duke Charles
  of, 73, 74, 79, 114; Archduke
  Charles of, 113; Duke Francis
  of, 98, 101
Louis XIV, king of France, 1, 67,
  70, 71, 83, 85–87, 89, 90, 118–
  119
Louis XV, king of France, 98, 99,
  108, 109
Louis XVI, king of France, 142–
  143, 146, 147
Louis XVIII, king of France, 159
Louis I, king of Hungary, 20–21
Louis II, king of Hungary, 24,
  26–29
Lower Austria, 31, 32, 116;
  Counter-Reformation in, 65,
  92; and division of Habsburg
  possessions, 47; local saints,
  92; Protestants in, 39, 65; and
  Serfdom Patent, 133
Ludwig (Louis) of Baden, 79, 80,
  82
Lusatias: Bohemia and, 14–15, 17,

24, 62; and Bohemian Protestant army, 50; diets, 28; and division of Habsburg possessions, 47; Protestants in, 53, 65; Saxony and, 62
Luther, Martin, 8, 42
Lutheranism, 8, 9, 38–42, 76
Lutherans, 41, 51–52, 57; Saxon, 41, 120
Lützen, battle of, 54
Luxemburg dynasty, 5, 14, 17

Mack von Leiberich, Karl, 150
Magenta, battle of, 157
Magna Charta, 19
Magyar language, 41, 119, 121, 141
Magyar nationalism, 120, 154
Magyars, 3, 12, 17–19, 35, 78, 95, 96, 120, 121, 141–142; Calvinist, 41, 46, 66, 120; Protestant Reformation and, 40, 41
Mansfeld, Ernst von, 50
Marchfeld, battle of, 3
Maria Theresa, 101–109, 111–112, 127, 142, 144; advisers, 102–103; alliance with Louis XV, 109; and Bohemia, 115–117; centralization and bureaucratization policy, 115–116; and Counter-Reformation, 102; economic program, 114–115; educational reforms, 117–118; fiscal policy, 112–113; germanization policy, 116–117, 130; and Hungary, 116, 118–123; military reforms, 113–114; and partition of Poland, 124–125; penal code, 130; personality, 101–102; social reforms, 114; and War of the Austrian Succession, 104–105, 107–109; and War of the Bavarian Succession, 126
Marian kingdom, cult of the, 92
Marie Antoinette, 143
Marie Louise, 157
Martini, Karl Anton, 128, 130
Martinic, Jaroslav, 49

Martinovics, Father Ignaz, 145
Mary II, queen of England, 86
Mary of Burgundy, 6–7
Matthias I, emperor, 47, 49–51
Matthias Corvinus, king of Hungary, 23, 24, 27
Maximilian I, elector of Bavaria, 47, 52, 53
Maximilian II Emmanuel, elector of Bavaria, 87
Maximilian III Joseph, elector of Bavaria, 107, 126
Maximilian I, emperor, 6–7, 157
Maximilian II, emperor, 30–31, 33, 39, 43–44
Mazarin, Jules, 56, 67
Medici dynasty, extinction of, 99
Mehmet (Mohammed) the Conqueror, 11, 22–23, 26
Mehmet IV, 72, 74, 79
Mehmet Köprülü, 67
Methodius, St., 12
Metternich, Clemens Wenzel von, 144, 156–160
Milan, 7, 53, 88, 108, 147
Military Frontier, 81–82, 95n.
Mohács, battle of, 26–29, 36, 37, 40, 65–66, 74, 125
Moldavia, 16, 21, 45n., 90, 100, 138
Montecuccoli, Raimondo, 68, 70
Montenegro, Turkish conquest of, 22–23
Moravia: Bocskay's raid of, 46; Bohemia and, 12, 14, 24; and Bohemian Protestant revolt, 50; diets, 14, 16, 28, 117, 140; and division of Habsburg possessions, 47; Great, 3, 12, 17; Hussite wars and, 16–17; Protestants in, 52–53; Silesia and, 17
Morosini, Francesco, 80, 83
Mozart, Wolfgang Amadeus, 128
Mukachevo, fall of, 74–75, 89
Mustafa Köprülü, 79, 82

Naples, 7, 71, 88, 89
Napoleonic wars, 143, 146–160; First Coalition, 146, 147;

Napoleonic wars (*cont.*)
Fourth Coalition, 158–159;
Second Coalition, 148; Third
Coalition, 150, 152
Nationalism: Czech, 117, 154;
German-Austrian, 153–154;
Magyar, 120, 154; Metternich
and, 157, 160
Near Eastern question, 85
Netherlands: Franco-Turkish
alliance and, 10; Habsburg
claim to, 6, 7; Peace of
Westphalia and, 56; Second
Coalition and, 148; Spanish
(*see* Belgium); War of the
Spanish Succession in, 88
New Russia, 136–137
Nicene Creed, 76*n*.
Nicola, Vasile (Horia), 134
Noburga, St., 92

Oliva, Peace of, 69*n*.
Order of St. Stephen, 119
Organization of the Kingdom of
Hungary, 75
Orthodox Church, 42, 66;
Eastern, 76*n*.; Greek, 41, 76;
Serbian, 81, 141
Orthodox Rumanians, 41, 81,
120, 126, 142
Orthodox Serbs, 79, 120, 121
Ostend company, 93, 115
Osterman, Andrey, 98*n*.
Otto I, emperor, 3, 13, 17
Otto II, emperor, 3
Ottokar II, king of Bohemia, 3
Ottoman empire, 1, 10–11, 35;
Austria and, 11, 85, 90, 91*n*.,
99–100, 137, 138; and the
Balkans, 11, 21–23, 79, 96; and
Bohemia, 11, 32; England and,
83; and France, 10, 26, 70, 83,
85, 90; Germany and, 32, 70;
growing decline of, 46;
Holland and, 83; Hungary,
wars with, 45, 69–70, 72–74,
94–97; millet system, 81;
Prussia and, 139; resurgence of
aggressiveness, 67; Russia and,

85, 90, 99, 124–127, 136–138,
152; Slavonia and, 18; trade,
93; and Venice, 90, 96, 97. *See
also* Turks
Oxenstjerna, Axel, 54

Palatinate, Spain and, 53
Parchevich, Peter, 79*n*.
Paul I, tsar of Russia, 148
Pázmány, Peter, 65–66
Peace treaties of: Aix-la-Chapelle
(Aachen) (1748), 107–108;
Amiens, 150; Baden, 88; Basel,
147; Belgrade (1739), 100;
Berlin (1742), 107, 112; Campo
Formio (1797), 147–148;
Constantinople, 90; Dresden
(1745), 108, 112; Füssen
(1745), 107, 108; The Hague
(1720), 98; Hubertusburg (1763)
111–112; Jassy (1792), 139;
Karlovci (Karlowitz) (1699),
82–85, 97; Kuchuk-Kainardji
(1774), 125–126, 136; Linz
(1644), 67; Lunéville (1803),
148–149; Mikulov (Nikolsburg)
(1621), 53; Paris (1763), 112;
Paris (1814), 159; Paris (1815),
160; Požarevac (Passarowitz)
(1718), 97; Prague (1635), 56;
Pressburg (1805), 152, 153;
The Pyrenees (1659), 67;
Ryswick (1697), 86; Schönbrunn (1809), 156; Sèvres, 85;
Svishtov (1791), 139; Szatmár
(1711), 90–91; Teschen (1779),
126, 136; Tilsit (1807), 152;
Utrecht (1713–1714), 88–89;
Vasvár (1664), 70; Versailles,
109–110; Vienna (1738), 98–99;
Vienna (1815), 159–160; West-
phalia (1648), 56–57, 63, 68;
Zsitva Torok (1606), 46, 66
Peninsular War, 154–156
Perpetual diet, 70*n*.
Pest, 123. *See also* Buda
Peter I, tsar of Russia, 79, 83,
85, 90, 98*n*., 99
Peter III, tsar of Russia, 111

Petrovaradin, battle of, 96, 97
Philip II, king of Spain, 9, 44, 51
Philip III, king of Spain, 52
Philip IV, king of Spain, 67
Philip V, king of Spain, 87, 88, 97–99
Philip the Handsome, 6–7
Philosophes, 102, 118, 128
Piccolomini, Enea, 79, 80
Piedmont-Sardinia, 105, 108
Pitt, William (the Elder), 110, 111
Pitt, William (the Younger), 137, 150
Pius IV, pope, 43
Pius VI, pope, 132
Poděbrady, George of, king of Bohemia, 23
Poland: Austria and, 98, 123–126, 159–160; and battle of Mohács, 27; Bohemia and, 12; Confederation of Bar, 123–124; cultural decline, 60; Deluge of, 58*n.*, 69*n.*; First Northern War, 69; France and, 10, 158; Greek Catholic (Uniat) Church, 76*n.*; Hungary and, 21, 22, 73, 74, 79; Hussitism and, 16; Jagellon dynasty, 7; partitions of, 123–125, 147, 156, 159; Peace of Karlovci and, 85; Prussia and, 123–125, 139, 147; Russia and, 123–125, 147, 159–160; socioeconomic structure, 125; and Sweden, 54, 69*n.*, 90; and Turks, 73, 74, 83. *See also* names of rulers
Poland-Lithuania, 7, 24, 58*n.*, 59
Polish nationalism, 154
Polish Succession, War of the, 98–99, 105
Poltava, battle of, 90, 98*n.*
Pompadour, Madame de, 109
Poniatowski, Stanislaw, 123
Potato War, 126, 136
Potëmkin, Grigori, 137
Pragmatic Alliance, 105; French defeat of, 107–108
Pragmatic Sanction, 92–93, 99, 101, 103–105

Prague, 29, 60; architecture, 15, 44–45; Charles IV and, 15; Clementinum in, 43; Conference of, 158–159; Defenestration of, 49; Hradčany castle, 44, 49; Peace of, 56; population (1800), 123; Rudolf II and, 44–45; St. Vitus Cathedral, 15; Silesian wars and, 105, 107; transferral of Habsburg court to, 44
Prague, University of, 15, 62, 140
Pressburg (*see* Bratislava)
Protestant Reformation, 16, 38–44. *See also under* names of countries
Protestantism, 10, 39–40, 42, 43, 46, 51, 63, 65, 71, 76
Protestants, 38, 60–61; English-speaking, 43. *See also under* names of countries
Prussia: area (1740), 104; army, 104; and Austria, 103–105, 107–114, 123, 124, 126, 139, 146, 147, 158; England and, 109–111; and France, 143, 146, 152; and Poland, 123–125, 139, 147; population (1740), 104; Silesian wars, 104–105, 107, 110–111; and Sweden, 123; treaties of Tilsit and, 152; Treaty of Versailles and, 110; and Turkey, 139. *See also* names of rulers

Queen Anne's War (*see* Spanish Succession, War of the)

Radetzky, Josef, 159
Rákóczi, Ferenc I, 70, 72, 89
Rákóczi, Ferenc II, 88–91
Rákóczi, György I, 66, 67
Rákóczi, György II, 69
Rastadt: Congress of, 147–148; Treaty of, 88
Reichenbach: Convention of, 139, 141; Treaty of, 158
Renaissance, 38
Rhine River, 54, 67, 86, 98, 103, 105

Rhodes, Turkish seizure of, 26
Richelieu, Cardinal (Armand du
    Plessis de Richelieu), 54, 56
Riegger, Paul Josef, 128, 130
Royal absolutism, 8, 9, 30, 57,
    61, 68
Royal Hungarian Bodyguard, 119
Royal Hungary, 33–38; Counter-
    Reformation in, 45; and
    Croatia, 37; religious freedom,
    46
Rudolf I of Habsburg, emperor, 3
Rudolf II, emperor, 44–45, 47, 49
Rudolf IV Habsburg, 4, 5, 14
Rumanian nationalism, 154
Rumanians, 19n., 35, 36, 41, 42,
    66, 78, 81, 95, 120, 126, 142
Russia, 1; attacks against
    Crimean Tartars, 79–80; and
    Austria, 85, 98, 100, 104–105,
    109–111, 123–127, 136–137,
    155, 158; and Bulgaria, 124;
    colonization of Siberia, 94; and
    England, 109, 110, 137, 150;
    and France, 147, 148, 150, 152,
    158; Moldavian campaigns,
    90, 100, 138; Muscovite, 10, 74;
    New, 136–137; and Poland,
    123–125, 147, 159–160; and
    Polish succession, 98; and
    Serbia, 152; and Sweden, 90,
    123, 137; and Turkey, 85, 90,
    99, 124–127, 136–138, 152. *See
    also* names of rulers
Ruthenes, 18, 76, 95, 120–121,
    125, 126
Ruthenia, 18, 74–75, 96

St. Gotthard, battle of, 70, 74
St. Petersburg, 109, 124, 125, 127
Salzburg, 149, 152
Sardinia, 97, 98
Sava River, 22, 27, 79–82, 99–100,
    137, 156
Savoy, duke of, 87, 105, 108
Savoy, Prince Eugene of, 83,
    88, 95–99
Saxe, Maurice de, 107–108
Saxons of Hungary, 18–19, 35,
    36, 41, 78, 120–121, 142

Saxony, 62, 107, 108, 110, 111
Schwarzenberg, Karl, prince,
    158, 159
Scientific Revolution, 44, 60
Scotland, rebellion in, 108
Seckendorff, Friedrich von, 99
Senta, battle of, 83, 97
Serb Privilege, 80–82
Serbia: and Austria, 80, 138,
    157–158; Habsburg advance
    in, 79, 97, 99, 138; Hungary
    and, 21; Russia and, 152; Serb
    Patriarchs, 80–81, 99–100;
    Turkish conquest of, 11, 21–23
Serbs of Hungary, 35, 80–82,
    95, 121, 140–141
Serfdom Patent, 133–134
Seven Years' War, 108–114, 123
Siberia, Russian colonization of, 94
Sicily, 7, 97–99
Sigismund I, emperor and king
    of Hungary and Bohemia,
    5, 15–17, 21–22
Sigismund I Jagellon, king of
    Poland, 7
Sigismund III Vasa, king of
    Poland, 52n.
Silesia: Bohemia and, 12, 14,
    17, 24; and Bohemian
    Protestant army, 50; diets, 28;
    and division of Habsburg
    possessions, 47; Hussite
    movement and, 17; and
    Moravia, 17; Protestants in, 53
Silesian wars, 104–105, 107, 110–111
Slany Kamen, battle of, 82
Slavata, Vilém (William), 49
Slavic tribes, 11–12
Slavonia, 18, 19, 33, 81, 85
Slovak nationalism, 154
Slovakia, 18, 19, 22, 33, 40, 43,
    95, 96
Slovaks, 19n., 40–41, 95, 121
Slovenes, 4, 40, 46
Society of Liberty and Equality,
    145
Sofia, regent of Russia, 79
Solferino, battle of, 157
Sonnenfels, Josef, 128, 130
Sopron, 72, 75

Spain: and Austria, 104;
Bourbons, 108; Catholics in, 8;
England and, 67; France and,
26, 67, 87, 98, 146, 147, 150;
Habsburg claim to, 7; and
Palatinate, 53; and War of the
Polish Succession, 98. *See also*
Habsburg empire; Habsburgs
and names of rulers
Spanish Succession, War of the,
83, 87–90, 103–105
Spis (Zips, Szepes), 21, 124
Stadion, Count Philipp, 144,
153–157
Stahrenberg, Rüdiger von, 73
Stanislaw II Augustus, king of
Poland, 123–124
Stanislaw I Leszczyński, king of
Poland, 98, 99
Stephen I (saint), king of
Hungary, 17–18, 118
Stephen Báthori, king of Poland,
45
Stuart, Charles Edward (the
Young Pretender), 107–108
Styria, 3, 4, 31, 40, 116, 147
Suleiman I (the Magnificent),
26, 31–33, 35, 72
Suvorov, Alexander, 138, 148
Swabians of Hungary, 121
Sweden: army, Bohemian
refugees in, 63; and Denmark,
90; and England, 150; France
and, 10; and Poland, 54, 69*n*.,
90; Prussia and, 123; Russia
and, 90, 123, 137; and Seven
Years' War, 111; and Thirty
Years' War, 54, 56. *See also*
names of rulers
Swieten, Gerhard van, 118
Sylvester II, pope, 17–18
Sylvester, János, 41
Szekels, 18, 35, 41, 78, 142
Székesfehérvár, 20, 29
Szelepcsényi, György, 71
Sziget, fortress of, 33, 96

Talleyrand-Périgord, Charles
de, 148–149
Tarashevich, Vasil, 76

Tartars, 18, 79–80
Temesvár, 85, 97, 140–141
Thirty Years' War, 41, 49–57,
66–68, 103; aftermath of, 58–67
Thököly, Imre, 72–74, 77, 79,
89, 91*n*.
Thugut, Johann, 147
Thurn, Heinrich Matthias von,
49–52
Tilly, Jan Tserklaes, 52, 54
Toleration, Patent of, 131, 135,
138, 140
Tranovský, Jiří (George), 41
Transylvania, 18, 19, 27, 32, 33;
and Bohemia, 52; Counter-
Reformation in, 45–46, 78;
diet, 35–36, 41, 45, 77, 78, 140,
142; ethnic groups, 120, 121;
Greek Catholic (Uniat)
Church, 78; Habsburg control
of, 77–78; Habsburg oc-
cupation of, 45, 46; Horia's
revolt, 134; and Hungary,
77–78; independence, end of,
67, 69; Leopold I and, 77, 78;
Leopold II and, 142; Magyar
nobles in, 96, 142; military
frontier, 81–82; Orthodox
Church, 41, 42, 66, 78, 81; as
Ottoman protectorate, 36;
partition, period of, 36;
political autonomy, 77, 78;
Protestants in, 41–42, 78;
Rákóczi's reforms, 66; religious
freedom, 41–42, 45, 66, 77, 78;
Rumanian cultural revival
in, 66; Saxon towns, 96;
Serfdom Patent and, 133–134;
silver mines, 20; Turkish
invasions of, 69, 77, 79;
Ukranian Cossacks, invasion
of, 52*n*.
Trent, Council of, 38, 39, 65
Trieste, 4, 7, 93, 115, 156
Trnava, University of, 66, 119
Trubar, Primož, 40
Turkey (*see* Ottoman empire)
Turkish Hungary, 33–35, 37, 94;
conquest of, 76–77; Magyar
nobles, flight from, 96;

Turkish Hungary (*cont.*)
  religious freedom, 45
Turks, 1, 10–11, 22–23;
  Albrecht II and, 5; Belgrade
  occupation, 22, 23, 26, 27, 72,
  74; Buda occupation, 20, 32, 33;
  Bulgaria destroyed by, 11,
  21, 35; crusades against, 21, 22;
  Esztergom occupation, 66;
  France and, 10, 26; and
  Habsburg Balkan policy, 82;
  Holy League and, 74, 79, 83,
  90; Hungarian invasions, 11,
  22–23, 26–27, 31–35, 40;
  Peace of Zsitva Torok and, 46;
  Poland and, 73, 74, 83;
  Rhodes seized by, 26; Serbia
  destroyed by, 11, 21–23, 35;
  Transylvanian invasions, 69, 77,
  79; Vienna sieges, 31–32, 72–74
Tuscany, 99, 108, 148, 149, 159
Two Sicilies, Kingdom of, 99
Tyrol, The, 4, 5*n*., 31, 39–40,
  92, 113, 154

Ukraine, The, 73, 74
Ukranian Cossacks, 52*n*.
Unitarians, 38, 41–42, 78
Upper Austria, 31, 116;
  Counter-Reformation in, 65,
  92; and division of Habsburg
  possessions, 47; local saints, 92;
  Protestants in, 39, 65; and
  Serfdom Patent, 133; Silesian
  wars in, 105, 107

Valmy, French victory at, 146
Venceslas, St., 12, 92
Venceslas IV, 92
Venice: Charles VI, alliance
  with, 96; and Coronation of
  Maximilian I, 6; Dalmatia and,
  18, 21, 85; and Holy League,
  74, 90; Hungary and, 21;
  Napoleon's conquest of, 147;
  Turkey and, 90, 96, 97
Verböczy, István (Stephen),
  25–26, 29
Vienna, 3, 4, 7, 9, 29; architec-
  ture, 4, 68–69, 92; central

offices, 30; Church of St.
  Stephen, 3, 4, 73; Congress
  of, 159–160; Franco-Bavarian
  advance toward, 105; General
  Hospital, 128; Hofburg, 3, 44,
  69; imperial offices, 36, 49;
  imperial patronage, 59–60;
  Jacobin plot, 144; Jesuits in, 39;
  municipal bank of, 115;
  Napoleon's occupation of, 150,
  155; Oriental Academy, 115;
  Pazmaneum, 66; population
  (1800), 123; stock exchange,
  115; Theresianum, 119;
  Turkish sieges of, 31–32, 72–74
Vienna, University of, 4, 39, 65,
  73, 128; medical school, 118
Vladislav II, king of Bohemia
  and of Hungary, 7, 24, 27
Vladislav II, prince of Bohemia, 13
Vlahs, 35

Wagram, battle of, 155
Wallachia, 21, 79, 97
Wallenstein, Albrecht, 53–54,
  56, 64, 68
Wallis, Olivier, 99
Wellington, duke of, 154
Westminster, Treaty of, 109
White Mountain, Battle on the,
  52–53, 61, 62, 71, 75
Wiener Neustadt, military
  academy at, 113
William III, king of England, 86
Wittelsbach dynasty, 107, 126
Wittenberg, 38; ninety-five
  theses of, 8
Wladyslaw III, king of Poland
  and of Hungary, 22
World War I, 146*n*.
Worms, Diet of, 8
Wycliffe, John, 15

Zápolyai, János (John), 25, 27, 29–33
Zápolyai, János Zsigmond (John
  Sigismund), 32–33, 45
Zrinyi, Ilona (Helen), 72, 74, 89
Zrinyi, Miklós, 96
Zrinyi, Nicholas, 33
Zrinyi, Peter, 70–72

182